VEILED HALF-TRUTHS

VEILED HALF-TRUTHS

*Western travellers' perceptions of
Middle Eastern women*

SELECTED AND INTRODUCED
BY
JUDY MABRO

I.B. Tauris & Co Ltd
Publishers
London · New York

First published in 1991 by
I.B.Tauris & Co Ltd
45 Bloomsbury Square
London WCIA 2HY

175 Fifth Avenue
New York NY 10010

Paperback edition published in 1996

In the United States of America
and in Canada distributed by
St Martin's Press
175 Fifth Avenue
New York NY 10010

Grateful acknowledgement is made for permission to reprint
Excerpts from *In Search of the Forty Days Road* by Michael Asher, Longman
Excerpts from *A Cure for Serpents* by the Duke of Pirajno, Eland 1985
Excerpt from *Arabian Sands* by Wilfred Thesiger, Penguin 1987

British Library Cataloguing in Publication Data

Mabro, Judy
    Veiled half-truths. Western travellers' perceptions of Middle
    Eastern women.
    1. Middle East. Society. Role of women.
    I. Title
    305.420956

ISBN 1 86064 027 3

Library of Congress Catalog Card Number: available

Printed and bound in Great Britain by
WBC Print Ltd, Bridgend

*For Felicity, Floreeda, Frances, Nevine and Nyla
with love*

CONTENTS

ACKNOWLEDGEMENTS

The ideas of many authors have helped me in compiling the anthology, but I would particularly like to acknowledge Malek Alloula, *The Colonial Harem*, Sarah Graham-Brown, *Images of Women*, Rana Kabbani, *Europe's Myths of Orient*, Edward Said, *Orientalism*, Anne Summers' W.E.A. class in Oxford on women in nineteenth-century England, Lynne Thornton, *La Femme dans la peinture orientaliste*, and the writings of countless feminists from many countries.

Where the title of a book is given in French, the translations are my own, but I would like to thank Robert Mabro for help and for listening to interminable pieces being read out, whenever I found something that incensed me even more than usual. I would also like to thank Léonie Archer, Marion Farouk Sluglett and Charles Webster for reading a first draft of my introduction; Mourad Wahba for drawing my attention to several texts; Camillia Fawzi El-Solh for passing on interesting articles and books; Kathleen Howey for translating Italian sources; Diane Ring at the Middle East Centre Library, St Antony's College, Oxford; and Père Maurice Martin at the Collège de la Sainte Famille, Cairo, who enabled me to read a large number of books in a very short space of time, by knowing what I wanted to read before I did myself.

Most of all my thanks go to Anna Enayat of I.B.Tauris, whose idea it all was and who understood that hassling people is counter-productive.

PREFACE TO THE SECOND EDITION

There are two things to be said about this anthology. First, it is not a selection of readings about the lives and thoughts of women in the Middle East, but concerns the way in which Western travellers, mainly in the nineteenth and early twentieth centuries, chose to depict these women in their travel books, guides and memoirs. It is also concerned with fact and fiction regarding the position of women in European societies at that time – the ideas which travellers took with them about women's place in society. For this reason, the material has been arranged around the observers' ideas and prejudices.

Secondly, this anthology does not pretend to be an objective selection of readings – what anthology can honestly claim that? It is a highly personal and subjective choice (taken from about one-third of the books I read), which nevertheless reflects the way in which women in the Middle East and North Africa have been portrayed in the West. The legacy of these writings can be found in newspapers, magazines and films today.

As in earlier centuries, writers remain fascinated by the veil and by the imagined lives of Muslim women. This was very evident when the marriage was announced in 1995 of former world cricketer and playboy, Imran Khan, with a young English heiress, Jemima Goldsmith. Some of the reporting can only be described as apoplectic. Despite the fact that the couple would be leading a privileged life in Pakistan, photographs and head-lines proclaimed that Jemima would be living in the backstreets of Lahore, in a state of virtual slavery, veiled from head to toe. The old confusion of images from the *Arabian Nights*, applied indiscriminately to a wide geographical area, was nicely repeated

in a Spanish magazine which showed her wearing a Pakistani
shalwar and kameez and described this as traditional *Arab*
dress.[1]

Three circumstances in the world in 1995 are of particular
relevance to the way in which Western travellers and the media
perceive and portray Middle Eastern women: the growth of
activist Islam in the world, the run-up to the 1995 UN World
Conference on Women in Beijing, and the increase in tourism
to countries with a majority Muslim population – in particular
Egypt, Jordan, Turkey, Tunisia and Morocco.

The result of the first is that it is virtually impossible to
discuss any aspect of women's lives in the region without
considering the role of Islam. Indeed, to believe some conversations and media reports, every moment of a woman's life
there is in some way ruled by the religion. In fact, for the
women living in these widely varying communities:

legislation, customs and traditions, affected or inspired by interpreta-
tions of the Qur'an and the Shari'a, combine to define concepts of
female roles and status ... these concepts may vary from one class
or generation to the other as well as over time, just as they may differ
from one Muslim country to another. In addition, Muslim women's
lives and the choices they face are influenced as much by patriarchal
social arrangements as they are by religious ideology.[2]

Nevertheless, generalizations abound on the subject of women's
lives in Muslim countries, even though there are 51 very diverse
countries in the world describing themselves as Muslim (if we
take current membership of the Islamic Conference). Even
the 20 or so countries of the Middle East and North Africa
with which this anthology is concerned do not constitute the
homogeneous world that the political Islamists like to portray
and the Western world dislikes and fears.

Secondly, in the two decades between the first UN Conference on Women in Mexico in 1975 and the 1995 Beijing
conference, much attention has been paid by development
agencies to the position of women in Third World countries.
Women's organizations have often been highlighted as targets
for projects and a lot of information exists about women's
groups in Africa, Asia and Latin America. Indeed, in magazines

and on television women are frequently portrayed working together, setting up cooperative enterprises and so on. However, as Annika Rabo pointed out at a workshop held in Oxford,[3] Middle Eastern women have been largely ignored by these agencies (with the exception of Palestinian women, who have received attention through the existence of solidarity groups). The reasons for this, she suggests, are that most Middle Eastern countries receive relatively little or no international aid, and women are therefore not involved in the policy negotiations between development agencies and governments, and that many women's groups and organizations are either state controlled or informal.

However, the 1995 *Human Development Report*[4] highlights the issue of women's position in this region by concentrating on factors other than the income level of a society. This study revealed interesting variations in levels of adult literacy, education and participation in the non-domestic labour force. For example, in Bahrain, United Arab Emirates, Qatar, Libya and Jordan more females than males enrol in tertiary education; in Bahrain, the United Arab Emirates, Qatar, Kuwait and Lebanon nearly as many or more females than males enrol in secondary education. However, concerning paid employment, women's share of the adult labour force in Bahrain is 12 per cent, in the United Arab Emirates 9 per cent, in Qatar 7 per cent, in Kuwait 23 per cent, in Libya 10 per cent, in Lebanon 27 per cent. Women in the Middle East are still seen as symbols of underdevelopment by the West and symbols of tradition by the Islamist groups (and by their own governments in many states) in much the same way that they have been during periods of colonization or liberation in the nineteenth and twentieth centuries. The increasing level of female education, however, means that women are becoming more vocal about their rights and their role in society.

The third circumstance of relevance is the growth in tourism to countries referred to in this book. Since the nineteenth century travellers have visited Egypt, the Holy Land and North Africa, but the 1960s saw an explosion in the travel industry – of package holidays to Spain, to Greece and increasingly on a large scale to Turkey, Tunisia, Jordan and Egypt. To give an idea of the scale, even after a fall in numbers in the early 1990s because of threats by Islamist groups, the total number of tourist arrivals to Egypt in the six months to June 1995 was 1.3 million, and according to the minister of tourism it was expected to reach 3 million by the end of the year.[5]

Does this mean that Western travellers are now better informed about the countries they visit? Are they more prepared to overcome the prejudices that they bring with them, which the French traveller Volney warned about at the end of the eighteenth century? (see Introduction to this book, p. 27).

When fashion magazines and news programmes depict women in the Middle East, they frequently show them wearing a veil, which remains a powerful image. It is also, of course, an important symbol to the fundamentalist Islamist groups, who place great emphasis on the female dress code. In an article in *Cosmopolitan* magazine (June 1995), Lesley Abdela, the political editor, reported on a visit to Amman to meet Jordanian women:

This was my first visit to an Arab country. Like many other Westerners, my impressions of Middle Eastern women have been pre-formed by the media. Fashion and advertising images frequently show exotic-looking Arab women standing in billowing robes, staring dreamily across sand dunes. Television news coverage tends to portray them as Islamic fundamentalists, heads covered with the *hijab*, oppressed by patriarchal regimes.

After working with a group of Jordanian women on ways of participating more fully in public life she recognized that her preconceptions about Arab women were similar to those she held about nuns – that they were either 'passive god-followers or aggressive fundamentalists'. Both were wrong, she realized, for, 'like nuns', Jordanian women 'can be fun and have a great sense of humour'. They were also determined to be involved in the building and improving of their society.

What is surprising about this is that the political editor of the magazine, a woman, was herself surprised. It is also unfortunate that she leaves readers with the comparison with nuns towards the end of the article. It is a comparison that comes easily and has been used by many writers over the years, but it tells us nothing at all.

She could quite effortlessly have discovered how much Arab

women have achieved. In Egypt, for example, women work in a great variety of jobs. In addition to their traditional work in agriculture and selling produce, they work in factories and are also 'doctors, film-makers, politicians, economists, academics, engineers. Mostly, they are public servants, cogs in the country's bloated bureaucracy.'[6] Looking forward to the UN World Conference on Women in Beijing, the weekly *Al-Ahram* newspaper, published in Cairo, celebrates the 'feminist chain' in Egypt which began in the final decades of the nineteenth century and continues to this day: 'In virtually every walk of life, and across a wide spectrum of opinion, there are women advancing the twin causes of gender and nation.'[7] In the strict Wahhabi state of Saudi Arabia during the Gulf war, 47 women took part in a demonstration in November 1990 seeking the right to drive a car. They all had international driving licences and were professional women, although most were dismissed from their jobs as a result of the action.

Concerning the Islamic world more generally, it is worth recording that at this time (August 1995) Turkey, Bangladesh and Pakistan all have a woman prime minister.

Having recognized these achievements of Arab and Muslim women, it is equally important to identify the multiple constraints under which they live and the dilemma of Muslim women's human rights, which is the cause of increasing conflict today:

Islamist intransigence forces Muslim women to fight for their rights, openly when they can, subtly when they must. The struggle is multifaceted, at once political, economic, ethical, psychological and intellectual.[8]

In Algeria today, for example, women are being killed because they are women – because they do not wear the veil, because they are related to policemen or soldiers. Two women in Turkey were recently shot dead by male relatives because they were 'dressed revealingly'.[9] Such stories are numerous, but the various ways in which women stand up and fight for their rights are not as well reported as the atrocities committed against them.

A recent French edition of *Marie Claire* magazine (August 1995) celebrated the coming Beijing women's conference by selecting 100 women from around the world who are fighting in different ways for women's human rights. From the region of the Middle East and North Africa 15 women were chosen, who bear no resemblance to the stereotypical passive woman in veil or flowing robes. It is worth mentioning a few of them.

Khalida Messaoudi, a maths teacher in Algiers, has regularly denounced the assassinations and rape of women and has received death threats as a result. *Leyla Zana*, a Turkish member of parliament, has been tortured and condemned to 15 years in prison for denouncing the crimes of the state against the Kurds. *Wassila Si Saber*, an Algerian journalist who published the story of an 18-year-old girl, was kidnapped by Islamic fundamentalists along with other women, raped, beaten and starved. *Linda Matar* in Lebanon is fighting for the abrogation of discriminatory laws which permit women to be killed by their family to preserve its honour. *Hakima Himmich*, a Moroccan doctor, set up the first Moroccan association to fight against AIDS and directs a service to care for those who are HIV positive. *Mevlude Genc* is a Turkish woman living in Germany; her children and grandchildren were burned to death in their home by fascists. She nevertheless preaches peace between Turks and Germans. *Mehranguiz Kar*, an Iranian lawyer who regularly defends women, has been constantly insulted and humiliated. *Fawzia Talout*, the editor of Morocco's only feminist magazine, led a campaign to regulate repudiation. *Maryam Zakout*, leader of the Palestinian feminist movement Khan Yunis, has drawn attention to daily problems such as domestic violence and low pay which are normally overlooked in the political struggle. *Toujan al-Faisal*, the first woman MP in Jordan, was elected in 1993 after being condemned to death by an Islamic tribunal in Amman.

Many people believe that social change in the Middle East will come from women and that in situations of extreme turmoil they become more active. For example, despite the terror in Algeria women have been organizing demonstrations calling for peace and an end to the killings. In the words of a male government official, 'Women are the only men in this country. They are struggling to live, whereas most men have to all intents and purposes given up the fight.'[10] Governments censure or ban women's groups when they demand their rights and challenge patriarchal structures.

This is not new either. Fatima Mernissi states that throughout the history of Islam, it has been a tradition for Muslim sovereigns facing riots or popular revolt to ban women from leaving their homes.[11] In the nineteenth century Lucie Duff Gordon described how when the Sultan was on a visit in Egypt, the Pasha ordered all the women of the lower classes to remain indoors. For, as she said: 'Arab women are outspoken, and might shout out their grievances to the great Sultan.'[12] The great sultans today still fear that women will shout out for change, and they react in the same ways.

Notes

1. *Semana*, 9 August 1995.
2. Camillia Fawzi El-Solh and Judy Mabro (eds), Introduction to *Muslim Women's Choices: Religious Belief and Social Reality*, Oxford: Berg Publishers, 1994, p. 1.
3. Paper delivered at the Workshop on 'Women Organized in Groups in the Middle East: Issues and Constraints', Centre for Cross-Cultural Research on Women, University of Oxford, held on 23 and 24 June 1995.
4. Published for the United Nations Development Programme by Oxford University Press, Oxford, 1955.
5. *Financial Times*, 21 July 1995.
6. Geraldine Brooks, *Nine Parts of Desire: The Hidden World of Islamic Women*, London: Hamish Hamilton, 1995, p. 178.
7. *Al-Ahram Weekly*, 20–26 July 1995, p. 15.
8. Mahnaz Afkhami (ed.), Introduction to *Faith and Freedom: Women's Human Rights in the Muslim World*, London: I.B.Tauris, 1995, pp. 1–2.
9. *Guardian*, 3 August 1995.
10. Quoted in *Index on Censorship*, July/August 1995, p. 95.
11. *Islam and Democracy: Fear of the Modern World*, London: Virago, 1993, p. 154.
12. *Letters from Egypt*, p. 53.

INTRODUCTION

Muslim women have been the subject of much discussion in the Western press recently, particularly when a few girls in France and England demanded the right to wear a headscarf in school. The long acrimonious debate in France and the shorter one in England reflect the Western view that the sole cause of Muslim women's oppression is their religion. That racism in Europe could be a contributory factor in these instances was not given the consideration it deserves. Europe has always 'known' that Muslim women are particularly oppressed, for it has been described for a very long time in Western travel books and literature, and depicted in art. This is taken as an unquestioned fact, there for all to see in the veil and the institution of the harem – and reactions to both are as strong today as ever they were.

The veil, as it is called in the West, although it may sometimes be a scarf covering the head, is such a powerful symbol that it can blind people into false generalizations. A set of ideas about Islam and Muslim women quickly come to the surface. For example, when a male reporter from the *Guardian* investigated the case of the two schoolgirls wearing the headscarf in Altringcham he asked to speak to their father – presumably because he knew that Islam is a male-dominated religion and Muslim women are passive beings. He was told by one of the girls that her father was busy, but she offered to help. 'Fatima then helped me for 40 fully assertive minutes. She is only 15, but her fluency and confidence would be remarkable in someone twice her age; she is her own woman and knows what she thinks' (*Guardian*, 19 January 1990).

In May 1989 a television programme on Afghanistan

included an interview, also by a man, with some women students at Kabul University. Living in a war-stricken country, these young women stated that their overriding desire was for peace, and if compromise was necessary to achieve this, then so be it. The interviewer was shocked. Surely these young women, the product of communist rule, should find women's position more important than peace. 'But would you *really* be prepared to wear the veil?' he asked. They all replied that, if that could contribute to peace in the country, they would.

During the UN decade for women, 1975–85, Western feminists began with a myopic emphasis on such issues as clitoridectomy or the veil, telling Middle Eastern and African women that these were the pivotal issues in the struggle for women's liberation in their countries. By the end of the decade there was the beginning of a recognition that things were not so simple; that it was not the place of a Western woman to decide what was the pivotal issue for a Middle Eastern or African woman; and that by throwing off the veil or the fetters of genital mutilation women would not suddenly acquire the economic independence, food and peace which many of them considered to be the issues that should be dealt with first.

For centuries Europe has been both fascinated and repelled by the veil and the harem, symbols which, on the one hand, have prevented the observer from seeing and communicating with women and produced feelings of frustration and aggressive behaviour. On the other hand, they have provided men with a fantasy and dangled the promise of exotic and erotic experiences with the 'beauty behind the veil' and the 'light of the harem'. Female observers, as we shall see, have been as ambiguous, as hostile and as Eurocentric as men in this respect, if for different reasons.

It is worth stating at this point that by concentrating on the harem and the veil, Western travellers often failed to understand aspects of the life of Middle Eastern women. First, the harem as it was understood in the West was extremely rare and would have appeared just as 'exotic' to the majority of Middle Eastern women who lived in rural areas, were poor and did a large proportion of the agricultural labour. In towns also, many women worked to contribute to the family budget.

The word 'harem' simply means the segregated part of the house where strange men do not have access. As we shall see later, its connotations in Europe have been very different.

Secondly, the assumption made by travellers that veiled women were necessarily more oppressed, more passive, more ignorant than unveiled women led to exaggerated statements about the imprisoned existence of women in 'the Orient' as compared to the total freedom enjoyed by women in Europe. Of course women were oppressed in both societies to a greater or lesser extent, but by commencing with assumptions that a Western lifestyle was of necessity superior, travellers failed to recognize the similarities in the situations of the two groups of women.

In reading for this anthology I became particularly interested in the multitude of travel books by little-known writers which poured from the presses in the nineteenth and early twentieth centuries. Europeans were curious to learn about 'other peoples', but only at a level that would confirm their belief in the superiority of their own culture. Their travel books and magic-lantern shows served as the equivalent of today's television documentaries. Indeed, so many books were published on the Middle East and North Africa that many authors began by apologizing for bringing out yet another. Rightly so, for there was much repetition and, no doubt, plagiarism. The diversity of life in the region was – and frequently still is – ignored. A global attitude was adopted; ignorance and fear of the different dictated an approach which concentrated on external signs. Such was the fascination with the Orient, and particularly with the women there, that even scholarly books on archaeology, for example, felt obliged to comment on the subject. Publishers sometimes included sensational drawings of women in an effort to sell a book.

When these travellers, tourists, archaeologists, geographers, naturalists, artists and others arrived in North Africa and the Middle East they saw veiled women for the first time. Today most people will have seen veiled women in European cities and the following reaction, in an article in *Marie Claire* magazine in September 1988, is perhaps a common one. It plays on the age-old assumptions about Oriental women handed down by Western travellers:

Most Westerners' experience of the veil comes from seeing collections of small, dumpy women, covered from head to toe in what appears to be linen dyed a blotchy charcoal, roaming slowly through the department stores of capital cities. They look incongruous and bizarre heaving in and out of limousines that seem, in London, to be parked permanently outside Marble Arch's Marks & Spencer, but in their own country, these women can be stunningly beautiful; as mysterious, graceful and exotic as the dry desert plateau of the Arabian peninsula itself.

It seems to me that the author is saying several confused things about veiled women: that they may not all be as exotic and beautiful as Western fantasy has depicted them, that they *can* be stunningly beautiful, mysterious, graceful and exotic – in which case they should reveal themselves, preferably in their natural habitat where they do not appear incongruous and bizarre. In other words, the author is concerned with the women solely as sex objects and is reinforcing the mystique because this is a topic that sells well. Reading this article, which is entitled 'Arabia, Behind the Veil' and is accompanied by sensational photographs in keeping with a fashion magazine, I was struck by the similarity to the reactions of so many nineteenth-century tourists in Algeria, Egypt and other parts of the Middle East, who wrote at length about the appearance and sexuality of the women they encountered or dreamed about.

 Setting forth with ideas about Oriental women culled from romantic novels and poems, travel books and biblical stories, the immediate response of many, after the first excitement at being back in the days of the *Arabian Nights* or the Bible, was one of aggression, often manifest in extremely uncivilized behaviour – trespassing in houses, spying on women on terraces or bathing in rivers, demolishing whole cultures as decadent, in one case paying for a girl to be circumcised in order to see what it was all about. They felt hostile towards the closed houses and cities and veiled women which excluded them, the Western observers, and which could even reverse the roles of observer and observed, for of course the women behind the barred window and the eye behind the veil were not deprived of vision. As Malek Alloula wrote of French photographers in Algeria:

These veiled women are not only an embarrassing enigma to the photographer but an outright attack upon him. It must be believed that the feminine gaze that filters through the veil is a gaze of a particular kind: concentrated by the tiny orifice for the eye, the womanly gaze is a little like the eye of a camera, like the photographic lens that takes aim at everything.

The photographer makes no mistake about it: he knows this gaze well; it resembles his own when it is extended by the dark chamber or the viewfinder. Thrust in the presence of a veiled woman, the photographer feels photographed; having himself become an object-to-be-seen, he loses initiative: he is dispossessed of his own gaze. . . .

The photographer will respond to this quiet and almost natural challenge by means of a double violation: he will unveil the veiled and give figural representation to the forbidden. (*The Colonial Harem*, p. 14)

In this book Malek Alloula is looking at the many thousands of postcards produced by the French in Algeria, which were said to depict local women, manners and customs. Frequent use was made of windows with bars to make it abundantly clear to the viewer that these women were imprisoned. Pornographic representations of women's bodies denied them all but their sexual nature while establishing that the photographer had succeeded in his trade, he had unveiled the veiled – although these photographs were taken in studio settings with models:

In this manner the theme of the woman imprisoned in her own home will impose itself in the most 'natural' fashion. . . . If the women are inaccessible to sight (that is veiled), it is because they are imprisoned. This dramatized equivalence between the veiling and the imprison-ment is necessary for the construction of an *imaginary scenario* that results in the dissolution of the actual society, the one that causes the frustration, in favor of a phantasm: that of the harem. (Ibid., p. 21)

In just the same way, nineteenth-century travellers (both male and female) wrote obsessively about the harem and veiling; images of prisons and shackles were used all over the

place, however irrelevant. A wall, the tinkling of an ankle
bracelet, a window shutter all invoked ideas of imprisoned
women and an aggressive reaction to the closed system of life
in 'the Orient', so unlike the friendly, outward-looking life of
the West. Being unable to enter into the family – which
apparently any foreign traveller would have easily been able to
do in Europe – moral judgements on polygamy, the harem, the
'immorality' of women (over-sexed, no moral principles,
lesbian tendencies, and so on), their deplorable attitude to
motherhood, their stupidity, poured from the pens of writers.
Such attitudes were the result of ethnocentricity and a belief in
the superiority of the European race. Indeed, descriptions of
life in Africa and Latin America would have retailed the same
things about women. But the fact that women were 'hidden' in
the Middle East provoked a special reaction, and the focus of
this was the harem. When reading all the allegations of gross
immorality, it should also be remembered that the women who
appeared to have the most freedom and were most visible to
travellers, were the prostitutes and public dancers.

Much Western literature referred to the harem as though it
was present everywhere in the Middle East as depicted in
Orientalist paintings and descriptions of the seraglio in
Istanbul. This was the equivalent of presenting daily life at
Buckingham Palace and portraits of Victorian aristocratic
ladies as typical of English family life, manners and customs.
Before departing from home European tourists 'knew' that the
harem was a lascivious world where beautiful, sensual and idle
women were cooped up together, lying around on sofas all
day, smoking pipes, waiting for the master to come and choose
one of them and, if not chosen, indulging in indescribable
activities together – or in some cases described in great detail.
In fact, the majority of women in the region lived in villages.
While their lives were known to be completely different, and
were often written about at length because it was easier to
observe, this did not obtain any greater respect for them (or
the urban poor women who worked outside the home). Either
writers indulged in fantasies about dusky maidens at the well,
recalling Rebecca or the Virgin Mary, or these women were
dismissed as ignorant and degraded, almost beasts of burden.
And the generalizations about imprisoned women continued.

Although in the nineteenth century sufficient evidence had accumulated to establish that – apart from in the seraglio and other large harems – Muslim women were free to come and go from the house and exercised considerable authority within it, many Europeans stuck confidently to the idea that the condition of women was deplorable and the harem a place of depravity. The word 'harem' (coming from 'haram', forbidden) means either the rooms of a house where women and children spend their time – and from which men are excluded apart from the husband and certain close relatives – or the women of the house. However, the first edition of *Roget's Thesaurus* in 1852 had the word 'harem' entered under 'impurity', along with words synonymous with brothel. This continued as the sole entry until a 1952 Everyman's edition of the thesaurus included 'apartment' as a second entry. A 1962 edition removed 'impurity' as an entry for 'harem' and replaced it by 'womankind' and 'love-nest'. Recent editions have more accurately placed 'harem' under 'womankind' and 'seclusion', although as late as 1972 an *Everyday Roget's Thesaurus* (London: Galley Press) retained the original single entry of 'impurity'.

Only women travellers have been able to visit harems, and their reactions are complicated and often extremely critical. I am not thinking here of women such as Lucie Duff Gordon, who lived in Egypt for seven years until her death there from consumption in 1869, but of the increasing number of tourists who were taken on an organized trip to a harem in the second half of the nineteenth century. What followed was often a very short visit, marked by mutual incomprehension and a stilted conversation through an interpreter. The travellers rarely thought in any depth about the effect of their presence on the proceedings, which had by definition meant that they were not observing normal daily life – they had become a part of what was happening. Some writers ridiculed the reactions of the women they were visiting to show how childish and ignorant they were. Many felt qualified to make confident judgements. If the women were not as beautiful and depraved as they had believed, then they were certainly uneducated, bad mothers and to be pitied for the tedious lives they led. Some women were so well informed in advance that they refused to make a visit on principle. E. H. Mitchell reacted in this way in 1891, commenting that she would

have paid a call if it would have helped 'our poor sisters' to
escape from their captivity, but to go and see them in their
detestable prison was more than a Christian should have to bear
(quoted by Lynn Thornton in *La Femme dans la peinture
orientaliste*). Harriet Martineau, the English fighter for women's
rights, did visit two harems and commented simply that she could
not 'think of the two mornings thus employed without a
heaviness of heart greater than I have ever brought away from
Deaf and Dumb Schools, Lunatic Asylums, or even Prisons'
(*Eastern Life*, vol. II, p. 147).

In fact, from as early as the 1860s middle- and upper-class
women in Egypt were writing and producing books which were
circulated in the harems, and by the last decade of the century
women's journals were also produced. These decades were what
Margot Badran describes as a period of 'invisible feminism',
when women's voices were not heard by the outside world
because of female seclusion and the segregation of the sexes.
Certainly, a very few Western travellers were able to hear what
was going on or to read the published writings of nineteenth-
century Arab women – poetry, stories, articles on the relationship
between men and women in society, biographical dictionaries of
women, and so on (Margot Badran and Miriam Cooke, *Opening
the Gates*). Egyptian middle- and upper-class women joined in
nationalist demonstrations against the British in Egypt in 1919
and soon after many stopped wearing the face veil.

Writing on the attitudes to the harem of American women in
the 1980s, Leila Ahmed found that most 'knew' that Muslim
women in particular are oppressed while freely admitting that
they knew nothing about Islam or Middle Eastern societies. She
discusses different ways of looking at the harem:

The harem can be defined as a system that permits males sexual access
to more than one female. It can also be defined, and with as much
accuracy, as a system whereby the female relatives of a man – wives,
sisters, mother, aunts, daughters – share much of their time and their
living space, and further, which enables women to have frequent and
easy access to other women in their community, vertically, across lines,
as well as horizontally. ('Western Ethnocentrism and Perceptions of the
Harem', *Feminist Studies*, 8: 3 (1982))

The West has always preferred the first definition, of course, and when women have been depicted by artists in groups together the Turkish bath has been a typical setting. It is remarkable how few Orientalist paintings before the end of the last century have shown women as mothers, compared to the large number of portraits of Western women with their children around them. This is partly because painters could paint things in an 'exotic' setting which they would not have got away with in a domestic one: 'A provocative, barely clothed girl in an Algerian doorway was exotic; the same girl in the same attitude in a Parisian doorway would have been obscene' (Peter Gay, *The Bourgeois Experience*, vol. I, p. 392).

However, such attitudes were reinforced not only by perceptions of 'Oriental' women but also by the prevailing European ideas of women's role. The developing bourgeois ideology was based on an opposition of two spheres – the male, public sphere of alienated labour, the female private sphere of self-sacrificing, nurturing, non-alienated labour. The whole structure depended on enforcing the ideals of mono-gamous marriage and women as passive sexual beings. To have depicted harem dwellers as ordinary women who cared for their children and looked after the home as did women in Europe would have undermined the whole basis of Western family life. In a century of constant flux, with middle-class culture (as Peter Gay describes it) 'eclectic with tensions and contradictory impulsions', it was vital to maintain these separate spheres, which were under constant threat.

The nineteenth century was a time when people had to adapt to so much change in their daily lives that they tried to freeze things into compartments to reduce their bewilderment. In-dustrialization, transport, political upheaval and change, increas-ing overseas trade, colonialism, periods of boom and depression, struggles between philosophy and religion on the continent, between science and religion in England, all served to transform society and make people simultaneously arrogant and insecure about their place in the world. Humankind had to adapt to a new sense of time brought about by the introduction of trains, fast steamers and a postal service as well as geological and ar-chaeological studies in the first half of the century and Darwin's *The Origin of Species* in 1859, only a few years after the 1851 exhibition in the Crystal Palace, the high point of the century:

It was ironic that a society which regarded itself as the unique climax of civilization should have sponsored the diggings which shattered that comfortable illusion.

The cultural stream to which the Victorians belonged was merely one of history's many, and perhaps not even the most accomplished, let alone the most enduring. Certainly Judaeo-Christianity could no longer be thought of as having continuously occupied the center of the world stage; it was a mere incident in a complex drama reaching back over long ages. (Richard D. Altick, *Victorian People and Ideas*, pp. 99–100)

As domestic production had begun in the mid-eighteenth century to give way to factory production, so the bourgeois ideology of separate spheres developed. Newly rich families built villas where women were secluded and stopped working in the public sphere. The powerful idea of 'refinement' prescribed that middle-class women should emulate those of the upper class – that they should not indulge in paid employment except when absolutely unavoidable. The way they passed their days learning female accomplishments and visiting back and forth among each other has been written about in many novels of the time and is well known. Whatever education they acquired was extremely limited and only intended to make them into good wives and mothers, and whatever sexuality they were acknowledged to possess was for the same end.

In the earlier part of the eighteenth century women had not been perceived in this way, however: 'As late as the 1740s woman was *consistently* represented as the site of wilful sexuality and bodily appetite. . . . women were associated with flesh, desire, and unsocialized, hence susceptible, impulses and passions' (Mary Poovey, *Uneven Development*, pp. 9–10). From the mid-eighteenth century on this image of woman was slowly transformed into the domestic ideal, the angel in the house, preserving the home as a refuge from the harsh world outside. Jean-Jacques Rousseau in his influential *Émile* (1761) set out a suitable education for Sophie, his ideal woman. This, he wrote, ought to be wholly relative to men: 'To please them, to be useful to them, to make themselves loved and honoured by them, to educate them when young, to care for them when grown, to counsel them, to console them, and to make life agreeable and sweet to them.' Such ideas were reinforced in the nineteenth century by Darwinism, which maintained that woman's special evolution made her an organism adapted to child-rearing, but otherwise frail and ill-adapted to intellectual pursuits. Of course the earlier image, which demanded that women must always be both controlled and protected by men, never quite disappeared, and of course the new image was only an ideal. Sexual desire was acknowledged to exist in some women but they were considered to be 'immoral', either lower-class – factory girls, for example, were considered to be of low morals and could not be accepted as domestic servants – or 'exotic' women, such as gypsies and women from other races, or simply insane. Nevertheless, this bourgeois code of values was assumed to be good for the middle class and therefore good for everyone else – particularly since it left men free because of their 'stronger passions'.

When travellers to the Middle East compared the lives of women there to those in Europe they were not comparing like to like. Almost invariably they were speaking of middle-class European women, and even then it was a less than honest comparison. It is clear that many writers knew nothing about the daily lives and degradation of working-class women in Europe. When confronted with veiled and 'imprisoned' women, many male writers yearned to see and possess them while stressing how different were their own womenkind. Female writers were apt to give glowing descriptions of the equality enjoyed by themselves, ignoring the boredom, frustration and misery which many of them suffered in their own society – and which was often their reason for travelling.

Indeed, some had problems doing even that, unless they had a male companion. In her book *Through Algeria* published in 1863, for example, Mabel Sharman Crawford has an introductory chapter entitled 'A Plea for Lady Tourists', where she complains that:

whilst it may be freely admitted that masculine eccentricity or originality of character is to be admired, very few will allow that any departure from ordinary rule is approvable, or even justifiable in a woman. We can applaud our grandmothers for overstepping the

conventional proprieties of their day, or we can recognise the right of
Chinese and Turkish ladies to go about with uncrippled feet and
unveiled faces. But, clearly as we can see the follies of our ancestors,
or those of contemporary nations, we cling with unreasoning
reverence to every restriction on feminine liberty of action imposed
by that society amidst which we live.

What she is criticizing is the maintenance of the rule that 'no
lady should travel without a gentleman by her side' and its
effect on further confining single women. She continues:

And if the exploring of foreign lands is not the highest end or the
most useful occupation of feminine existence, it is at least more
improving, as well as more amusing, than the crochet-work or
embroidery with which, at home, so many ladies seek to beguile the
tedium of their unoccupied days.

In the European male view of the world, women and natives
were often 'portrayed and treated as children in need of the
protection and care of male/imperial authority by virtue of
their weaknesses, innocence and inadequacy' (Joanna de
Groot, ' "Sex" and "Race": The Construction of Language and
Image in the Nineteenth Century'). If European men recognized the right of Turkish women to go about unveiled, as
Mabel Sharman Crawford said, but struggled hard to keep
their own women within set boundaries, this was because they
were attempting to use Turkish – or other Oriental – women
to subvert the social system while pretending to liberate them
from their own men. Native women were seen as the
repositories of traditional or ancestral values, with whom it was
necessary to collaborate in order to establish a Western-style
family life, which was evidently superior to all others.

Women travellers, however, were sometimes torn between
identifying with their race or their gender. Treated by the local
people as though they were men, usually spending considerably more time talking to men than women, they often
seemed to be seeing women through male eyes. On other
occasions, when they did visit women at home and found them
apparently bored, imprisoned and ignorant, it may have
reminded them too much of their own domestic situation. As

will be seen later they frequently described the women they met as children, in the same way that men did. Women who stayed in a country for a longer period or worked as missionaries, for example, sometimes became sympathetic to the problems of poor women. However, they failed to recognize the real causes of the problems, which were frequently lack of clean water and medical help rather than the ignorance and immorality of women. In just the same way in Europe the middle class tended to brand all working-class women as bad mothers and housewives because of their alleged gin-drinking, moral depravity and inability to manage money.

Feminists were as guilty of Eurocentric and colonialist attitudes as anyone else, and when Arab women began to be involved in nationalist struggles European women were often quick to point out how wrong they were. For example:

O ye women, so splendidly, so nobly fighting for freedom, forget for the time all political strife. You have a task infinitely more important than the self-government of your country. Forget everything save wiping out polygamy, this hideous blotch besmirching your country's good name. (Trowbridge Hall, *Egypt in Silhouette*, p. 64)

Reading the mass of generalizations written about women in North Africa and the Middle East one is struck by the easy acceptance of what local men told travellers about women, the facile value judgements and preconceived notions and the refusal to recognize the enormous variety of situations in which women lived, apart from the obvious town and rural differences, or the most glaring differences of wealth. Sarah Graham-Brown has commented on this as follows:

As will become apparent, there were many variations in women's social and economic roles, according to their age and class and to the particular circumstances of their own families and communities. The public/private dichotomy often employed in descriptions of these roles may not prove to be the most illuminating way of seeing them. As anthropologist Roxan Dusen suggests, it may be more useful to examine what she calls the 'social horizons' of particular groups of women. These horizons were set by a variety of factors, most importantly by economic circumstances and by social constraints imposed according to male notions of what constituted proper behaviour for women in that community. (*Images of Women*, p. 86)

When travellers met a woman who did not conform to their idea of submissive, Oriental women they usually reported it as an exception that proved the rule, in much the same way that men dealt with what they called 'deviating' women in Europe (in reality the majority). A good example appears in the letters of M. Michaud and M. Poujoulat from Egypt in 1830–1. Entering a village home, a fellah (peasant) woman was heard shouting in a rage at her husband, and this voice of authority in a Muslim woman was considered most surprising, since the Koran says that women must be obedient! However, the interpreter was reassuring, stating that this 'was not the rule, but the exception to the rule; Egyptian women in general are as submissive as slaves' (*Correspondence d'Orient*, p. 83).

In the recent play *M. Butterfly*, the opera star, Song, asks why women's roles are always played by men in the Peking Opera, and then gives the reply: 'Because only a man knows how a woman is supposed to act.' Men have always known how women should act, different women, different styles, but determined by men, whether in the East or the West. Reading travellers' descriptions of the life of 'Oriental' women in the last century the most striking thing is the high level of hypocrisy about women's position in the West. Whatever the external appearances and different ways of organizing the family, how great were the differences in women's lives in the two regions – allowing for the different economic and political situations? Was Christianity what made the situation of European women so different, recognizing – as many authors claimed – woman's real worth? Before reading what writers had to say about Oriental women, we should first look at the position of women in Europe and the ideas about woman's nature that travellers carried with them.

With the bourgeois ideology of the nineteenth century increasingly confining women to the home, an effort was made to achieve a neat opposition of male/female, public/private spheres, by invoking woman's maternal 'instinct' to define her whole being, which not only made her nurture children but also gave her a moral influence by virtue of her loving and self-sacrificing nature. Many men would have found it easy to agree with the painter Delacroix when he wrote in his diary after his visit to Algeria: 'It is beautiful! Just like the time of Homer! The woman in the gynaeceum looking after the children, spinning wool or embroidering beautiful materials. This is woman as I understand her' (quoted by Assia Djebar in *Femmes d'Alger dans leur appartement*).

Of course, to maintain this structure of separate (but equal) spheres throughout society was not possible – it would always remain an ideal. Neither was it desirable for the economy, since women's labour was vital in the workforce, however much this was resented and opposed by men in some trades. Nevertheless, the long discussions about woman's position could ignore this as long as the basic structure was not threatened. As the century proceeded the idea of the two spheres was increasingly under threat, and Mary Poovey (*Uneven Developments*) has used 'border cases' to demonstrate the challenges and changes which were occurring in England. In the meantime, however, many middle-class women lived unnaturally restricted and secluded lives, and many put enormous energy into charitable endeavours. This was acceptable since it took place in the wider 'domestic' sphere and they did not receive money for their labour, rather it reflected their self-sacrificing nature. Less fortunate sisters became impoverished and were forced into low-paid posts as governesses, for example, where their position was ambiguous. Indeed, this is one of the border cases which Mary Poovey uses to demonstrate the threat to the binary structure.

Separate but equal was how the two spheres were portrayed. Rarely could this have been done in such a misogynist way as in Pierre-Joseph Proudhon's writing in 1846:

As for me, the more I think about it, the less I can justify the destiny of woman outside the family and the household. Between harlot or housewife (housewife I say, and not servant) I see no halfway point: what is so humiliating about this alternative? In what respect is the woman's role, charged with the conduct of the household and everything that pertains to consumption and to savings, inferior to the man's role, whose own function is to direct the workshop, that is to say, the government of production and exchange? (Susan Groag Bell and Karen M. Offen, *Women, the Family, and Freedom: Documents,* p. 191)

However, many women accepted this definition, for there was a strong belief among the middle and upper classes in woman's special mission. When travellers in North Africa and the Middle East told the people they met about the perfect equality to be found in Western marriages they may have believed it at the time or were making a generalization based on a limited experience. In reality, much of the criticism they levelled at the societies they visited could also be levelled at their own.

Women in nineteenth-century England were considered to be a problem. First, they did not always accept their allotted place in society and, secondly, there were just too many of them for a society based on monogamous marriage, the sanctity of the home and dependent women. The actual situation was far removed from this. In 1849, Henry Mayhew had drawn attention to the incidence of prostitution among needlewomen in London, pointing to low wages and destitution as the cause. At a meeting of about 1,000 slop-workers which he organized that year, Lord Ashley and Mr Sidney Herbert (reformers) walked on to the platform unknown to Mayhew and announced that emigration was the answer to the problem. Apparently, there was an excess of 500,000 women in England and Wales and, fortunately, exactly the same number too few in the colonies (E. P. Thompson in the introduction to *The Unknown Mayhew,* p. 25). The census in 1851 showed that at age thirty 25 per cent of women in England and Wales were unmarried and 2 million out of 6 million in Britain were self-supporting. (It also showed that at age thirty almost the same percentage of men were unmarried.) The 'problem' was discussed by W. R. Greg in 1862 in his essay 'Why Are Women Redundant?' These women, he argued, were 'the evil and anomaly to be cured' and his cure too was the removal of 500,000 to the colonies, which would eliminate 'surplus' women. As late as 1913 Sir Almoth E. Wright, a staunch anti-feminist, was recommending 'surplus' women to emigrate or move down into a humbler social class and earn a living (*The Unexpurgated Case Against Woman Suffrage*, p. 70).

W. R. Greg had suggested that emigration would also solve the problem of prostitution, which was widespread in Europe. In his study of the London poor in the 1880s, Charles Booth reported on this:

Mingled with the more regular members of this varied group of women, there are in each class some who take to the life occasionally when circumstances compel: tailoresses or dressmakers, for example, who return to their trade in busy times; girls from low neighbour-hoods who eke out a living in this way; or poor women, neglected wives, or widows, under pressure of poverty; or worst of all, such as are driven to this course by a bad husband or a bad father. (*Charles Booth's London* (ed. Fried and Elman), pp. 193–4)

In France also, female impoverishment plus the double sexual standards for men and women, the demand that men should come into marriage 'experienced', created a huge prostitution industry. Working-class and immigrant women from the colonies were supposed to ensure the purity of bourgeois wives and daughters.

In his novel *One of Our Conquerors* (1891), George Meredith depicted an 'Oriental Rajah' on a visit to London walking around the streets at night. He remarked that, 'Monogamic societies present a decent visage and a hideous rear.' The 'hideous rear' consisted of many levels, from the fashionable prostitute who was carefully secluded and did not solicit, to the poorest and most degraded. In the following passage, Dr Iwan Bloch, a sexologist of the late nineteenth century, is describing drinking and cabaret saloons in Germany and France where 'secret prostitution' took place:

by their mysterious-looking interior; by the heavy curtains, which produce semi-obscurity; by small very discreet *chambres séparées*, lighted by little coloured lanterns and with erotic pictures on the walls; by their Spanish walls and their enormous couches – [they] obtain the appearance of small lupanars. (*The Sexual Life of Our Time*, p. 341)

They might also be said to obtain the appearance of harems in the popular imagination.

The bourgeois ideology, then, relied on turning a blind eye to real life. Double sexual standards acknowledged men's 'stronger passions' but denied women's sexuality except as a passive partner in marriage or as an outlet for men in prostitutes. Iwan Bloch referred to prostitution as 'a haunting shadow [which] accompanies the so-called conventional marriage – a shadow growing ever larger the more strictly, exclusively, and narrowly the idea of the "marriage" is conceived' (op. cit., p. 202).

Given that women were not merely passive sexual beings and that, once married, they were constrained on all sides, by the law and society's attitudes, to remain in their marriage, there were many casualties. From the beginning of the nineteenth century the science of gynaecology developed as a separate medical specialism, defined in 1849 as 'The doctrine of the nature and diseases of women' (Ornella Moscucci, *The Science of Woman*, p. 7). This new specialism treated (and treats) woman as a special case because of her reproductive role and helped to legitimate views of different roles in society for men and women. Increasingly the 'casualties' were attended by these male specialist gynaecologists and by psychiatrists. Medical men were aware that women often demonstrated sexual passion at what they termed 'inappropriate' times, such as childbirth, or during depression. This was considered to be an illness requiring treatment, for if mothers or unmarried women were allowed to act as assertive sexual beings, then monogamous marriage was in danger. In the middle of the century there was a great debate in the medical profession over the use of chloroform in childbirth, one of the reasons being that under its influence women were sometimes excited into sexual passion. W. Tyler Smith, who later helped to found the Obstetrics Society, had this to say:

I may venture to say, that to the women of this country the bare possibility of having feelings of such a kind excited and manifested in outward uncontrollable actions, would be more shocking even to anticipate, than the endurance of the last extremity of physical pain. (Quoted by Mary Poovey, op. cit., p. 31)

Post-natal depression, called puerperal insanity, accounted for 7–10 per cent of female asylum admissions at times in the nineteenth century, and here again physicians were shocked to find women flaunting their sexuality. Menstruation and the menopause were also diagnosed as problems by many members of the male medical profession, for female sexuality was regarded as an illness to be cured. Dr William Acton in the mid-century gave his views on woman's sexual nature: 'The majority of women (happily for them) are not very much troubled with sexual feelings of any kind. What men are habitually, women are only exceptionally' (quoted by Peter Gay in *The Bourgeois Experience*, vol. I, p. 153).

The exceptions were obviously mad, according to physicians like Dr Acton, although the cures they recommended might suggest that the madness was on their side. W. Tyler Smith, for example, had a cure for sexual desire in the menopause: injections of iced water into the rectum, introduction of ice into the vagina, and the application of leeches to the labia and cervix. Menstruation was considered to be disruptive to the brain and doctors recommended delaying it by keeping teenage girls in the nursery, making them take cold baths, avoid feather beds and novels, eat no meat and wear drawers. In 1851 Edward J. Tilt stated that delayed menstruation was 'the principal cause of the pre-eminence of English women, in vigour of constitution, soundness of judgement, and . . . rectitude of moral principle' (Elaine Showalter, *The Female Malady*, p. 75). When the patient was not considered to be too serious, various of the above treatments were used, but a more serious case would be put in an asylum as well. One member of the Obstetrical Society of London in the 1860s became convinced that masturbation was the cause of madness and therefore practised clitoridectomy 'to help women to control themselves' (ibid.). However, he was not alone in performing this treatment, as the following horrific story shows. In 1894, in Ohio, a nervous seven-year-old girl under treatment for masturbation was finally subjected to clitoridectomy. The operation was 'a success': she stopped masturbation, for as she said, 'You know, there is nothing there now' (Peter Gay, op. cit., vol. I, p. 304). In the United States and Britain in the 1880s gynaecologists happily removed healthy ovaries to deal with such conditions as incipient insanity and epilepsy (Ornella Moscucci, op. cit., p. 105). With attitudes like this around it is not surprising that reactions to 'Oriental sensuality' were so strong and mixed.

Images of madwomen were frequent in Victorian novels and in the later decades of the century anorexia, hysteria and nervous diseases were increasing. Women confined to bed and 'nervous' women were also familiar figures in novels and everyday life. Rest cures, rather than a more active and fulfilling life, were the recommended solution, in fact some members of the medical profession stated that it was *because* women tried to break out of their ordained roles that they became hysterical. In addition, physicians were convinced that the instability of the female nervous and reproductive systems made them more vulnerable to derangement than men. It was widely accepted that moral depravity, wilfulness, and egoism were common to all hysterical women. The following assessment by physician Sir George Savage is a typical nineteenth-century opinion: 'The characteristic of all hysterical cases is the tendency to laziness, want of will, getting into bad habits (etc)' (quoted by Michael Clark in 'The Rejection of Psychological Approaches to Mental Disorder in Late-Nineteenth-Century British Psychiatry').

The effect of an enforced rest cure and the instruction to 'pull herself together' on a woman who wanted 'congenial work, with excitement and change' was tragically depicted by Charlotte Perkins Gilman in a short novel, *The Yellow Wallpaper*, based on her own experience in America with a 'nerve specialist' – who advised her to devote herself to domestic work and never attempt writing again. Charlotte Brontë at one point in her life was prevented from writing because of domestic tasks and developed a hysterical form of near-blindness. Florence Nightingale also suffered a period of depression and in her autobiographical novel *Cassandra* she described a society where mothers and daughters were confined in 'the prison which is called a family' (quoted by Elaine Showalter, op. cit., p. 63).

Many women in Britain, France and the USA were working for money, whatever the current views on the matter. It was accepted that working-class women could work outside the home – indeed, the lifestyle of the upper and middle classes depended on this. In England, domestic service was the largest employer of women in Victorian times, and both there and in France the service had been feminized. However, if a lady was forced to earn her own livelihood it was universally considered to be a misfortune, and she would have a hard struggle. If she wanted to work simply through choice, the struggle would be even harder. When the young Charlotte Brontë sent some of her verse to the poet Robert Southey for an opinion in 1837 he admitted she had talent but discouraged her from continuing:

Literature cannot be the business of a woman's life, and it ought not to be. . . . The daydreams in which you habitually indulge are likely to induce a distempered state of mind; and in proportion as all the ordinary uses of the world seem to you flat and unprofitable, you will be unfitted for them without becoming fitted for anything else. (quoted by Rebecca Fraser in *Charlotte Brontë*, pp. 109–10)

When Charlotte published *Jane Eyre* in 1847 it had an immediate success, but dissenting voices soon began to point out that the heroine did not display the characteristics of the feminine ideal. Jane Eyre was proud and showed feelings of passion and anger, none of which was acceptable in an age dominated by the Evangelicals. At this point it was not known that the author was a woman, for it was published under the name of Currer Bell. Certainly, many male writers had their work censored for 'offending public morals' with their depiction of women and interaction between men and women. In the year 1857, Flaubert was charged with this offence in France in connection with *Madame Bovary* and Charles Baudelaire for his poems *Les Fleurs du Mal*. In the same year the Obscene Publications Act was introduced in Britain. In the 1870s and 1880s Thomas Hardy had novel after novel edited or rejected: *Far from the Madding Crowd* had lines deleted by the editor, and no magazine would accept *Tess of the d'Urbervilles* in its unexpurgated form. An episode in *The Mayor of Casterbridge*, when a man sold his wife, particularly shocked Victorian sensibilities. Critics accused him of passing the bounds of credible fiction. However, wife-selling did take place in nineteenth-century England, frequently in cattle markets, and popular custom often demanded that the woman be led there in a halter. (Samuel Pyeatt Menefee in *Wives for Sale* documents 300 *recorded* cases between 1800 and 1900.)

The list of books which 'offended public morals' in Britain was long, and the power of the circulating libraries in determining what people read was enormous. What 'offended public morals' in the works mentioned was the depiction of women characters who were a threat to the ideal of the angel in the house – women who were strong-minded, independent, passionate. Concern was frequently expressed about the effect of such books on girls at the age of puberty, and in fact one of the suggestions for delaying menstruation, referred to earlier, was for girls to avoid reading novels.

However, if women succeeded in getting their writing published, they could earn the same as men did – although the use of male pseudonyms seems to have been necessary from the 1840s. Payment for a novel could be the equivalent of a governess's annual salary, while these were so low that an advertisement for an *unpaid* nursery governess was answered by 300 women in the 1860s (Josephine E. Butler, *The Education and Employment of Women*, p. 3). It was not until the 1890s that employment opportunities for middle-class women in Britain (or France) began to widen. For much of the century, therefore, many young ladies might have identified with this description of their life in 1865:

here I sit, with health, strength, and knowledge, and able to do nothing, *nothing* – at the risk of breaking my mother's heart! . . . here am I, able and willing, only longing to task myself to the uttermost, yet tethered down to the merest mockery of usefulness by conventionalities. I am a young lady forsooth! (Charlotte M. Yonge, *The Clever Woman of the Family*, p. 3).

Educated many young ladies may have been, but their education was usually confined to 'suitable' subjects and their outlook on the world could be very limited. If they came from a strict religious family, their situation might be even worse – reading would be censored, as would works of art and any forms of entertainment. In France, there was an ongoing struggle to break the clerical influence over women, and girls' lycées were established to this end in 1880, but again with a restricted syllabus, suitable for a bourgeois lady.

Victorian travellers were inclined to believe that if the life of a middle-class European, Christian woman was at one end of a continuum, then the life of the equivalent Oriental, Muslim woman was at the other. Given that the life of the latter was not the *dolce far niente* that they described and that that of the former was under considerable restraints until the end of the century, they were not as far apart as people liked to stress. Poor women in both countries worked hard both inside and outside the home, and the fact that one wore a veil did not necessarily make her a greater 'drudge'. Women were no more passive victims in one society than they were in the other.

When Lady Mary Montague was pressed by the women in a Turkish bath to take off her clothes and join them, she undid her blouse to show them her corset. This led them to believe, she said, that she was imprisoned in a machine which could only be opened by her husband. Both groups of women could see each other as prisoners – and of course they were both right.

Few travellers to the Middle East or North Africa ever found themselves in a position where they could really communicate with women living there, and even fewer had any interest in learning how *their* society was perceived by the people they were observing. Very soon after the Napoleonic invasion of Egypt, the chronicler al-Gabarti wrote down his reactions to the events which had so drastically disturbed the harmony of daily life. Conquering armies have never been remembered for the consideration they showed to women – on the contrary they usually leave a legacy of rape and prostitution. Al-Gabarti reported the effect of the army's presence in Cairo:

During this year [May 1800–May 1801] local morals began to be affected by licentiousness. The French women who came with the army went about the town with their faces uncovered and wearing brightly coloured silk dresses and scarves. They rode about on horses and donkeys wearing cashmere shawls around their shoulders; they galloped through the streets laughing and joking with their guides and with the people of the lower class.

This indecent freedom pleased the badly brought up women of
Cairo, and as the French were proud of their submission to women
and lavished gifts upon them, the women began to enter into
relations with them. At first they were quite circumspect, but after
the Cairo revolt when Boulaq had been taken by assault, French men
began to seize the women and girls who pleased them, dress them in
the style of their country and make them change their ways.

From then on licentiousness spread rapidly throughout the town;
many women, who were drawn by a love of riches or by the gallantry
of the French, followed the example of the women of Boulaq. The
French in fact held all the money in the country, and seemed to be
entirely submissive to the women, who might sometimes even hit
them with a slipper. Many Frenchmen asked for the daughters of
Cairo notables, who would agree to the match either through avarice
or because they wanted protectors in the army. Although the French
were obliged to make the two professions of faith, this cost them
nothing for they were people of no religion. (Quoted by Charles Vial
in *Le Personnage de la femme dans le roman et la nouvelle en Égypte
de 1914 à 1960*, pp. 4–5)

What disturbed al-Gabarti of course was the fact that
French soldiers were corrupting Egyptian women, drawing
them out from their traditionally secluded life, encouraging
ideas of freedom. Whether European or Arab, men have
always tried to control their own women. However, the
passage also demonstrates how French soldiers were imposing
their own values on Egyptian society – and certainly not from
any desire to improve the position of women there. It also
places European allegations about the immorality endemic to
Islam in a different light. It is easy enough to rape a woman
and then call her immoral.

By the time Lucie Duff Gordon went to live in Egypt in
1862, Egyptians had been given ample opportunity to observe
the English and French. Coming from a radical background in
England and having developed a marked sympathy for the
Arabs, she passed many hours in conversation with the people
in Luxor. She discovered that what most shocked Egyptian
men about the English was their treatment of women. Not
because they allowed them too much freedom, but because of
the way Englishmen talked about women among themselves,

their hard and unkind treatment of their wives and women in general. In a letter home she wrote:

How astonished Europeans would be to hear Omar's real opinion of their conduct to women. He mentioned some Englishman who had divorced his wife and made her frailty public. You should have seen him spit on the ground in abhorrence. Here it is quite blackguard not to forfeit the money and take all the blame in a divorce. (*Letters from Egypt*, p. 176)

While both European and Arab men believed that women were the weaker sex, the judgements they made differed:

It is impossible to conceive how startling it is to a Christian to hear the rules of morality applied with perfect impartiality to both sexes, and to hear Arabs who know our manners talk of the English being 'jealous' and 'hard upon their women'. Any unchastity is wrong and *haram* (unlawful) but equally so in men and women. Seleem Effendi talked in this strain, and seemed to incline to greater indulgence to women on the score of their ignorance and weakness. (Ibid., pp. 135–6)

Lucie Duff Gordon was careful to emphasize that this conversation related to Arabs and may not have been true of Turks. It may very well not have been true of all Arabs, but it is worth remembering the position of 'the fallen woman' in English society.

In his book *Sketches of Persia* (1845), Sir John Malcolm used a dialogue form to demonstrate how English and Persian men viewed the way the other treated their women. He began the dialogue by making 'a violent attack' on the condition of women in Persia by comparison with the 'civilized nations of Europe'. Conceding that legitimate wives and daughters did have rights, he asked about the fate of the children of slaves and other members of the harem. The Persian, in reply, asked what happened to illegitimate children in England and quoted a book by Meerza Aboo Talib, who had travelled in England and reported that 'a great proportion of your females and their offspring are in a much more degraded state than any in our country'. 'But perhaps', said the Persian, 'Aboo Talib has exaggerated, which travellers are in the habit of doing.'

The conversation continued. Sir John Malcolm deplored the fact that Persian women could not acquire 'that knowledge of the world which is necessary to enable them to perform their duties'. The Persian took over:

'I do not exactly know,' said he, 'what you mean by a knowledge of the world; nor do I distinctly understand the benefits you expect them to derive from such knowledge. We consider that loving and obeying their husbands, giving proper attention to their children, and their domestic duties, are the best occupations for females.'

As Sir John Malcolm replied, this made them either slaves of their husband's pleasure, or drudges performing the work of the house. This is quite true, but it is not a description of women's duties that many European men would have disagreed with.

While travelling in North Africa, Matilda Betham Edwards went out walking with some young French women she had met. Their mother requested that she see them safely home, for it was not *comme il faut* for them to walk around the streets alone with so many officers in the town.

Here was a parody on European emancipation of thought! We were pitying the seclusion and trammels of Moorish ladies, and found that young Frenchwomen of twenty-three and twenty-four are not trusted alone beyond their own garden! Surely an Arab satirist might make something of such a state of things! (*A Winter with the Swallows*, p. 116)

Another traveller, John Reynell Morell, heard much spoken against the Arabs by the French in Algeria, but warned his readers about blindly accepting such attacks.

In receiving these and other statements of French writers about the Arabs, it is necessary to observe great caution, as it is in the interest of the conquerors to represent their victims in the most odious light possible, in order to justify their own injustice and cruelty. (*Algeria*, p. 303)

Finally, the French scholar Volney, who set out on his journey to Egypt and Syria at the end of the eighteenth century, spent more time preparing himself than most travellers. In order to understand the nature of the population of a country, he said, it was necessary to live there, learn their language and practise their customs. But this was still not sufficient for travellers to acquire a real understanding.

Not only must they contend with all the prejudices that they will encounter, but they must overcome those that they bring with them: the heart is partial, habits are strong, facts are insidious and illusion is easy. The observer must therefore be cautious but not faint-hearted, and the readers who can only see through the eyes of the intermediary, must keep an eye on both the judgement of the guide and their own judgement. (C.-F. Volney, *Voyage en Égypte et en Syrie*, p. 399)

Few travellers have ever been able to fulfil the first list of requirements, much less the second. To face up to the prejudices that they brought with them, was not one of the helpful hints given to nineteenth-century travellers, and this anthology shows just how little most authors attempted the task. As readers we can follow Volney's advice, however, by keeping an eye on the judgement of both the authors and of ourselves.

Chapter 1

'ALL WE HAVE WILLED,
OR HOPED, OR DREAMED'

When I first started reading for this anthology I was struck by the number of people who recalled the *Arabian Nights* stories when they first began their journey. I started making a note of these references but soon gave up, for that would make an anthology in itself. References to stories from the *Thousand and One Nights* appear in many nineteenth-century novels, as do general allusions to things 'Oriental' (Rana Kabbani, *Europe's Myths of Orient*). The image of the flamboyant, erotic and cruel Orient was applied indiscriminately to a large geographical area. In Mrs Gaskell's novel *Cranford*, for example, the arrival of Mr Peters from India caused great excitement in the village, for he told 'more wonderful stories than Sinbad the Sailor' and was considered to be as good as an Arabian Night for an evening's entertainment. Reading travellers' accounts I was surprised that they recalled the *Arabian Nights* not just when they arrived in Baghdad but wherever they found themselves in the Middle East or North Africa – whether a city, a village or the middle of a desert. Indeed, the images from childhood were so strong, as was the desire to escape from the reality of their own stifling society, that other travellers found the atmosphere and characters of these stories in Uganda, India, Yugoslavia (Dea Birkett, *Spinsters Abroad*, p. 45).

The following extracts are a very small sample of one idea of the East that travellers took with them when they set out on their journeys. The extract from the novel *Askaros Kassis the Copt* (published in 1870) was written by a former US consul-general in Cairo who claimed that his official position and long residence there gave him special knowledge. Although this piece is spoken in the novel by an American visitor to Cairo, in the preface to the novel de Leon himself records that 'The realities of the East are stranger than the dreams of the West.'

I remember wishing as a child that the 'Arabian Nights' were all true; little dreaming how I should one day discover nothing to be truer than poetic fiction. For, as Browning says, –

> All we have willed, or hoped, or dreamed, of good shall exist,
> Not its semblance, but itself;

and I was no sooner in Algeria than I seemed to hear story after story added to the Thousand and One, all as new, as true, and almost as wonderful.

Matilda Betham Edwards, *A Winter with the Swallows*, 1867, p. 1

The reader, perhaps, is weary of the frequent reference in travellers' tales to the popular work just named, but in truth it is not easy to avoid it. In a Mahommedan city – such is the conservatism of the Moslem character – you are at every turn brought into contact with the facts of the 'Arabian Nights'. Almost every object you see illustrates some story, or clears up some difficulty. . . .

In fact, you are surrounded by the properties and dramatis personae of the 'Thousand and One Nights.' The old familiar figures of your fancy have become realities, bringing with them recollections of how and where you first made their acquaintance: of the shady side of the haycock, where you first met Camaralzaman and Badoura; of the nook in the shrubbery where the blackbird found you deep in the story of the Magic Horse, and never suspected you were alive till you turned the leaf; even of that sick-room, which to this day connects the adventures of Sinbad the Sailor with the flavour of arrow-root, where you forgot that there were such things as sunshine and merriment out of doors, over the beneficent pages of the schoolboy's Bible.

John Ormsby, *Autumn Rambles in North Africa*, 1864, pp. 252, 254

The young girl turned her bright eyes, full of animated interest, upon the elder maiden, as she exclaimed:

'Oh, aunt! is not this wonderful? Does it not look to you like a page torn from the Arabian Nights? Why, these are the very people there described – the one-eyed water-carrier, the veiled woman, the old story-teller under the tree, and the wicked black man from the Hareem!

Edwin de Leon, *Askaros Kassis the Copt*, 1870, p. 18

Here lived all those whom His Highness delighted to honour. Here was the great family of the Seraglio. What memories may be recalled! what wondrous scenes have here been enacted! what visions of lovely daughters of the Caucasus and the Archipelago, the mountain, the desert, and the sea! Mussulmans, Christians, Jews and others, won in battle by Pashas, presented by Princes, or stolen by corsairs, pass like shadows under those silvery domes. To get within the gates of the Old Seraglio may almost be said to be a dream of one's life after reading the 'Arabian Nights' description of the homes of Caliphs and Sultans.

William J. J. Spry, *Life on the Bosphorous*, 1895, p. 10

Yes, I was in Bagdad, the fairy city of boyhood's dreams, the glittering home of pomp and pleasure, where the fair Zobeide dwelt in a palace with spangled floors and marble stairs with golden balustrades; where there was a riot of broidered sofas, damask curtains, silk tapestry, purple robes from the most famous looms of the East; where a joyous group of bejeweled dancing girls were wont, to the sound of harp and lute and dulcimer, to carol away, with voices as melodious as that of Israfel, the cares and ennui of their pleasure-sated mistress.

Willingly I yielded myself to the hynoptic influence of the *spiritus loci*. In fancy I saw Aladdin with his wonderful lamp; the one-eyed calenders as they told their fascinating tales; the fishermen as they deluded the heavy-witted jinn; Harun-al-Rashid and Jaffer as they wandered under their double-collared cloak through the somber streets of the capital; the radiant homes of wealth and luxury, which gleamed with the subdued light of a myriad golden lamps and reechoed with the heart-easing strains of sweet music and the gladsome voices of midnight revelry.

Reverend J. A. Zahm, *From Berlin to Bagdad and Babylon*, 1922,
p. 428

When Gertrude Bell first went to Persia as a young woman, she wrote in a similar vein and was drawn to the 'spirit of romance' for which she was searching and which she discovered there. When her early account was reprinted in 1928 with the title *Persian Pictures*, E. Denison Ross wrote in a preface of the magic influence which the *Arabian Nights* 'exercises over us all'. It was not until later in her life, he said, that Gertrude Bell was obliged 'to treat these picturesque and romantic denizens of Oriental towns and deserts as ordinary mortals'. The following extract from a letter to a cousin is from her early trip in 1892.

What else can I give you but fleeting impressions caught and hardened out of all knowing? I can tell you of a Persian merchant in whose garden, stretching all up the mountain side, we spent a long day, from dawn to sunset, breakfasting, lunching, teaing on nothing but Persian foods. He is noted for his hospitality; every evening parties of friends arrive unexpectedly 'he goes out, entertains them,' said the Persian who told me about it, 'spreads a banquet before them and relates to them stories half through the night. Then cushions are brought and carpeted mattresses and they lie down in one of the guest houses in the garden and sleep till dawn when they rise and repair to the bath in the village.' Isn't it charmingly like the Arabian Nights! but that is the charm of it all and it has none of it changed.

The Letters of Gertrude Bell, 1947, p. 32

The next two pieces by French authors at the end of the century tackle the idea of 'Oriental' women head on. The first reflects the talk of the barrack-room, while the second warns European men of the inaccessibility of these exotic beings.

The Kasbah!
    This magic word intrigued me when I was a child. It pursued me over the years, evoking so much mystery, such hazy and disturbing images. When it was spoken it had a special sound, and whenever it was mentioned by my father's orderlies they always laughed and winked in a special way. The Kasbah! I only knew that bloody fights between Arabs and soldiers took place there at night, and also that women were to be found there. Which women? I had no idea. Undoubtedly they were unnatural creatures, quite different from all

other women. I imagined a den of danger and enchantment, straight
from the Arabian Nights. . . .

                                          L'Algérie de nos jours, 1893, p. 28

It remains for us to say something of the women, and what we are
going to say will not conform to the ideas held in France about
Oriental women. Whatever has been written about the Orient,
French men happily believe that they will meet the famous
odalisques, as beautiful as the morning star and just waiting to be
loved. The European man thinks that he will find in Africa beautiful
palaces with a balcony over the door to the street, where a charming
prisoner will be waiting for a gallant French knight in shining armour
to rescue her. They forget that the harems are well guarded and that
the *moushrabias* at the windows make it impossible to communicate,
even to exchange glances.

                                          Léon Michel, *Tunis*, 1883, p. 171

Robert Hitchens published an account of his trip to the Holy
Land in 1913, a romantic over-blown description of the magic,
fairy-tale scenes he encountered, with frequent allusions to
veiling and mystery. Here, he is quite specific about the desires
of European men for 'exotic' women.

Again and again, as I wandered alone in the oasis, where the women
in dim purple and black, their heads bound by red and orange
handkerchiefs, their breasts covered with masses of beads and
amulets, glide noiselessly by on naked feet, carrying between their
lips those wonderful mauve roses of Jericho, I thought of Haiti, of
villages under the Blue Mountains of Jamaica, where life always
seems a dream, at least to the Western man.

                                    Robert Hitchens, *The Holy Land*, 1913, p. 185.

In 1984, *In Search of the Forty Days Road* by Michael Asher
was published, an account of his extraordinary journey across
the desert in Sudan. He describes how he met the 'survivors of
a lost world', and as always one wonders at the use of this
term. Lost to whom? Did they know they were lost? However,

the following extract is an interesting analysis of his feelings about the Arabs before he set off to Sudan, his realization that these images were a creation of his own culture, and his subsequent discovery that the desert camel-men in fact corresponded quite closely to his earlier imaginings. In this, as in earlier books by men for whom the desert held a great fascination, women appeared infrequently, merely to give a little colour to the desert. In these first musings, however, we are left only with an image of 'trains of women in vampire-like masks' encountered in the streets of London.

When I first went to the Sudan, I never dreamed that I should find there the survivors of a lost world. I thought I knew the Arabs: that word lay in the sump of my memory, where it had been since as a child I had read the simplified *Arabian Nights*, as a youth I had seen *Lawrence of Arabia*, and as a young man I had read the poetry of James Elroy Flecker. I did not know, however, that the images which these romantic works conveyed were composites, created through the rose-tinted glasses of my own culture. They had little connection with the real figures which loomed up dimly behind the celluloid strip and the romantic phrases ...

As I settled down in Dongola, I saw this world from my door every day. It seemed a place of mystery, fearsome, infinite, as alien to men as the surface of the moon. Yet I knew that men lived there, for I had seen camel herds, great mobs of loose-limbed beasts crawling over the flat sands like giant insects. In their wake came fierce-looking men who rode masterfully on enormous bull camels, cracking rawhide whips and chanting odd songs: the breath of an alien domain. The lives of these camel-men were quite different from those of the river tribesmen amongst whom I lived. They did not shun the desert, for their lives were centred on the well and the camel, lives of constant movement over the vast plains of their homelands.

When I learnt that these camel-men were 'Arabs', the word immediately triggered off a complex series of associations in my mind. There were memories, recently formed, of hordes of white-robed figures sweeping, not over the desert, but along the streets of London in summer, wearing spotless white headcloths, and followed by trains of women in vampire-like masks. These images were coupled with vague pictures of oil derricks, concrete palaces and squadrons of gauche American cars. But these memories had submerged a far older stratum of associations – the vivid childhood characters of the *Arabian Nights*, mysterious, hawkish men in furled turbans with viciously curved daggers, camel-riders, their faces swathed in white cloth, carrying ancient and ungainly flintlocks, black tents in the desert, dim figures moving beneath the palms at an oasis – ghosts which still lurked in the darker recesses of my memory. These ghosts, I thought, belonged to a world created by childish fantasy, a world which, if it had ever existed at all, had long since faded.

I knew that the other, latter-day world did exist in the Sudan. There were rich merchants who flew regularly to Paris and London, just as there were diesel lorries, TV, telephones and discotheques in the country. I soon realized, however, that these things were as alien to some sections of the population as cornflakes and pork pie, and with delight and amazement I discovered that these desert camel-men of the Sudan seemed to correspond much more nearly to the earlier stratum of my imagination.

Michael Asher, *In Search of the Forty Days Road*, 1984, pp. 18–19, 29–30

Over the years, travellers to the Orient have set out in search of many things in order to escape from reality. Charles Payton went to North Africa to find the simple life and a health cure, while Marius Bernard described the attractions of Algiers in overtly sexual terms. Evelyn Waugh called his first travel book *Labels*, 'for the reason that all the places I visited are already fully labelled'. How much his description of widows on cruises reflects their state of mind, and how much his sense of humour, is a matter of conjecture.

I had longed to look on Oriental barbarism; to squat cross-legged and smoke the *chibouk* of friendship with the turbaned Muslim; to live for awhile in some land where postmen, tax-gatherers, and telegraph boys should 'cease from troubling' – where railways and Hansom cabs should be replaced by camels and dromedaries – and, above all, where I could bask in almost perpetual sunshine, and be relieved for a restful space from all fear of bronchitis, rheumatism, and catarrh.

Charles A. Payton, *Moss from a Rolling Stone*, 1879, p. 1

Algiers! Such a musical word, like the murmur of the waves against the white sand of the beach; a name as sweet as the rippling of the breeze in the palm trees of the oases! Algiers! So seductive and easy-going, a town to be loved for the deep purity of her sky, the radiant splendour of her turquoise sea, her mysterious smells, the warm breath in which she wraps her visitors like a long caress! A town where everyone is in his element – the artist in love with the colour and light, the scholar who is fascinated by the marvels of nature and the study of man, the philosopher who wishes to study religions and customs, the politician who is inquiring into difficult and compli-cated questions, the archaeologist who is examining the remains of earlier times, the man about town who is drawn by the pleasures and the festivals, and anyone who is bored by the monotony of life and comes to find rest, gaiety, a life of freedom.

Marius Bernard, *D'Alger à Tanger*, n.d., p. 1

These widows, then, read the advertisements of steamship companies and travel bureaux and find there just that assembly of phrases – half poetic, just perceptibly aphrodisiac – which can produce at will in the unsophisticated a state of mild unreality and glamour. 'Mystery, History, Leisure, Pleasure', one of them begins. There is no directly defined sexual appeal. That rosy sequence of association, desert moon, pyramids, palms, sphinx, camels, oasis, priest in high minaret chanting the evening prayer, Allah, Hitchens, Mrs Sheridan, all delicately point the way to sheik, rape, and harem – but the happily dilatory mind does not follow them to this forbidding conclusion; it sees the direction and admires the view from afar. The actual idea of abduction is wholly repugnant – what would the bridge club and the needlework guild say when she returned? – but the inclination of other ideas towards it gives them a sweet and wholly legitimate attraction.

Evelyn Waugh, *Labels*, 1986 (1st edn 1930), pp. 41–2

Almost as frequent as allusions to the *Arabian Nights* in travel books were biblical images. Photographers and artists toured Palestine producing pictures of daily life which were used to illustrate editions of the Bible. Travellers then saw scenes from daily life identical to those in their copy of the Bible, and concluded that life had not changed for the last 2,000 years. Quotations from the Bible about a woman at the well or grinding corn, a man ploughing a field and so on, served to reinforce this idea. Excursions to the Holy Land were organized by Thomas Cook, which enabled visitors to renew their faith and further convince themselves of the superiority of Christianity. Once again, this is a very small selection from a commonplace of Holy Land travel books.

Florence Nightingale set off on a journey on the Nile in 1849 when she was aged twenty-nine. This was a difficult year for her, struggling to find a real purpose to her life without causing offence to her parents. During her stay she developed a strong dislike of Islam. 'What chance is there', she asked, 'for a nation whose religion is enjoyment?' Her very first impressions, however, were sent home soon after her arrival in Alexandria.

Yes, My Dear People, I have set my first footfall in the East, and oh! that I could tell you the new world of old poetry, of Bible images, of light, and life, and beauty which that word opens. My first day in the East, and it has been one of the most striking, I am sure, – one I can never forget through Eternity.

Florence Nightingale, *Letters from Egypt*, 1987 (1st edn 1854), p. 21

Matilda Betham Edwards, who found the *Arabian Nights* in Algeria in the first extract in this chapter, also had childhood Sundays recaptured for her when she went out to the countryside. Walter Harris, recounting his travels in Morocco, produced an amazing description of Bedouin women, intertwining biblical images and romantic fantasy. Sir Frederick Treves, touring Palestine on the eve of the First World War, tried hard to ignore the evidence of change and keep women in the image of Rebecca and Mary. At the same period, Maude Holbach toured the Bible lands and produced an interesting justification for using centuries-old biblical language to describe life there. Kathlyn Rhodes' story for school girls was set in Egypt and published as late as 1937. Despite the fact that they were travelling in a train, the English girl found the 'pictures' outside to be just like the Old Testament.

In the country it is not so much the Arabian nights, as the Bible and the Koran, of which you are reminded. Hundreds of texts that brought little or no meaning as I heard them Sunday after Sunday in my childhood became suddenly new, and true, and beautiful, thus illustrated. The most trifling incident recalls some beautiful pastoral. The most simple feature in a landscape strengthens some familiar, though hitherto imperfect simile.

Matilda Betham Edwards, *A Winter with the Swallows*, 1867, pp. 22–3

A wonderful life these Bedouins live, wandering from place to place, a month here, a year there, a week somewhere else. Passing their days as their ancestors passed it when Rebecca was found at the well, simply pastoral, simply poetical, simply filthy. O dirt, what would artists do without thee? What an addition thou art to the picturesque! Wash the Bedouin lady, undo the tangles of her hair, give her clean clothes and a dress improver, and all her beauty is gone. It is one of the most poetical sights in the world, an Arab 'duar' at nightfall. The sun has set, yet the Eastern sky is a blaze of crimson and silver with the afterglow. Slowly winding their way from the well are the women and girls, bearing on their heads their heavy pitchers. Over the hill-top come the lowing kine and the bleating herds, driven by little boys, who dance along to the music of their reed pipes, not shrill and harsh, but with soft, low-sounding strains. From the 'ghimas' can be heard the sound of the corn-mill as the women sit and turn with never-ceasing arm the heavy stone, while here and there from the encampment a thin coil of blue smoke ascends pillar-like into the breathless air. Glorious must be the life of a Bedouin.

Walter B. Harris, *The Land of an African Sultan*, 1889, p. 56

Looking across the plain from the carriage window, there may not be a modern building in sight. The primitive villages differ probably but little from the village of the days of Christ, if only the kerosene tins would be turned into water jars of earthenware. . . . On the ancient roadway – a mere track of foot-stamped mud – a woman will be riding on a donkey; the outline of her head is very gracious as it is seen through the hood she wears. She might have come from some old Italian picture showing the journeyings of the Saints.

Sir Frederick Treves, *The Land That Is Desolate*, 1913, p. 24

The waters of the Nile were my first introduction to Bible lands, and suddenly, though I had much neglected to study it for many years, Bible language flowed to my lips to express the common scenes of everyday life. No other language seemed to fit the picture! As amid the hills and valleys of Westmorland you are irresistibly impelled to quote the nature-loving poet who dwelt there – as Tennyson's verses best describe the lonely fens of his native Lincolnshire, or Matthew Arnold's the 'city of the dreaming spires' and its adjacent water-ways; so if you have anything of the poet's soul, and learned the Bible in childhood, your spirit will find utterance in Scriptural language in the East – even amid the apparently incongruous surroundings of a crowded Nile pleasure steamer, or a tourist-filled hotel – how much more, then, if you escape into the solitude of the desert, or the lonely shores of the Lake of Galilee!

Maude M. Holbach, *Bible Ways in Bible Lands*, 1912, pp. ix–x

We have at home a big old Bible, with lots of coloured pictures in it, and when I was quite small I used to love looking at them – all the Old Testament characters, Joseph, Abraham, and so on, wearing long robes and riding along very dusty-looking paths on donkeys, while little children, in long garments like night-dresses, ran about and played in narrow streets with stalls on either hand. There were pictures of villages too, with women going to the wells for water, carrying pitchers on their heads, and there was always a very blue sky overhead. Well, the pictures we saw from the windows of the train were just like those in our big illustrated Bible.

Kathlyn Rhodes, *A Schoolgirl in Egypt*, 1937, p. 22

The last piece in this chapter comes from a book published by the Religious Tract Society in 1915. Arthur Copping expressed surprise that Egypt was so Egyptian. In a wonderful moment of concealing from himself the train in which he was travelling, he was able to tell his readers that life was quite unchanged.

My western soul feasted on the romance of the East.
And now Egypt was mine to see.
It was a landscape, not of grass and trees, but of dry mud and greyness, with occasional areas of green crops. It looked like part of another world, and very old. *I had never dreamt to find Egypt so*

Egyptian. Here and there one saw the people, in dark flowing draperies, the men bare-legged. Upright, impassive, and full of grave dignity, they moved slowly in a line along the roads and across the land – strings of men, women, and camels. And certain patriarchs, bearing long staves in their hands, rode on asses, like figures in a dream.

Moreover, the train itself being invisible from the train, there was no sign of modern Western influence. Some of the empty land was faintly coloured with moisture, and the wetting of it was plainly visible as a great national industry. Those picturesque creatures – it was not difficult to realize – were engaged in an occupation as old as history. [my italics]

Arthur E. Copping, *A Journalist in the Holy Land*, 1915, pp. 13–14

When reading these 'descriptions' of people and societies, it is important to remember a point already alluded to in the Introduction – the enormous popularity of travel books in the nineteenth and early twentieth centuries, when people were thirsty for knowledge of 'other peoples'. Sitting at home in Europe reading about the characters from the *Arabian Nights* and the Bible who allegedly populated the countries of the Middle East and North Africa, it was easy to develop a sense of superiority. Oriental women became doubly inferior, by virtue of being both women and Oriental. Such attitudes were of course extended to Asian, African and Latin American women as well, by other travellers.

Chapter 2

HIDDEN MYSTERIES

Arriving in the Orient, travellers were thrilled by the spirit of romance and the impenetrable mysteries. The idea of hidden treasures excites people only as long as they believe that they will find the key to possess them and, if successful, the treasures are as rich as they had believed. The first obstacles which the newly arrived, highly inquisitive traveller en- countered were walls and veils. Given their fantasies concern- ing what lay behind, they quite naturally were frustrated at being excluded – even more so, when they discovered that they, .the would-be observers, were being observed from behind shuttered windows and veils. Many writers became very hostile towards the 'closed societies' in which they found themselves, and developed great theories about the relative merits of Islam and Christianity, of Eastern and Western life, using images of dark prisons to depict the former, and light, open buildings the latter. The veil was used to indicate Islam's particular subordination of women, ignoring the fact that in a number of societies Christian women and houses were indistinguishable from those of Muslims. The following piece, written in 1854, is an example of this type of philosophizing.

An imperfect idea of this antagonism may be given by saying that eastern life is poetry, and western prose. The fascination of the fabulous and the hues of romance will ever gild the battlements of Damascus, and hover round the minarets of Cairo, casting into a stern shade and pallid twilight the dismal machinery of Teutonic and Scandinavian poetry. To the sunshine of imagination, Saladin, Alraschid, and the Mameluke Beyes will ever carry off the palm from Round Tables and the aureole of Roncesvalles. There is a wealth of wonder, a gorgeousness of tint in oriental life and thought, that can never square with doublet, point lace, trunk-hose, or inexpressibles.

Chivalry and gallantry first passed from Saracen tents under the crests of northern barons, and inspired the rugged breasts of steel-clad Goths with gentleness in bravery. Thus, to the airy minaret, the tinkling fountain, the tapering date, and Ali Bey on his barb, belongs the diadem of fancy. Yet the Westerns shall have their due, and in the workshops of Manchester and the ateliers at Paris, I ween that you shall find miracles that put Aladdin's lamp to the blush. Look, however, to the Vulcan, and your lamp goes out, for you shake hands with ragged socialism and hoarse radicalism.

The mind of man leaves its stamp on his greatest as well as smallest creations, and his clothing, his thatch, in short, all that reflects him, is an image of, and correspondence to, his character, modified by time and space. Hence the social state of a people can be gathered from its architecture and its tailoring, which also give the key to the climate that it inhabits, to its dominant pursuits, and national propensities.

The great contrast of Moorish and European houses is a type of their national antagonism. The latter are impelled by a vague instinct of association to issue from the castellated isolation of families in the dark ages, and to live together in vast agglomerations of humanity, where the individual and the family become fractions of the social body. Such agglomerations are no doubt without any form or organisation, and only cemented by physical position; but they form the natural and necessary bridge from the hostile isolation of barbarism to the complete association of humanity, to which all the higher tendencies of modern civilisation are pointing. A Moorish house shews at one glance its great distance from this consummation. Generally small, they can only hold one family; and whilst our European houses give free admission to the light of heaven through large and numerous windows, the Moor gropes about in a perpetual twilight, his walls presenting the appearance of a prison.

These two facts are symbolical of the great characteristics of eastern and western life. The more progressive race, leading a more public life, required vaster and more comprehensive edifices, embracing numerous groups, who find daily the advantage and amenity of a greater social approximation between the members of society, accepting material association in the first instance as a prelude to the general extension of this great principle to more elevated interests. But in oriental life, where man has never conceived of a higher association than that of private families in the most imperfect form, through the slavery of woman, no other dwellings could be expected than houses uniting the character of castle and dungeon.

It is natural to infer from their residences that one of these hostile races is inquisitive, sociable, and accessible, on seeing the number of windows in their houses; nor can we wonder at the Arab captives at Marseilles comparing the French dwellings to large ships pierced with port-holes. And do not the long bare walls, with a few rare pigeon-holes and barred openings, announce a people careless about every thing beyond their family group, disdaining to look abroad, and anxious to hide the mysteries of the household from the profane crowd? The inquisitive and restless citizen of the West required the broad daylight and a wide horizon to look about him, learn the news, and see what was going on; but a jealous nation, shut up in individualism, could not endure to lay bare the privacy of its seclusion to neighbours and strangers; patriarchalism could not brook the fraternising co-operation of our social life.

John Reynell Morell, *Algeria*, 1854, pp. 94–6

The next pieces, written over a period of almost a hundred years beginning in 1828, reveal the feelings of insecurity which travellers experienced. Edmondo de Amicis, who visited Morocco in 1877, was an established travel writer whose book on Constantinople was translated into English from the *fifteenth* Italian edition. In the extract below, he was in fact describing a visit inside a house. He made much of the dark and dirty atmosphere of the place, and was entranced by a black slave girl – a 'seductive female creature'. However, his moment as a spectator was ruined when he realized that he had become the spectacle for a gallery full of veiled women. This was also true of Alexandre Dumas and his companion, travelling in 1830, who were inside a tent when the women devised an ingenious way of observing them.

More than one of the writers likened the towns to the women, using the image of the veil to indicate the act of concealment. Robert Hitchens compared Damascus and Jenin to Eastern sirens beckoning on Western men, and in a flight of fantasy was even drawn to conceive of the mountains of Moab as a tantalizing female.

Some half dozen times, perhaps, in the course of my musing peregrination, my observations were enlivened by the sight of sundry black eyes that (wondering, no doubt, at what I could be doing in those unfrequented quarters) were seen peeping through the white *yashmaks*, and the thick lattices (so appropriately denominated in French *jalousies*) that shut up every *shahnishin* of a Turk's house. Once or twice my ears were greeted with a titter from my concealed observers, – pleasant sounds, as they showed, at least, all gaiety had not fled from the place.

Charles MacFarlane, *Constantinople in 1828*, 1829, pp. 32–3

While they were performing this first service, I examined with great interest the inside of one of the tents which has not changed since the time of Abraham, and from which Ismail carried the tradition of the land of Canaan to the depths of Arabia Petraea.

I was watching one of the brown sides made from the wool of a black sheep, when suddenly I thought I saw the blade of a dagger pass through the material. It slid down, cutting the wool approximately two inches, then it vanished. It was followed by two, delicate tapering fingers with red painted nails, holding apart the edges of the material which the blade had just separated. Then a black, shining eye appeared between the two fingers; it was the Arab women who, desirous of seeing the Nazarenes without being seen by them, could find no better way of satisfying their curiosity without disobeying the law, than by making this small opening to which a new eye appeared every five minutes all the time we were sitting in the tent of Toualeb.

Alexandre Dumas and A. Dauzats, *Quinze jours au Sinaï*, n.d., pp. 170–1

As we approached, it seemed really as if we had at last discovered the Eastern city of our dreams – the city where barbers are philosophers, and pastry-cooks are the sons of kings; where Efreets may safely come disguised as woodmen, and beautiful spirits live undisturbed in wells. A massive archway of foliage led to the gate, with a raised threshold formed by a palm-tree, opening through walls over which crowd to view white houses not to be explored – and this is the great secret of the strange impression produced – but by the imagination. A humming crowd filled the first shortroofed street, where are the government offices, with sallow Coptic clerks looking through the unglazed lattice windows; and rows of naboot-armed men sitting without – constables, special or otherwise, ready to do the bidding of power. Beyond was a quiet open space, with a white tomb shaded by a sycamore; and beyond this a labyrinth of narrow lanes, with houses all turned, as it were, back outwards, and showing no sign of the life that swarms within. Most inhospitable and churlish is the aspect of these Egyptian country-towns. The streets are for the most part mere slips between dead walls, commanded by a series of high-placed loopholes. If you see an eye now and then, you do not know whether it is that of a houri, languishing and love-sick, or a robber about to take a shot at you.

Bayle St John, *Village Life in Egypt*, 1852, pp. 123–4

Damascus is like the women I see every morning passing in front of our camp, covering their embroidered dresses with a miserable cotton veil. They hide their treasures and show themselves in a dismal light to the European who meets them for the first time. The low houses without windows form the dirty, narrow alleys. In them we only come across mangy dogs sleeping across our path, or some women who glide along the walls as though to avoid our gaze.

S. A. R. le Comte de Paris, *Damas et le Liban*, 1861, p. 9

We have been to take tea at the house of the Moor Schellal. We entered by a narrow corridor into a small dark court, but beautiful – beautiful and filthy as the filthiest house in the ghetto of Alkazar. Except the mosaics of the pavement and pilasters, everything was black, encrusted, sticky with dirt. There were two little dark rooms on the ground-floor; round the first floor ran a light gallery, and on the top was the parapet of the terrace. The big Moor made us sit down before the door of his sleeping-room, gave us tea and sweetmeats, burned aloes, sprinkled us with rose-water, and presented his children to us – two pretty boys, who came to us white with terror, trembling like leaves under our caresses. On the opposite side of the court there was a black slave-girl of about fifteen, having on only a sort of chemise, which was open at the side as far up as the hip, and confined round the waist with a girdle, the slenderest, the most elegant, the most seductive female creature (I attest it on the head of Ussi) that I had seen in all Morocco. She was leaning against a pilaster with her arms crossed on her bosom, looking at us with an air of supreme indifference. Presently there came out of a small door another black woman, of about thirty years of age, tall in stature, of an austere countenance, and robust figure, straight as a palm-tree; who, as it seemed, must have been a favourite with her master, for she advanced familiarly, whispered some words in his ear, pulled out a small bit of straw that was stuck in his beard, and pressed her hand upon his lips with an action at once listless and caressing that made the Moor smile. Looking up, we saw the gallery on the first floor and the parapet of the terrace fringed with women's heads, which instantly disappeared. It was impossible for them all to belong to that house. The visit of the Christians had no doubt been announced in the neighbourhood, and friends from other terraces had come over to Schellal's terrace. Just as we were gazing upwards, three ghost-like forms passed by us, their heads entirely concealed, and vanished through the small door. They were three friends, who, not being able to come by the terraces, had been forced to resign themselves to enter by the door; and a moment after, their heads appeared above the railing of the gallery. The house, in short, had been converted into a theatre, and we were the spectacle. The veiled spectators prattled, and with much low laughter, popped up their heads, and withdrew them again as if they had flown away. Each one of our movements produced a slight murmur; every time one of us raised his head there was a great tumult in the first row of boxes. It was evident that they were much entertained, that they were gathering material for a month's conversation, and that they could scarcely contain themselves for delight at finding themselves so unexpectedly in the enjoyment of so strange and rare a spectacle! And we complacently obliged them for about an hour – silent, however, and much bored, an effect produced, after a time, by every Moorish house, however courteous its hospitality.

Edmondo de Amicis, *Morocco*, n.d., pp. 317–18

There is something special about the silence – a feeling of life surging up behind the closed houses, the narrow barred windows. Through the walls murmurs can be heard of plaintive women's songs, of arguments. Sometimes in an open courtyard you can see a group of squatting Moorish women, fat, lewd, and painted like barbaric idols.

And still you go up and up, staircase after staircase, turning after turning. The women in white who are coming down stare at you with a look that is lascivious and yet full of irony.

L'Algérie de nos jours, 1893, p. 28

Thrown out into the sea, its houses lie close-packed one against the other, an irregular jumble of roofs, but all straight, flat, and the colour of desert sand. There are no trees in the city itself, nowhere a patch of green. Countless windows, mere bare slits, close-barred and shuttered, look out from the walls and behind the narrow railed-in verandas, like sightless eyes that see nothing and give no index of the soul behind. For this is the first dominant impression of Bushire – even before one sets foot on Persian soil – that one has run one's head against a dead wall. Its utter secretiveness baffles at the outset, and throws one back against oneself. It seems to cry aloud that it will tell you nothing; that all that matters is hidden and close-guarded; that you are a stranger and can never enter into its inmost heart and thoughts. It is all shut in, silent and reserved, like a Persian woman with her veil drawn close around her.

F. B. Bradley-Birt, *Through Persia*, 1909, pp. 24–5

Other women flitted about in the street. The night had fallen, and they came from the trapdoors in the walls, and moved like ghosts on a stage. Sometimes they were alone, sometimes they were accompanied by girls of their household, sometimes by an ebony-complexioned Soudanese. They stood in groups apart from the men, and their *gandouras* showed harmoniously against the dark background of the night. It was all romantic. Some of them removed the veil in the shelter of the dusk and revealed their charms. But as I wandered by, their veils were dropped. A side-glance, and each woman peeping over the veil seemed to be looking at me with great liquid eyes, fixing upon me the bold glance of one conscious she could see without being seen. Often I felt there was something uncanny about those great eyes of the solemn women, always bright and always black. Big, unblinking, dreamy, sensuous eyes which filled one with a nervous curiosity as to what their owners were thinking about.

John Foster Fraser, *The Land of Veiled Women*, 1911, pp. 75–6

Quite suddenly, as you turn out of the French highway, you find yourself in the Orient, almost before you miss the familiar sounds of the Western life you have left. One begins the ascent of these winding streets, which are not so much streets as stairs, with the sensation of invading another world. Houses edge these tortuous ways, which seem to possess none of the characteristics of human habitations. Their windows are mere cracks in the surface of their walls, inaccessible and iron-barred as is the low door hidden in a shadowy corner. Sometimes the houses touch each other, forming a vault over the ladder-like street; sometimes a dark passage, suggesting the entrance to a dungeon, opens into a sort of bazaar, where objects of which one can scarcely guess the utility are exposed for sale. Merchants who look like mummies crouch in the midst of their motley wares. Strings of pepper-pods and dried fish hang beside silken robes and embroidered sandals; sacks of green henna, destined to dye slender fingers and feet, are flanked by fragments of red flesh and chaplets of orange blossoms. And the whole street exhales the hot, indescribable odour of the East – the scent of organic matter in decay mingled with the aroma of many flowers.

Figures, whose outline is as indefinable as the architecture of their houses, flutter round this curious merchandise, which responds to most of their limited needs. Great eyes, ringed with *kohl*, pierce the white veils that cover the women as a calyx its flower. They barter for the objects of their desire in twittering tones that suggest the voices of birds. . . .

Thus upon these labyrinthine ways you may meet every degree of poverty that rags and dirt can express, a poverty which implies, however, neither sorrow nor shame. The Oriental standard of comfort is not ours; the luxuries for which we strive he disdains. That man in the shabby burnous, whose whole appearance suggests indigence, may well conceal a fortune behind the battered door that closes upon him like the gate of a prison. Sequestered within those inviolate walls are the two great mysteries of the East – its women and its wealth. Both are jealously guarded from the eye of the stranger; both are in the most literal sense of the word interred, for the manner of the Moor betrays nothing concerning the extent or quality of his possessions.

Roy Devereux, *Aspects of Algeria*, 1912, pp. 6–8

As Damascus, seen from afar, has a fairy look of almost piercing, yet delicate, romance, so tiny Jenin, in its different way, has a fairy look, with its small minaret, its cupolas, its flat roofs peeping over the trees. Long I gazed at it that day and that evening till the darkness fell, yet never ceased to feel its summons, which was like the voice of an Eastern siren, whispering: 'Come, I will show you romance. In my strange ways there is fascination. Among my shadows, where my fountain falls, beauty lies in hiding.'

Robert Hitchens, The Holy Land, 1913, p. 144

Whereas the other ranges of mountains that guard the valley of the Jordan and the Dead Sea are stern and terrible, cruel in their fierce nakedness, the mountains of Moab seem always to hold themselves apart in a mood of exquisite reserve. Always a kind of lovely veil seems floating before them, through which, though they are often seen distinctly, they present themselves with a species of noble restraint, suggestive of a strange purity and dignity which may rightly be worshipped, but which must never be too nearly approached. And yet with this austerity there is blended a romance which is poignant. No other mountains are romantic as are the corrugated mountains of Moab. No other mystery is akin to their mystery, as they watch over the Dead Sea at the frontiers of the land to which 'He led them forth.' And as behind the blue hills of Judaea the sun goes down, and the last rays fade from the waters of Elish's Fountain, and the green cloud of the tangled oasis darkens into a sombre hue, in which grey and brown are mingled with black, in which the bright hues of the flowers are swallowed up, and the cypresses come to their own, the mountains of Moab seem to retire, folding softly their veil about them, into some region unknown to man, beyond our voices and the wandering of our feet, but to which our deepest longings draw mystically near.

Robert Hitchens, The Holy Land, 1913, pp. 194–5

The last four pieces in this chapter are all by women. Gertrude Bell in this extract from her early work (first published in 1894) was still full of the romance of the East and likens it to a flirtatious veiled woman. Helen Gordon travelled with her friend Lisette to Algeria in 1912, and these are her first reactions to Algiers. Frustrated at the culs-de-sac and blank walls she encountered, she looked up at the shuttered windows and met what she called an empty gaze. This ability to ascribe loss of vision to the woman behind the shutter or the veil was not unique to her by any means, as we shall see later. Lucie Margueritte writing in 1937, is more open about her reactions to being observed, while Colette plays with language and attempts to come to terms with life behind the 'prison' walls.

Such were the expectations of Europeans that few of them appear to have been willing to accept that ordinary human beings, living ordinary daily lives, were the reality to be found. If they did not find what they were seeking, they were quick to express their disappointment very harshly.

The East is full of secrets – no one understands their value better than the Oriental; and because she is full of secrets she is full of entrancing surprises. Many fine things there are upon the surface: brilliance of colour, splendour of light, solemn loneliness, clamorous activity; these are only the patterns upon the curtain which floats for ever before the recesses of Eastern life: its essential charm is of more subtle quality. As it listeth, it comes and goes; it flashes upon you through the open doorway of some blank, windowless house you pass in the street, from under the lifted veil of the beggar woman who lays her hand on your bridle, from the dark, contemptuous eyes of a child; then the East sweeps aside her curtains, flashes a facet of her jewels into your dazzled eyes, and disappears again with a mocking little laugh at your bewilderment; then for a moment it seems to you that you are looking her in the face, but while you are wondering whether she be angel or devil, she is gone.

She will not stay – she prefers the unexpected; she will keep her secrets and her tantalizing charm with them, and when you think you have caught at last some of her illusive grace, she will send you back to shrouded figures and blank house-fronts.

Gertrude Bell, *Persian Pictures*, 1928 (1st edn 1894), pp. 34–5

As soon as we were sufficiently rested we began to explore the town, which bewildered me at first and I felt in a maze; for the little alleys exist only to oblige the houses crowded together in a mass built, apparently, anywhere, facing this way, or that, without rhyme or reason. Often we chose out a promising passage only to find our progress suddenly stopped by the door of some private abode, or by a blank wall. What lay behind? Looking up at a barred aperture, perhaps only the vacant stare of emptiness met our gaze; but we might be rewarded by the glimpse of a braceletted arm, or a half-veiled face, speedily withdrawn.

> Helen C. Gordon, *A Woman in the Sahara*, 1915, p. 7

Under the arcades of the Avenue de France the veiled women of the common people go into the shops. Beside these women wrapped up from head to toe, whose eyes cannot always be seen but are always seeing, I have the feeling of being naked.

> Lucie Paul Margueritte, *Tunisiennes*, 1937, p. 67

The secret alleyways of Fez. Secret? Perhaps the real secret of this town is that it conceals nothing. Everything that it seems to hide tempts you: high walls of pinkish clay, closed doors with two door knockers (one at the level of the horse rider, the other for the pedestrian), which tap against the nail-studded panels; gardens which are imprisoned, inaccessible, divined, fabricated, and which flaunt flowers and bright leaves at the top of the gaols. But every time that one of the doors opens we are disappointed: a morose child with a runny nose stares and says nothing; a woman with red-stained heels washes clothes; a long-suffering donkey waits, standing in its own excrement, a little more pain, still a little more....

> Colette, *Notes marocaines*, 1958, pp. 44–5

Chapter 3

DEATH OUT FOR A WALK

Blighted hopes and disillusionment came quickly where women were concerned, and the writings of travellers recorded more about their own state of mind than anything else. The title of this chapter comes from Guy de Maupassant, who travelled around North Africa towards the end of the last century. Arriving at Kairouan in the desert during a downpour of rain, the city slowly emerged:

And what a sad city lost in the desert, in this arid, desolate solitude! In the narrow, winding streets the Arabs watch us pass from the shade of the street stalls, and when we meet a woman, a black spectre between the walls, which the downpour of rain has turned yellow, she looks like death out for a walk. (*La Vie errante*, 1890, p. 204)

Images of ghosts and death were used in profusion when writing about women in the streets, and since cemeteries were places where groups of women met together, much was made of this. Wrapped in black or white, they could be depicted as inert or insubstantial beings, lacking existence, completely passive; somehow invisible, because not seen. In this way women were dehumanized, deprived of all character or action. These writings are the predecessors of Michael Asher's 'women in vampire-like masks' in the streets of London.

The square on which my window looked, and which, open on one side, revealed the scene of which I write, was crowded with a bewildering variety of the most brilliant costumes. The splendid

dresses of Moors and Jews mingled with the numberless varieties of
the uniforms of French soldiers; while the rainbow mass was relieved
by the graceful simplicity of the Arab bernouse, and the mournful
white of the shrouded Moorish women, who seemed already half
buried from life and clothed in the garments of the grave – where,
even if the spirit lingered by the mouldering form, they could scarce
feel less lonely and hopeless than they at least appear to the eyes of
the English stranger.

George MacDonald, 'An Invalid's Winter in Algeria', 1864, p. 794

and, lastly, fair Mauresques, enveloped in snowy attire, who, were it
not for the beautiful eyes whose sparkle cannot be veiled, might be
mistaken for ghosts passing to and fro silently and mysteriously
among the human crowd, but taking no part in its affairs.

Reverend E. W. L. Davies, *Algiers in 1857*, 1858, pp. 77–8

Behind them, – is it a mummy or a ghost? – a Moorish lady shuffles
along in her comical and ungainly dress of full white trousers,
reaching to the ankle, and white shawl of woven silk and cotton,
wrapt around her so as to form hood and mantle in one.

Matilda Betham Edwards, *A Winter with the Swallows*, 1867, p. 12

In a shady grove in front of the town a man with a full beard and
expressive features is seriously and quietly spreading a carpet on the
ground; his head is covered with a large roll of linen, the turban; his
body, bronzed of a deep brown colour, is enveloped in a full toga
with wide sleeves, reaching down to his feet; he takes off his red
slippers, steps devoutly and composedly on the carpet, turns his face
towards the south-east according to an invariable rule, and prostrates
himself before the Almighty. In another spot sits or squats a son of
the country, who in contemplative mood imbibes from a long pipe
and a tiny cup the permitted luxuries of tobacco and coffee. Round
the walls of the house before us a ghost-like being steals, the whole
figure from the crown of the head to the feet – which are alone
visible – carefully enveloped in a wide mantle, which falls in
numerous folds; we are told that it is one of the fair sex.

C. B. Klunzinger, *Upper Egypt; Its People and Its Products*, 1878,
pp. 2–3

We are still going up. We are in the cool shade among the wonders of the native quarter. What men and women we see in the streets! Negresses wrapped from head to toe in large blue and white checked draperies go about with huge loads on their heads, their arms slightly thrust back from the body to balance it. Moorish women like ghosts, veiled with a handkerchief and quite lost in huge calicoe trousers, shrouded in the floating white haik which their invisible hands hold to their chest; like dominos at a masked ball they pass in silence, and glide along the walls like phantoms, white against white.

Marius Bernard, *D'Alger à Tanger*, n.d., pp. 37–8

To complete the gloominess of the picture, the women, who are the flowers of our crowds, are in Persia black, shapeless phantoms stealing silently along in the shadow of the walls. . . .

In the crowd were a number of the black phantoms; they were true daughters of Eve, some of them, for they lifted the white veils, which hung over their faces a little, to watch. But no torturing of my imagination could poetise creatures as void of form as the earth on the day of its creation.

Eustache de Lorey and Douglas Sladen, *Queer Things About Persia*, 1907, pp. 2, 3

Of colour there is almost none. The women creep furtively through the byways clad from head to foot in a long black shroud-like garment drawn closely round them, unrelieved save for a white patch of gauze across the eyes, and disclosing nothing of the figure within, save the feet clad in ungainly bright yellow top-boots. It is the most unpicturesque, ungraceful costume that the most jealous of husbands could devise. No stranger may look upon the Persian woman and see the beauty that many a poem and romance would lead one to believe lies hid behind those close-drawn veils.

F. B. Bradley-Birt, *Through Persia*, 1909, p. 42

Equating veiled women with death and phantoms was so commonplace that other images had to be found to attract the attention of the reader, or publisher. Writers had to scan their minds, or other travel books, for the perfect simile and produced extraordinarily demeaning language. Richard Burton was not, of course, an average tourist, but the following extracts from his report of his pilgrimage in 1852 say much about his attitude to women generally, and Eastern women specifically.

Living in rooms opposite these slave girls, and seeing them at all hours of the day and night, I had frequent opportunities of studying them. They were average specimens of the steatopygous Abyssinian breed, broad-shouldered, thin-flanked, fine-limbed, and with haunches of a prodigious size. None of them had handsome features, but the short curly hair that stands on end being concealed under a kerchief, there was something pretty in the brow, eyes, and upper part of the nose, coarse and sensual in the pendent lips, large jowl and projecting mouth, whilst the whole had a combination of piquancy with sweetness. Their style of flirtation was peculiar.

> Sir Richard F. Burton, *Personal Narrative of a Pilgrimage to al-Madinah and Meccah*, 1907 (1st edn 1855), vol. I, p. 59

Having dismounted, we gave our animals in charge of a dozen infant Badawin, the produce of the peasant gardeners, who shouted 'Bahhshish' the moment they saw us. To this they were urged by their mothers, and I willingly parted with a few paras for the purpose of establishing an intercourse with fellow-creatures so fearfully and wonderfully resembling the tailless baboon. . . . Their mothers were fit progenitors for such progeny: long, gaunt, with emaciated limbs, wall-sided, high-shouldered, and straight-backed, with pendulous bosoms, spider-like arms, and splay feet. Their long elf-locks, wrinkled faces, and high cheek-bones, their lips darker than the epidermis, hollow staring eyes, sparkling as if to light up the extreme ugliness around, and voices screaming as though in a perennial rage, invested them with all the 'charms of Sycorax'. These 'Houris of Jahannam' were habited in long night-gowns dyed blue to conceal want of washing, and the squalid children had about a yard of the same material wrapped around their waists for all toilette.

> Sir Richard F. Burton, *Personal Narrative of a Pilgrimage to al-Madinah and Meccah*, 1907 (1st edn 1855), vol. I, pp. 406–7

Burton was not alone in characterizing women as animals – the following passages use images of horses, ducks, gorillas, ants and rabbits. I have included the piece by Colin Thubron,

written in 1967, since he brings up once more the impression
of a duck.

The personal ornaments of the wealthier classes are extremely
splendid and elegant; but nothing is more revolting than the
appearance of such as roam the public streets. In addition to the
squalid rags which clothe the rest of their figure, a linen mask hangs
from the nose, resembling in colour and substance the graceful
pendants that are occasionally borne by the hackney-coach horses in
London.

T. R. Joliffe, Letters from Egypt, 1854, vol. II, p. 9

The custom, universally adopted by Oriental ladies, of riding astride
like a man, is certainly the most ungraceful that can be conceived.
Enveloped in the ample folds of a blue cotton cloak, her face (as
required by the strict injunctions of the Koran) concealed under a
black or white mask, her feet encased in wide, yellow boots, and
these in turn thrust into slippers of the same colour, her knees nearly
on a level with her chin, and her hands holding on by the scanty
mane of the mule – an Eastern lady is the most uncouth and
inelegant form imaginable. On foot, too, her appearance is not much
improved; for the awkward boots and slippers compel her to slide
and roll along in such an ungainly manner as forcibly to remind the
beholder of a duck waddling to a pond, or of a bundle of clothes on
short thick stilts. To complete the picture, it must be left to those
European ladies who have had the fortune to gain admission to the
privacy of a harem, to state whether the tone and conversation of
their Mohammedan friends is more polished and elegant than their
external appearance; many a fair form is concealed beneath a rough
exterior; but, if we may judge of the fair sex of Islam by the native
Christian ladies, I fear the answer will not be satisfactory.

William Kennett Loftus, Travels and Researches in Chaldaea and
Susiana, 1857, pp. 68–9

There is much destitution among the tribes of this province and in
Oran. A great deal is done for them each year at Algiers in the way of
subscriptions and bazaars, and yet beggary is alarmingly on the
increase, probably because they begin to learn – the miserable
wretches – that they will not be allowed to starve. Munching her
crust in the midst of the unsavoury throng was one woman whom it

was painful to look at, so near did she come in baseness of countenance to the recognised type of the gorilla: a broad, flat face, utterly devoid of intellect, and fearfully developed in the sensual department. The only scintillation of humanity shone out of her eyes. I was all but converted to the Darwinian theory on the spot.

> The Hon. Lewis Wingfield, *Under the Palms in Algeria and Tunis,*
> 1868, vol. II, pp. 184–5

The cotton bazaar is a little disappointing for although damask derived its name in the past from Damascus it is probable that the damask to be now seen in the city is derived from Manchester. This bazaar, which appears to be the Galeries Lafayette of Damascus, is ever filled with native women, waddling about confusedly like ants in a disturbed ant-heap. They serve to show that the great passion of women, the passion for shopping, is as intense in the unregenerate female as it is in the most advanced. Some women were pecking eagerly about among the bales like fowls in a newly discovered pasture; others turned the cottons over hurriedly as if they were hunting for a mouse. In the matter of bargaining the Moslem lady is hampered by her veil, the veil both muffling the shrillness of her speech and at the same time checking the volume of it. I imagined that one woman, who was shaking like a cinematograph figure and was screaming the while, must have been stabbed by the shop-walker but the dragoman assured me that she was simply declining to pay what was the equivalent to the final halfpenny in the account and was calling somewhat freely upon Allah ('whose name be exalted') in connection with this righteous matter of discount.

Sir Frederick Treves, *The Land That Is Desolate,* 1913, pp. 234–5

The most curious and, to me, most pitiful part of that promenade, was the attitude of the poor little women we came across from time to time. They were all rolled up from top to toe in cream coloured *melh'afa,* which looked rather like sacks. Had there only been long upstanding loops near the head, their resemblance to rabbits would have been complete, especially as their movements were hampered by the folds of their long draperies which, presumably, they dared not lift up from around their feet, even in their haste to hop away. . . .

In my present surroundings there was no room for doubt that this social tradition held all the poor little rabbits fast in its grip. Faffa

and Nanna, Betti, Chacha and Hanna, as they are most appropriately
named, darted into doorways; hid and crouched in any available
nook, or angle; hopped nervously round corners, or pressed
themselves against some house, their veiled faces close to the wall,
their backs to us, who all passed on paying no heed to them
whatever. As well as curiously pathetic, it was also very comical and I
could not forbear making some comment on these ridiculous antics
to Sedd-el-Kedim, who remarked with a solemn and severe
countenace:– 'Of course they hide themselves: they are ashamed!'

Helen C. Gordon, *A Woman in the Sahara*, 1915, pp. 159–60, 163

A woman went incognito beneath the all-enveloping *izzar*. Her yellow
boots, as she walked splay-footed in baggy trousers, enhanced her
appearance of a monstrous duck. Beneath the cloak, perhaps, a gold-
edged veil fell below her eyes, or she wore the flower-painted shroud
which may still be seen in Arabia and old Jerusalem.

Colin Thubron, *Mirror to Damascus*, 1986 (1st edn 1967), p. 140

The next two pieces, both written in 1888, describe Egyptian
women as balloons. In the third, John Foster Fraser brought
out all the invective he could lay his hands on to abuse
Tunisian Jewish and Muslim women.

Here is to be seen every shade of complexion in every variety of
Oriental costume. There are men in flowing robes of the softest and
most harmonious colours, wearing on their head the kaffieh, or the
fez, the white turban, or the red tarboosh. Women are here in black
veils, which cover all their face but their eyes, and wrapped in
garments of dark blue or of black cotton. Yonder is a lady with a veil
of white muslin, seated astride on a fine white donkey, which is led
by a servant richly clad, the lady herself wearing such a large silk
cloak, and so arranged, that she looks like nothing so much as a
distended bubble or an inflated balloon.

Reverend Charles D. Bell, *A Winter on the Nile*, 1888, p. 21

Camels pass, laden with wares from Mocca and Barbary, gingerly
placing their feet in the mud to the warning 'Hat' of the driver;
donkeys laden with balloon-like women, who sit cross-legged on the

very summit of the saddle, crowded with sail formed by their black *fadlas*, and held on by sympathetic donkey-boys.

C. F. Moberly Bell, *From Pharaoh to Fellah*, 1888, pp. 48–9

If you love fat women, come to Tunis.

Real fat, podgy, waddling, wobbling women – not ladies just inclined to stoutness.

The Tunisian – Moslem or Jew – likes bulk. He likes his wife to look like an overcharged balloon. He likes her to be so fat that she hobbles and rolls.

The Tunisian woman is Humpty-Dumpty and Daniel Lambert reincarnated as one person. No scraggy, angular, Gothic-framed females for the Tunisian! A beauty specialist who tried to sell anti-fat in Tunis would have her establishment wrecked for attempting to diminish the mammothian loveliness of the fat Fatmas of the land.

Any itinerant showmen, despondent about the circumference of their fat exhibits, can go to Tunis and hire a ship-load. Only a showman must not try to carry too many Tunisian women in one ship. They would sink the ship.

A Tunisian girl is slim like other girls. As she reaches the marriageable age she takes no exercise. She gorges on *kous-kous*, which is farinaceous and flesh-producing. The bigger and flabbier she is, the more like a prize-fed pig she becomes, the more lusciously alluring is she in the eyes of Hamid. The Tunisian when he marries does not want learning. An athletic, golfing, hockey-playing, tennis-whacking girl would be indecent. He likes nice eyes. But he must have fat.

Most Mohammedan ladies shield their charms of countenance with a soft white veil falling from just below the eyes. The female Moslem of Tunisia has hers swaddled in black. It is just as though, before she went forth to the *souk* to market, her husband tightly tied her head in a black bag, so tight that the bag split and she can peer through the split.

John Foster Fraser, *The Land of Veiled Women*, 1911, pp. 188–9

Other writers happened on the idea of likening women to moving bundles of clothes, with odd disembodied limbs sometimes in view. Clothes can be looked at as containers, 'storage spaces for emotional, mental, spiritual strength'

(Fran Cottel, artist, on her work). Here women have been deprived of everything save the container. C. B. Klunzinger, walking around a town in Upper Egypt, described women as walking suits of clothes and reported hearing 'an invisible female voice issuing from a house'. Salvatore Aponte was ashamed to admit that, although the women of Sanaa were said to be beautiful and pleasing, he could not confirm this from personal knowledge. Instead, he wrote: 'Sometimes, as in those lively animated cartoons, a little pile of multicoloured clothes walks among the Arabs; and then one can say, "That is a woman." More one cannot say' (*La vita segreta dell'Arabia felice*, 1936, pp. 66–7).

Here we have a *hareem* out for exercise, looking like moving bundles of rags, their bright, dark eyes being the only part that denotes humanity, excepting perhaps the shapes of their legs, which stand out in bold relief when the wind catches them, as they ride after the manner of their lords. Every person of good breeding and morals studiously avoids their gaze as they pass – so what an advantage it must be to squint!

J. W. Clayton, *Letters from the Nile*, 1854, pp. 59–60

Another case of the same sort I might make something of if I had a talent for romantic fiction. This time it was one of those bales of linen, with two black eyes at the top, that represent a Moorish woman, who took an interest in my proceedings. If I could only have represented her as young and lovely, escaped from the harem of some cruel and elderly Moor, and with large tearful eye imploring the sympathy of the Christian, what a valuable incident it would have been, and how well 'Fathma the Victim' would have read at the top of this page! But truth compels me to say that there was nothing in the lady's expression or appearance to warrant any pleasant theory of this kind. In her 'soft black eye' I could discover no particular expression save one of ordinary dull curiosity. I have a shrewd suspicion she was at least middle-aged, and I know that her nose, the only feature I can give an opinion on, showed through the muslin bandage of her face very like a small pudding in a bag ready for boiling.

John Ormsby, *Autumn Rambles in North Africa*, 1864, pp. 27–8

The women also ride on donkeys, and look very funny when so mounted. They sit astride the animal with short stirrups and knees stuck up, looking like a bundle of clothes with a head stuck on the top.

Sir W. G. Armstrong, *A Visit to Egypt in 1872*, 1874, pp. 6–7

We now step aside into a dark and narrow lane. Our way twists and turns, so that in its course it follows all the points of the compass. Without plan or guide we fearlessly wander about in the labyrinth. Pistol and dagger we may allow quietly to rest in our pocket; the poor people who have settled here have none of the Graeco-Alexandrian bandit proclivities about them. They are rather inclined to suspect us of such a character, timidly retiring from us, while the little children regard us with mistrust and terror, and run off screaming.

After a time the street forks, and we turn to the left by way of experiment. An invisible female voice issuing from a house suspiciously asks us what we want. We find we are caught in a *cul de sac* and turn back. We now come upon a creature entirely enveloped in a large brown or striped gray cloth, and as our glance lights upon it it darts in at an open door. Another creature of the same kind that does not at once find a place of refuge squeezes itself close to a wall till we have passed by, drawing the cloth together firmly over its face. Turning a corner we suddenly come upon a third, and catch a glimpse of the face, but quick as lightning its head is shrouded in its mantle. Wishing to behave with propriety we behave as if we had seen nothing, and turn aside to let it pass. After a few minutes both of us – we and this being – seized with curiosity, turn around at the same moment; our eyes again meet, and the two large black beaming orbs betray to us that under the uneasy covering a heart warm as our own is beating, perhaps beating for us. Wherefore then this fear, this flight, this anxiety; what crime have we committed; are we robbers or enemies; are we hunters laying our plans to catch the gentle gazelle? Modesty will have it so; we are men, and unbelievers to boot, and the creature we have just seen is a woman. We meet quite a drove of such modest walking suits of clothes, who lay their heads together, like cows before a wolf, and form a square against us with their backs. The veil which the bolder ladies of the capital wear, and which allows the eye, the mirror of the heart, to be seen, is not worn by the fair sex in the provincial town, and they have always their hand ready at both sides of the slit in front of the face, in order that they may at once conceal their features with their outer wrapper in times of danger, that is when a man's form becomes visible. A woman that does not do this is certainly of doubtful character, or else we have become intimately acquainted with her, and have seen her fully on some former occasion as in attending her medically, in which case veiling before us is no longer thought of. It is not the case that good-looking women are ready to let themselves be seen, while old ones, on the contrary, when neither dangerous nor likely to run any danger, are not so particular.

We were surprised at the walking suits of clothes, but we now light upon one riding. The ladies of the East are still as good equestrians as formerly in the time of the Virgin Mary, and sit so firm and secure on the saddle of their donkeys, with stirrups buckled high up, that the business of suckling is never interrupted even while they are riding.

C. B. Klunzinger, *Upper Egypt: Its People and Its Products*, 1878, pp. 40–2

Douglas Sladen and Norma Lorimer both hit upon the image of a ship in full sail to describe Tunisian women, others thought of witches or the Klu-Klux Klan. Once again, this is a small selection from such outpourings.

The women are far more Oriental than the men. They all adhere to their national costume. A lady hardly ever leaves her house, and in the Medina, the Arab quarter, a man may not go on his house-top, lest he should overlook his neighbour's wife. Not long have the Arab ladies of Tunis been able to see a doctor. The highest rank you meet in the streets are the wives of rich tradesmen, splendid patches of Eastern colour, for they wear thick black veils, embroidered with all the colours of a Roman scarf, without eye-holes, over their faces, and they can only see to walk by holding out the bottom in both hands a foot in front of their bodies. As they bear down upon you, like an antique galley with a silken sail, you know that you have entered the Gate of the Orient. They, too, are hedged in by conventions, for they may not stop to shop or talk – a prohibition which they, and even ladies, are beginning to defy, when sale days are on at the Petit

Louvre. The city Arab women of the lower class are no less Eastern
than their sisters. They dress their whole persons in white, and wind
a black scarf round their faces, without holes for eyes or mouth,
except the chink between two folds.

From a few yards off they look like negresses, a piece of gentle
irony, since negresses, like the Bedouins, excuse themselves from
veiling. The lower-class Arab woman is really very funny; for though
she covers her face so jealously, she thinks nothing of showing her
skinny legs as high as her knees, and the effect of the incongruity is
heightened, if she is a country-woman, by huge silver anklets.

The Arab women of all degrees, in their outdoor dress, are mere
bundles of clothes; but this may be an artifice to conceal their
charms, though I doubt it, judging by the Arab women I have seen
accidentally or on postcards. Like the Jewesses, they show as much
leg as a fowl. You know that you cannot be in a Christian country, or
their lords and masters would very soon make them veil their legs
and let their faces take their chance – especially those faces.

Douglas Sladen, *Carthage and Tunis*, 1906, vol. II, pp. 324–5

My escort . . . told me that an Arab woman of the better class when
she goes out into the street (which she never does until she is quite
elderly and ugly, and even then *never* unaccompanied by her
servants) not only conceals her entire person in a seamless, shapeless
garment of white and hides her face under a black mask, but she
throws over her head a long, broad, brocaded scarf of rich and
brightly striped silk. She puts it on like a shawl around her neck and
shoulders and then turns the back portion of it up until it comes
right over her head, so that she can only see the actual ground in
front of her feet. To be quite correct the scarf is held out at arm's
length, at the point on each side where it doubles over. Attired like
this (and I have seen not a few) she looks like a ship in full sail as she
steers down the narrow white-walled street.

In this way her head is, as you will see if you have grasped the
idea, completely hidden. When you first see a vision of this sort
sailing along, you think that some simple person is playing at blind
man's buff, or that the face underneath the outspread canopy must
be horribly disfigured, or else rarely beautiful. Why the Arab man
permits his womankind to show their bare legs right up to their

knees and at the same time insists on their faces being completely covered, I can't imagine.

Norma Lorimer, *By the Waters of Carthage*, 1925, p. 70

In the crowd, too, are veiled women in black who would seem to be items detached from a funeral pageant, as well as bent old crones who, upon the addition of a conical hat, a red cloak, and a cat, would turn at once into witches.

Sir Frederick Treves, *The Land That Is Desolate*, 1913, pp. 52–3

The native women were, perhaps fortunately, unidentifiable. They did not wear the revealing and all but notional *yashmak* veil of the Turks, or the obscurer veil of the Egyptians, but were enveloped from head to foot in a billowing hood, rather like the uniform dress of the Klu-Klux Klan, except that the customary eye-holes were replaced by a little panel of closely latticed stuff. This garment covered everything but the hands and ankles and imposed a deterrently shapeless outline on the most willowy figure. The only women to dispense with conventional propriety were the local washerwomen, negress harridans of surprising inelegance, who wore only a short brown shift. By an unexpected play of priorities, they always chastely raised the skirt of this shift to cover their mouths when passing an unbeliever.

Laurence Grafftey-Smith, *Bright Levant*, 1970, p. 172

I must end this chapter with a small piece by Charlie Pye-Smith written as recently as 1987: 'Groups of young girls, walking arm in arm like links in a chastity belt, promenaded through the Western shopping centre, and the men of Alexandria, released from the day's work, flooded into the cafés' (*The Other Nile*, 1987, p. 28). The search for the clever simile continues. Why should a group of young girls linking arms together be likened to a chastity belt?

Chapter 4

LIFTING THE VEILS

A tourist in an Arabian port was once asked what he thought of the women. 'I never saw any,' he answered. Writers of travel books knew that their readers wanted an answer to this question, and they had to provide it – by whatever means. William Spry lived in Turkey for some time and published his recollections in 1895. The chapter on harem life was, he said, contributed by his wife, who had been able to visit many harems. It was presented in the form of a tour of the house of a wealthy Pasha.

The lingering groups turn inward from their walks, which, as they pass, gives me the opportunity of comparing and observing the faces of some of these beauties of the household.

Here are Circassians, whose fair skin and delicate colouring, blue-grey eyes, slightly arched noses, and almost golden-coloured hair go far to justify all I had from time to time heard of the beauty of the Circassian women.

Another beautiful woman passes. I am informed she is a Georgian. She is dark, with delicately-cut features, a lovely little mouth, and an ever-winning smile lighting up a charming face full of bright intelligence.

A tall, blue-eyed, dark-haired girl is pointed out to me. I learn she is of Persian origin, captured, perhaps, when young, from some distant hill tribe. What lovely eyes and deep fringe of silken lashes! What a combination of charms! A lovely face so full of intelligence. She holds her head high, and walks with a queenly step, as one of great importance.

Another, a moon-faced Turkish girl. I could not help noticing her well-formed figure was set off to perfection by the lovely draped costume she wore. Her bright eyes, long dark hair, the curved and pearly forehead and regular shaped nose, made a picture to dream of, and such hands – exquisitely small, soft and delicate.

Nature forms and colours the nose, the eyes, the foreheads and complexions of these ladies, but the character from the cradle onwards is moulded gradually to its inward changes, by surrounding circumstances, giving us the plastic and passionate breathing lines of the mouth and lips. How they came by these eyes 'that teach us what the sun is made of' the vales of Georgia and Circassia can best tell.

William J. J. Spry, *Life on the Bosphorous*, 1895, pp. 148–51

Emmeline Lott was one of the many English ladies in reduced circumstances who were forced to become governesses. She had already delighted in the poem 'Lalla Rookh' by Thomas Moore. The publisher Longmans had commissioned Moore to write an Oriental tale, and 'Lalla Rookh' had an immediate success when published in 1817. The publisher had gauged public taste correctly and the poem was translated into many languages. Influenced by this romantic poem and carrying all the prejudices of a genteel European woman, Emmeline Lott set out in about 1860 to take up a position in Cairo as governess to the son of Ismael Pacha. On arrival she was shocked at the poor room allotted to her and the discovery that she was expected to eat her meals with 'two clownish disgusting German peasant servants'. Her two-volume account of her stay is vitriolic; the following extract is a small sample and a good contrast to the glowing observations on harem women in the preceding piece.

Black slaves were there, disgusting-looking negresses with low foreheads, sure sign of cunning, malice, deceit, and treachery, sunken over the eyebrows, not unlike those hideous-looking beings the Cretins, with large rolling, heavy, inexpressive eyes, the unmistakable mark of want of intelligence which renders women almost akin to animals; flat, mis-shapen noses, wide mouths, projecting jawbones, black broad lips, long fingered hands, filbert nails, orange-coloured by the use of *henna*, spindle legs, projecting heels, and not very large flat feet. The colour of their skin varied considerably. Some had bright glossy black, others rather brown, and all possessing bad teeth, a rare thing with the regular negress; and, to sum up all, their *tout ensemble* was very repulsive.

Their occupation during the best portion of the day consisted in lolling or rolling about the divans and mattresses which lay upon the ground, or squatting upon all fours, doubling themselves up like snips upon their boards or, clasped knives, which *pose plastique* I was for ever doomed to behold. These were proceedings far more appropriate to beasts than human beings.

Then my head ached again with the incessant clattering of the tongues of upwards of two hundred women and children, jabbering away like monkeys – some in Arabic, others in Turkish; while the Ethiopian, Nubian, and Abyssins constantly hooping and hallooing out most indecent language in their own vernacular, since they do not, like Europeans, consider that

Immodest words admit of no defence,
For want of decency is want of sense;
She that brings fulsome objects to my view,
As many old did do, and many new,
With nauseous images my fancy fills,
And all goes down as oxymel of quills;

made such a hubbub that it was like 'Bedlam let loose'.

Pray, kind reader, just picture yourself surrounded by such a motley group of beings, gabbling, chattering to me in their unknown tongues; (for at that moment I did not understand either Arabic or Turkish,) and making grimaces like monkeys from four o'clock in the morning until ten at night incessantly; and then you may form some idea of life in the Harem – that myth-like Elysium of the fertile imagination of both western and eastern poets.

Emmeline Lott, *Harem Life in Egypt and Constantinople*, 1865, vol. I, pp. 214–16

Many travel books contained a chapter entitled 'The Harem' or 'Manners and Customs'. This was the moment the reader had been waiting for – now for the women! The next two pieces are attempts to inform readers about Egyptian peasant women.

It is not in the Delta that one should look for models of beauty and grace. Generally the women's features are not very regular, they have a large mouth and a nose which is broad and flat. Their face is expressionless, they have a glassy stare and a brown complexion. The long dress they wear falls well over their body and when you see them from afar, carrying a waterpot on their head, you would easily think that they are nymphs of the woods and the springs. However, all illusions disappear when you come nearer. When they speak they make many abrupt gestures, the sound of their voice is shrill and the intonation is somewhat harsh.

M. Michaud and M. Poujalat, *Correspondence d'Orient 1830–31*, 1835, p. 82

There is something massive about the beauty of Egyptian country-women. Their faces are of a short oval, like that of the young Bacchus. The expression of their eyes, which have space to develop their voluptuous outline, crushed slightly, as in the case of the men, by a heavy lid and long lashes, is often stiffened, if I may so speak, by the black border of kohl. It would be difficult, however, to imagine more beautiful eyes than those that sometimes flash upon you in the villages. There is a promise of heaven in them; often belied, however, by the earthly reality of the full pouting lips of swarthy red. Except that in some of the larger curves there is too great an evidence of muscle, and that the breasts are early wearied with child-feeding, no forms can surpass those of the fellahas. Parisian *bottines* never confined such exquisite feet; and those hands that dabble in cow-dung would, in Europe, be caressed all day by lovers, and startle the artist as the revelation of his long-sought ideal.

Bayle St John, *Village Life in Egypt*, 1852, vol. 1, pp. 49–50

Later in the century Count Gleichen, a lieutenant in the Grenadier Guards who took part in the Camel Corps Expedition in 1884–5, shared his impressions of the people at a country fair near Dongola. Notice how the 'strikingly handsome men' are sparingly described as compared to the women – who apparently were universally ugly – and that we are told nothing about what the women were actually doing.

A most curious and original sight the fair presented. On a gravelly

slope sat multitudes of men and women, each with their basket in
front of them, containing dhurra, cakes, butter, oil, a variety of
vegetables such as 'bami', leeks, beans, and lentils, eggs, cucumbers,
cotton goods, both neat and gaudy (from Manchester), bread, string,
sheepskins, and cheese, but *no* koorbashes or water-skins. The babel
of tongues was something terrific of course chiefly proceeding from
the women, whose charms were arrayed in the native dress of grease
and dirty sheets. All the women were appallingly hideous, ranging
from the coal-black negress to the yellow nondescript, a mixture of
every race in Africa and Asia, and sometimes with a dash of Southern
Europe. Everyone had her hair done in the approved fashion, viz.
parted in the middle, and hanging down in little tight plaits,
ornamented with cowries and blue beads, and dripping with grease.
A strong contrast to these were their lords and masters, mostly
strikingly handsome men, who paraded about with great solemnity,
only unbending their dignity when a bargain affected their pockets.

Count Gleichen, *With the Camel Corps up the Nile*, 1889, pp. 50–1

Douglas Sladen included in his book *Carthage and Tunis* a
chapter by a woman who went on an organized visit to a
harem. I could just as well have placed this piece in another
chapter of this anthology, but because of the author's
expectations of finding Lalla Rookh and her reactions to the
women she actually met, I have included it here. Many
European visitors displayed the most appalling manners as
guests, a theme to which we will return in Chapter 12, but
E. M. Stevens was typical of this.

Our one experience of harems was not a happy one. A Jewish
Whiteley in the bazar (whose universal enterprise was proved by his
employing a Mahometan saint as a tout) asked us one day if we
should care to see the harem of one of the Bey's ministers. He knew,
he said, a French lady who would be pleased to take us to one. There
was no talk of payment; but we had heard vague tales that
magnificent presents were expected by the inquisitive but childish
little women, who were immured in splendid luxury by their lords
and masters. So we hesitated. The Jew waxed insistent.

'A magnificent harem, mesdames!'

'But is it not necessary to take presents?'

'No, no; only a trifle to the children.'

We yielded to the oily tongue of the Hebrew. In a few minutes, the interval being occupied by his ransacking his shop for temptations irresistible to us, and in eloquent entreaties that we should buy them at three times their proper value, a respectably-dressed Frenchwoman of the middle class came and took possession of us. Her manner was rather condescending, and we followed her meekly out of the shop and down the sunny little whitewashed street, with high walls, that led out of the souks. She was a friend of the minister's three wives, she informed us, and one, as we should see, was very beautiful and quite young.

Visions of a slender Lalla Rookh, attired in the marvellous embroideries and jewellery of the Orient, rose before us. Presently we knocked at a nail-studded door in the wall, which was pulled a crack's breadth open. After a query and answer in Arabic through the grudging chink, the door was opened, and, passing by a kind of ante-room on our right, we stepped into the *patio*. It was not unlike the courtyard of a Sicilian palace; it had a cool colonnade, and two storeys. There were a number of slatternly-looking women in it, and one or two children. They were mostly engaged in washing in one of the rooms which led off the *patio*, but they left their work to come and stare at us, and ask our cicerone a host of questions.

We did all we could under the circumstances – smiled politely, and patted the children, imagining that these were the minister's servants, though we thought it a little curious that one strapping young woman should be particularly introduced to us. She was a great, smiling, buxom, scarlet-cheeked creature of eighteen, with figure enough for a woman of thirty, and black eyes as big as half-crown pieces, fringed by heavy black lashes. Her bare arms were an enormous size. She wore full trousers and a tunic and some jewellery; her feet were thrust into shabby, heel-less slippers. There was nothing to suggest that her social position was one whit above the rest.

'We will go upstairs,' our cicerone said, and we followed her up the upholstered staircase which led to the women's apartments. A stuffed puma crouched at the top of the staircase, which led into a small reception-hall, opening into the women's apartments. It looked luxurious enough, and the slatternly disorder of the *patio* was not observable here; but we could not quite share in our cicerone's enthusiasm as she pointed out this or the other piece of inlaid mother-of-pearl, this bit of furniture, those hangings, that china. The ceilings, which were carved, painted, and gilt, were rich in effect, and generally speaking, what was Arab was good and beautiful, but what was European was cheap and nasty. . . .

Still the wives did not appear.

'Where are the wives?' we inquired.

'Ah it is the Feast of the Birthday of the Prophet this week, and they are busy preparing. They will be here in a moment.'

We waited patiently, and presently in came two young women, no better dressed than the girl who had met us in the courtyard, who came towards us with smiles. These were introduced as the wives. One was frankly ugly, the other was pretty in a sallow way; her two big black eyes burned in her head, and a trilby fringe was combed over her low forehead. There was a rather pretty, small boy with them, who stared at us with all his eyes. He was much better dressed than either of the two women, in an embroidered jacket and bright blue trousers.

It was rather an awkward moment. Our so-called hostesses knew no French, and we knew no Arabic except the greeting 'Beslemma'. Madame was willing to interpret, and we plunged desperately into the inquiry as to which of the minister's spouses was the mother of the child. The better-looking of the two owned to being its mother. More smiles, more pauses. We then praised the house, and this loosed the tongues of our hostesses.

We were subjected to quite a Shorter Catechism, – Where did we come from? Why were we not married? How old were we? and so on. Even our persons were subjected to minute scrutiny. Some ornaments that Miss L— wore, particularly a small Negro's head with ruby eyes which she had attached to her bracelet as a charm, were much admired, and so was a white-embroidered blouse which I was wearing, which they fingered and thoroughly examined. It was becoming embarrassing, and I resolved to turn the conversation to other channels. Remembering what I had been told of Arab compliments, I made up my mind to become as boldly personal as they had been, and turned to Madame.

'Please tell them how very beautiful we think their eyes,' I said.

Madame translated, and they replied.

'They say that the eyes of mademoiselle are just as beautiful.'

'My eyes are small,' I said humbly, rising to the occasion. 'They are not comparable in loveliness to theirs.'

Again our cicerone translated.

'They say that the eyes of mademoiselle make up what they lack in size by their sympathy and brilliance.'

This battledore-and-shuttlecock game of compliments might have gone on indefinitely, but we remembered that our men-folk were waiting. We had seen all that we wished, and had no desire to keep the ladies from their washing and cooking. So we bade them goodbye, and, as we passed downstairs, were shown the small, neat, bare room, covered with cool-looking matting, in which the 'brother of the minister' studied the law of Islam. Then we made our adieux in the court. We were well examined all over before we said our final goodbye, and slipped a franc or two into the fist of the small, pallid boy, who stood clutching at his mother's trousers. Then we followed Madame up the sunny street again.

'Which was the beauty?' Miss L— asked; and we learnt that it was the over-buxom, red-cheeked damsel whom we had taken for a servant! So much for our dreams of Lalla Rookh!

Chapter by E. M. Stevens in Douglas Sladen, *Carthage and Tunis*, 1906, vol. II, pp. 594–9

Much earlier than any of these writers, C. S. Sonnini was sent to Egypt by order of the *ancien* French Government and published his observations in year 7 of the Republic. An officer and engineer, member of several scholarly and literary societies, he gave his readers the benefit of his knowledge of the physical charms of Egyptian courtesans.

Even if it is true, as has been said, that in all places in Egypt of a reasonable size there are a large number of courtesans, it is not true that they are there to provide free pleasure for travellers; nor that they have been bequeathed to prostitution by charitable men; nor that travellers are taken by gallant messengers to a temple where young priestesses perform their acts freely. The praise which has been sung of their charms, their swinging stature, their beautiful hips, their ravishing loins, their sole wish to please and to seduce, is also a series of errors. Equally false is the spirit of generosity with which the dishonest conduct of these girls has been honoured – the idea that happy to be loved and chosen above their companions, they would not ask travellers for money.

The wretches found in the public places in Egyptian towns earn their living in the same way as the street-walkers in Europe, by selling a semblance of pleasure. They try to lure men, whom they arouse as well as they can, fleece them as much as possible and with as much skill as our prostitutes. On the other hand, you would search in vain among those of Upper Egypt for the ravishing beauty with which they have been attributed. You will only find poor women, mainly ugly and badly dressed, who are tiresome because of their impudence, which is so much more noticeable in these countries where they are the only women who go out with their face uncovered and talk to men in public; even more disgusting, they are afflicted with many terrible diseases. In a word, they combine all the horrors of libertinism without any of the attractions. This is the reality of these women, who can only be charming in the eyes of brutal men. Young men who may have been seduced by the false picture of Egyptian Venuses and want to come near to adore them, should have no regrets. They would find them disagreeable objects and most of the prostitutes of Europe would pass for goddesses by comparison.

C. S. Sonnini, *Voyage dans la haute et basse Égypte*, 1798, vol. III, pp. 146–8

William Perry Fogg and Rider Haggard travelling in 1874 and 1900 respectively, were both disappointed in their hunt for Eastern beauty and repeatedly said so. A. C. Inchbold, a woman, was the author of several books. Here she describes 'the feminine element present' at a wedding, distinguishing physically those who had had the benefit of a European training. Suzanne Voilquin, a Saint-Simonienne who lived in Egypt from 1834 to 1836, expounded a theory that Arab women all looked more or less the same.

The women wear the universal loose, baggy gown, of white or dark blue cotton, and over the face a white mask in which is a small open-work space for the eyes. The disguise is so complete, that one might pass his own wife or sister in the street without recognizing her. It is said that this offers the greatest facility for intrigue, to which these Mahometan women are very much inclined. In the bazaars, especially those devoted to silks and wearing apparel, you see great numbers of females chaffering with the shopkeepers. But the men pass them by without notice, as it is impossible to tell unless they choose to raise the corner of their veils, whether they are white or black, ugly or beautiful. At home in the harems, the wealthy ladies are said to be very richly dressed, with a profusion of jewels and ornaments. In my travels in Mahometan countries, I have never yet seen a really beautiful woman. Circassian and Georgian females, who are especially admired for their large, liquid black eyes, and long silken lashes, over which the Persian poets go into ecstasies, are but handsome-faced animals, without education or intelligence. Refinement and intellect are attractions to them unknown, and would be unappreciated by their sensual masters.

William Perry Fogg, *Travels and Adventures in Egypt, Arabia, and Persia*, n.d., p. 172

The collection of passengers on board was one of the most motley that ever I saw. Forward were many pilgrims travelling to Mecca, of whom presently. Aft, standing or sitting on the quarter-deck, were a party of American maiden ladies; Levantines in fezes; Turkish officers in rather shabby uniform; a Maronite priest with a tall cap; and four Turkish women wrapped in black robes, and wearing various-coloured *yashmaks*. In the case of the youngest and best-looking of the quartet, this veil was of a perfectly diaphanous material; moreover she found it necessary to remove it from time to time in order to admire the view. The other ladies who, to judge from their enormous size, must have been elderly, were more correct, and managed to study Lebanon through their *yashmaks*. But if they veiled their faces they showed not the slightest objection to the display of limbs which the female sex elsewhere conspires to hide. Thus the very stoutest of the family, for doubtless they shared the same harem, by the simple act of crossing them, revealed to the knee and higher the most gigantic pair of yellow-stockinged legs that it was ever my lot to contemplate. There she sat and mused, and there we stood and marvelled. Indeed my nephew, graceless youth, actually fetched a camera and photographed them. But, will it be believed, the modest instrument refused to act! Out of all the plates brought home this one alone proved absolutely blank.

H. Rider Haggard, *A Winter Pilgrimage*, 1901, pp. 195–6

My gaze was drawn to a brilliant scarlet silk garment enveloping a figure of matured ripeness, merely restrained in exuberant display by a narrow ribbon confining a waist of unguessed proportions. Through the folds of the skirt were indicated the stumpy little knees in a position the reverse of elegant. Travelling upwards the eye viewed a small flat head with plain features overhung by a straggling fringe, and eyes sunken and dull that squinted abominably. It was a married woman, her baby but a couple of months old. That was the face viewed by the unsuspecting husband when, the marriage ceremony completed, he had been allowed to feast his eyes for the first time on the fabled loveliness of his bride.

But this was not a fair type of the feminine element present. The type most prevalent was of medium height, of plump and pleasant symmetry of figure, deficient only through lack of physical culture. For colouring, a complexion of pale olive, eyes dark and large with a tendency to curve upwards at the corners like Japanese eyes. The nose was shapely though thick, the mouth straight in line, and unrelaxing except in obedience to mood or temper. The hair was black and straight, dressed high with coiled knot, and untidy fringe.

Easily could one pick out among the number those who had received advantage of some education under European training. Their figures were disciplined, they held themselves erect, and sat on chairs or stools. Their expression had depth. Faculties of observation and disposition, still latent in others, manifested by the dumb wistfulness of many a dark eye, had been called into action.

A. C. Inchbold, *Under the Syrian Sun*, 1906, vol. II, pp. 416–17

The first Arab women whom I saw frightened me ... but my eyes soon became accustomed to these types of ghosts, of whom one can only distinguish the eyes – generally very beautiful. The women are usually tall and their body, which has never been submitted to any kind of restraint, grows straight and supple like their beautiful palm trees.

Passing in front of each village we took great pleasure in seeing the women and young girls come to the river to draw water for the family. None of them left the riverbank without first throwing themselves naked into the Nile waters, diving and swimming with the agility of a fish, describing circles in the water. Their only worry is to keep their little black veil in place in front of their face, claiming that there is no real difference between any of them except in the features of their face. Therefore, if the face remains veiled, if the burka allows no feature to be seen, honour is kept. . . . It is a truly wonderful thing to see the speed with which these women chase each other, diving and escaping in order to chase again. The bronzed colour of their skin is not unpleasant to see. Arab women are not generally pretty; the pure oval face of a European is not found in any of them; their teeth are very white . . . their eyes are beautiful, black and shining, that is when they have managed to avoid the effects of ophthalmia in childhood.

The habit of walking barefoot and the arduous work which they do, makes their feet and their hands grow large, without being at all disagreeable; their arms are well developed, their movement, like their posture, is lively, noble, always appropriate to the sentiment they wish to convey.

How many times I have admired the noble bearing of these women when, delighted with their visit to the Nile, they return together to the village, carrying on their head a type of amphora full of water, their hands reversed behind at shoulder level, carrying smaller jars as well; then their flimsy veil is waving in the wind, their long blue dress draping the supple body so well. In these simple women of the people, in their attitude and bearing, you rediscover the grace and nobility of the laughing nymphs who blossomed in the pagan imagination.

One peculiarity of Arab women is the physical and moral uniformity which produces one single type. If I was rich I would submit this fact to careful examination; in the meantime I will leave it to the scholars to investigate, if ever these humble pages should come to the attention of one of this honourable group.

The life of these women has no variety, no change; their faces all have the same expression; as a result the type remains uniform; they have no freedom except to look. Look at their eyes, they are beautiful, expressive, full of provocative languor. As for their veiled features, they are not used in social relationships. . . . Oh, wise people, all this means that we must liberate our sex, so that we may see all these women blossoming in the sunshine of freedom in all the diversity of their nature.

Later, when I saw the fellah women of the towns, I recognized the truth of this first insight; in the town or in the countryside, among the mistresses and the servants, there was no variety in the type; they all had the same prejudices and the same boisterous gaiety.

Suzanne Voilquin in Rouchdi Fakker, *Aspects de la vie quotidienne en Égypte*, 1975, pp. 59–61

Some writers held a belief that the religion which women professed somehow affected their physical looks. A. W. Kinglake charged the Bedouin women with committing a cardinal sin by not putting more effort into appearing pretty. He reflected that if they became Christian, their looks might improve. The piece by Gertrude Bell is of interest because of the reference to the seclusion of a Christian woman, who was 'an exceptional beauty'.

The Bedouin women are not treasured up like the wives and daughters of other Orientals, and indeed they seemed almost entirely free from the restraints imposed by jealousy; the feint which they made of concealing their faces from me was always slight; they never, I think, wore the yashmack properly fixed; when they first saw me, they used to hold up a part of their drapery with one hand across their faces, but they seldom persevered very steadily in subjecting me to this privation. Unhappy beings! they were sadly plain. The awful haggardness that gave something of character to the faces of the men, was sheer ugliness in the poor women. It is a great shame, but the truth is that except when we refer to the beautiful devotion of the mother to her child, all the fine things we say, and think about woman, apply only to those who are tolerably good-looking, or graceful. These Arab women were so plain and clumsy that they seemed to me to be fit for nothing but another, and a better world. They may have been good women enough, so far as relates to the exercise of the minor virtues, but they had so grossly neglected the prime duty of looking pretty in this transitory life, that I could not at all forgive them; they seemed to feel the weight of their guilt, and to be truly, and humbly penitent. I had the complete command of their affections, for at any moment I could make their young hearts bound, and their old hearts jump by offering a handful of tobacco, and yet, believe me, it was not in the first soirée, that my store of Latakaea was exhausted!

The Bedouin women have no religion; this is partly the cause of their clumsiness: perhaps, if from Christian girls they would learn how to pray, their souls might become more gentle, and their limbs be clothed with grace.

A. W. Kinglake, *Eothen*, 1982 (1st edn 1844), pp. 133–4

Antoninus, the pious pilgrim of the time of Justinian, says that 'in this city the beauty of the Hebrew women is so great that no more beautiful women are found among the Hebrews, and this, they say, was granted them by the Blessed Mary, who they say was their mother.' The same is said in our own times of the Christian women of the town, and of those in Bethlehem also. Certainly their type of beauty is very superior to that of the peasant women of Moslem villages. The Nazareth girls are more Italian than Arab in feature, and often very comely; but there are many ways of explaining this besides the theory of Crusading ancestry. We must not forget that in Syria mixed types, half Aryan, have long existed, due to Greek, or Italian, or Frankish forefathers, and the blue eyes sometimes seen in Syria may be due to yet later admixture of European blood. More weight is, I think, to be given to such facts than to a comparison with blue and green eyes in the faded pictures at Karnak, which represent the Canaanites.

C. R. Conder, *Palestine*, 1889, pp. 94–5

There was an air of respectability about the place, which must certainly come from the presence of so large a Christian population. As we entered the village the people seemed more respectable, the filth, the squalor, so very prominent in most Eastern places, were wanting. As we came by the fountain, perhaps the very fountain from which Mary drew water, the women standing around formed a picturesque and not a disagreeable sight. Their bright faces were handsome, and to this day the reputation of beauty is well deserved by them. Thus did Mary stand many a night chatting with her neighbors, her bosom swelling with the consciousness that she was the mother of the Messiah.

Edward S. D. Tompkins, *Through David's Realm*, 1893, pp. 248–9

at ten the party broke up and Yusuf began spreading quilts for my bed. Then and not till then did I see my hostess. She was a woman of exceptional beauty, tall and pale, her face a full oval, her great eyes like stars. She wore Arab dress, a narrow dark blue robe that caught round her bare ankles as she walked, a dark blue cotton veil bound about her forehead with a red handkerchief and falling down her back almost to the ground. Her chin and neck were tattooed in delicate patterns with indigo, after the manner of the Bedouin women. She brought me water, which she poured over my hands, moved about the room silently, a dark and stately figure, and having finished her ministrations she disappeared as silently as she had come, and I saw her no more. 'She came in and saluted me,' said the poet, he who lay in durance at Mecca, 'then she rose and took her leave, and when she departed my soul went out after her.' No one sees Yusuf's wife. Christian though he be, he keeps her more strictly cloistered than any Moslem woman; and perhaps after all he is right.

Gertrude Bell, *The Desert and the Sown*, 1985 (1st edn 1907),
pp. 20–1

The next two pieces reflect a very frequently found attitude towards the physical appearance of North African Jewish women. When writing of Jewish women in Palestine, however, writers were often torn between anti-semitic feelings and a desire to find beauty in biblical terms. The third author in this group reflects these feelings – having been disgusted by the Jewish women in Constantinople he is entranced by the biblical appearance of those he sees in Syria.

The Jewesses are as frightful as those of Algiers, and the Moorish women are as frightful as the Jewesses. The opportunity of criticism is here more common; for the Mauresques of Oran, instead of covering the face up to the eyes from below with a haik, and letting a veil fall down to the eyebrows from above, wear no haik, but hold their veils about the whole of their faces with their hands, letting only a single eye appear. This normal appearance, however, involves for its preservation some fatigue and much attention; and it is sacrificed almost as often as not to the impulses of laziness, curiosity, or vanity.

Reverend Joseph William Blakesley, *Four Months in Algeria*, 1859,
pp. 164–5

Suddenly the narrow passageways are almost completely blocked by obese beings whose flanks and shoulders seem to touch the two walls as they sway along. They wear a pointed head-dress, often of silver or gold, a sort of witch's hat with a scarf falling down behind. Their monstrous body is a mass of surging, swollen flesh with a bright coloured blouse floating around it. Their shapeless thighs are confined in white trousers which cling to the body. The calves of their legs and their ankles, bloated with fat, inflate their stockings or, when they are dressed up, a sort of sheath of silver or gold material. They walk with small, heavy steps, wearing a type of slip-on shoe that makes them shuffle, since it covers only half the foot, and the heel flaps up and down on the street. These strange puffy creatures are the jewesses, the beautiful jewesses!

Guy de Maupassant, *La Vie errante*, 1890, pp. 146–7

Passing through the Jewish quarter we meet some young girls of distinctive beauty. Quite different from the hideous jewesses of Constantinople, these women have retained with wonderful fidelity the contour and expression of the face which typifies the Jewish type; just as we know from ancient documents, and from the models of the old masters, so I find it here. Large eyes, which are dark and gentle, delicate and almond-shaped, a grace which is imperious yet wild. When Esther faced the judgement of Ahasuerus she must have looked exactly like this.

Le Vte Eugène Melchior de Vogue, *Syrie, Palestine, Mont Athos*, 1876, pp. 30–1

Among the pages and pages of writing on women's appearance, much consisted of long and detailed descriptions of their dress, jewellery, tattooing and so on. The appearance of women in 'traditional' dress led travellers to believe that this represented a culture which had remained unchanged for centuries – eyes painted with kohl evoked Jezebel or ancient Egyptian goddesses, a flowing blue robe the Virgin Mary. The description by Eustache de Lorey and Douglas Sladen is a typical recitation of women's coiffure and make-up, detailed enough to be used by a stage designer. Isobel Burton brought her own cultural attitudes to colour and style in her description of the dress of Syrian women.

What is meant by 'making her eyes with paint', as the Hebrew has it? Simply that which has been and is still the favourite mode of beautifying the face among the ladies of this country. They 'paint' or blacken the eyelids and brows with *kohl,* and prolong the application in a decreasing pencil, so as to lengthen and reduce the eye in appearance to what is called *almond shape.* The practice is extremely ancient, for such painted eyes are found in the oldest Egyptian tombs. It imparts a peculiar brilliancy to the eye, and a languishing, amorous cast to the whole countenance.

W. M. Thomson, *The Land and the Book,* 1890, p. 461

What then are the special beauties of the Persian woman when stripped of the hyperbole of Oriental poetry? The accepted Persian type of beauty has a very full, oval face; big black almond-shaped eyes, which would be sufficiently bright and mysterious without the assistance of the everlasting kohl; heavy eyelids, which seem to drop under the long, full lashes that cast a shadow on the face; very regular arched eyebrows, the curves of which are elongated with paint and made to taper off on the temple, though they almost join over the 'birth' of the nose, where a blue patch cleverly adapted in the shape of a star separates them. The nose is small and aquiline, and is sometimes almost lost between the vivid crimson tulips on the cheeks, which, natural or otherwise, rival in intensity the brilliance of her sensual lips. The ground of her complexion is milky white; if Nature has not made it white, she makes it white for herself. On her cheeks the Persian woman wears another blue, star-shaped patch like that between her eyebrows. She seldom rests content with what Nature has done for her in the way of beauty. But a few years ago cosmetics went out of fashion, and the beauties of the harem lathered their faces with common soap and left it to dry, in order to make their skin shine, as if it had been varnished. It is acknowledged that many 'a full moon' did glitter more brilliantly; but the obvious inconveniences of the practice soon put it out of court, and the eternal cosmetics resumed their vogue.

The Persian woman has very fine hair; it is abundant and long, and generally jet black. But the fair Persian never hesitates to paint the lily; so, when she goes to the bath, she either dyes her hair with *vesmeh* to give it a blue tint, or with henna to make it auburn, or very often with both. But aureoline has no patronesses – the few women who are fair are ashamed of having golden hair, which is a feature not at all appreciated by their husbands. They, above all others, are devotees of dyeing. It is in the *hammam,* and there only, that the

Persian woman ever has her hair washed or dressed; in the intervals between going to the *hammam* it is not touched. At the same time she takes the opportunity of dyeing with henna the palms and fingers of her nice little hands, and the toes and heels of her dainty feet.

Her coiffure is very characteristic. A parting in the middle of her forehead divides her front hair, which falls in stiff, pomaded locks about five inches long on both sides of her face, forming love-knots upon her cheeks. Sometimes her front hair is cut in a straight fringe over her forehead; her black hair is divided into innumerable little tight plaits, terminating in ribbons, or sequins or tassels of pearls, which sweep the ground. As long hair is very much esteemed, the Persian women, like their enemies of antiquity, the Greeks, frequently lengthen their plaits with false hair, though they do not use horsehair for this purpose. . . .

Perhaps the reason why the Persian woman surrounds her face with the white cloud of gauze called *chargat* is that she may more exactly recall the circle of the moon at the fourteenth night. The *chargat* ought to frame the face in a circle as perfect as possible, showing the hair on the forehead like two raven's wings. It conceals the ears and binds the cheeks, letting the two love-knots escape. The ends of the veil meet under the chin, where they are caught together by a brooch, and hang down over the shoulder and throat. This gives the women of Persia the hieratic aspect of Egyptian divinities.

Eustache de Lorey and Douglas Sladen, *Queer Things About Persia*, 1907, pp. 104–6

The courtyards are full of gorgeous attendants. The orange, citron and jessamine trees, the balconies, and the trellis work are brilliantly illuminated. The women sit, as usual, in rows, cross-legged, upon the divans all around; they are splendidly dressed in every coloured silk, the bosom much exposed, and all are covered with jewellery, but especially worn on the head. They wear everything they have, regardless of colour, or 'sets' of ornaments, and they are very fond of sewing sets of earrings round their turbans – well they may, for the stones are gorgeous, though very badly set. This disregard of colour is not peculiar to jewesses, but extends through every class of Syrian women. If they can find two colours that 'swear', they are sure to put them on – a blue skirt and green jacket, with yellow head-dress; pink and red, blue and lilac, all is the same to them. They do not see it, and it has a garden-like effect, perhaps crowned with £20,000 of badly-set diamonds. Some of them are exceedingly pretty, but they have a habit which makes them all look alike, so much so that, pretty or ugly, until you get used to their faces, and are intimate with them, you can hardly tell one from another.

Isobel Burton, *The Inner Life of Syria, Palestine, and the Holy Land*, 1875, vol. I, pp. 142–3

One of the comments that writers often flung into a passage on dress (as the first piece here shows) was that, however fine women's robes, they would spoil their appearance by allowing the hem to sweep along in the dust. This charge was never levelled at men – but of course they were not expected to look as though they had stepped straight from an Italian painting. The governess Emmeline Lott went further still and proclaimed that, however exquisitely they may have decked themselves out, Eastern women would always be fundamentally unclean. In the third piece, the author applies this image to the whole of the East!

We met two travelling Bedawin, a man and his wife, on the way back to the village. The Bedawi walked ahead of the woman leading his horse, which was loaded with saddlebags and nondescript burdens of clothing and tent effects. His black keffiyeh drooped over his face, while over his shoulders hung the brown-and-black abba, dipping to the ground on one side, while dangling high in the air over the other arm. He scowled in passing. It was a swarthy, shining face, scorched by the desert sun, a rugged face lacking the classic delicacy of the pure Arab type.

The woman was dressed in the long Jericho or Bedawin dress of dark blue, with the sleeves forming a covering for her head. Her hair was of a rich, dusky brown, crinkled in small waves, parted and bushy at the temples, then hanging in two thick long plaits over her bosom. She had grey-blue eyes with dark lashes, the kohl-stained lids and sockets elongating and enlarging the form of the eyes. Her nose was small, and though wide at the nostrils, the bridge ran down the centre of her face into a delicate point. The upper lip was short, the lower pouted, while the blue tattoo marks round the mouth emphasised the inviting contour of lips and chin.

She was a beauty, in fact, tall, with statuesque bearing, sloping shoulders, and a high, swelling bust, over which the long drapery of the robe clung in classic folds. But round her bare feet the garment was bedraggled and torn; the long train proudly sweeping the dust behind the Bedawin belle was stained beyond recognition of its original colour.

A. C. Inchbold, *Under the Syrian Sun*, 1906, vol. II, pp. 441–2

It is almost impossible to imagine the celerity with which their Highnesses the Princesses, the whole of the ladies of the Harem, and the slaves, even down to the lowest scullery girl, effect their transformation from slatterns to 'Peris of the East', the instant that substitutes for the wires of the electric telegraph in the Harem announce the approach of H. H. Ismael Pacha. It seemed like a pantomimic feat; as if harlequin with his magic wand had touched them all with his galvanic battery, for in the twinkling of an eye their dirty, soiled, and crumpled muslins, their Monmouth Street and Petticoat Lane finery was exchanged for gorgeous silks and glittering diamonds. The transformation was not effected like that of harlequin, columbine, pantaloon, and clown, by a total change of garments, but by placing them over their habiliments.

Emmeline Lott, *Harem Life in Egypt and Constantinople*, 1865, vol. I, pp. 256–7

A typically Eastern city it has suddenly covered itself, at the imperious command of a King of Kings, with an outward Western veneer that sits as strangely upon it as a new transparent garment, thrown carelessly over an old and shabby garb. It is as if a woman in gaudy rags drew around her a gossamer cloak of fine and delicate thread. Asiatic the city deep down at heart must always remain, and Western influences sit but lightly upon it. The atmosphere of the East is in its very being unchanged and unchangeable beneath its outward covering.

F. B. Bradley-Birt, *Through Persia*, 1909, p. 274

As for the veil, which had so influenced Western images of Eastern women, travellers reacted in extraordinary ways. The same writer could in one breath deplore the constraints on women which the veil represented, and in the next breath recommend 'ugly' women to veil themselves. That the dress of

Western women – corsets and bustles, for example – might suggest containment and suppression never occurred to them, unless they had an experience like Lady Mary Wortley Montague in the Turkish bath (referred to in the Introduction to this book).

The veil seems to be the most important piece of their dress: their chief care is always to hide their face. There have been many instances of women who, upon being surprised naked, eagerly covered their faces, without shewing any concern about their other charms. The Egyptian peasants never give their daughters shirts till they are eight years of age. We often saw little girls running about quite naked, and gazing at us as we passed: None, however, had her face uncovered; but all wore veils. The veil, so indispensable a piece of dress with the female sex, is a long, triangular piece of linen cloth, fixed to the head, and falling down before, so as to cover the whole face, except the eyes.

M. Niebuhr, *Travels Through Arabia*, 1792, vol. I, p. 118

It is impossible to describe the misery of those mud huts which composed the several villages, and the singular state of wretchedness of the natives all along the banks of the Nile. Women, in particular, are most hideous and deplorable objects, having a handkerchief round the head, and only a loose, coarse, blue night-gown thrown round the body, and a long black cloth or veil to conceal most part of their faces, which is drawn to and fro like a curtain, and that part in front of the mouth brown with saliva. I observed many washing their miserable rags in the Nile, when they appeared to exercise a great degree of caution in hiding every part of the countenance, when it was supposed they were looked at attentively by strangers, and in fact equally ashamed to show their face as our fair countrywomen would be at being caught in a state of *déshabillé* at their own toilet.

William Rae Wilson, *Travels in Egypt and the Holy Land*, 1823, p. 77

And how pretty they look, these women draped like phantoms in their black silks. Their long veils do not completely hide them, as do those of the Moslems. They are simply placed over their hair and leave uncovered the delicate features, the gold necklet and the half-bared arms that carry on their wrists thick twisted bracelets of virgin gold. Pure Egyptians as they are, they have preserved the same delicate profile, the same elongated eyes, as mark the old goddesses carved in bas-relief on the Pharaonic walls. But some, alas, amongst the young ones have discarded their traditional costume, and are arrayed *à la franque*, in gowns and hats. And such gowns, such hats, such flowers! The very peasants of our meanest villages would disdain them. Oh! why cannot someone tell these poor little women, who have it in their power to be so adorable, that the beautiful folds of their black veils give to them an exquisite and characteristic distinction, while this poor tinsel, which recalls the mid-Lent carnivals, makes of them objects that excite our pity!

Pierre Loti, *Egypt*, n.d., p. 111

The females here wear in the street a peculiar black mask of thinly woven horse hair. It effectually conceals the face, but allows the free circulation of air, and through it they can see all that passes before them. Behind this friendly screen, youth and age, deformity and beauty, are alike safe from prying curiosity or insulting stare. I have sometimes laughed, when an accident has deranged one of these veils, to see behind it a face blacker than the mask itself.

William Perry Fogg, *Travels and Adventures in Egypt, Arabia, and Persia*, n.d., p. 223

We now return to the hall where we first undressed, enveloped in silk and woollen cloths, incense is burned about us, cups of very hot and rather bitter coffee are handed to us, and narghilehs are placed in our mouths. A woman advances and kneads you like bread; you fall asleep during the process, which has almost the effect of mesmerism.

When you awake you will find music and dancing, the girls chasing one another, eating sweetmeats, cracking nuts, and enjoying all sorts of fun. . . . You are quite right, it is not all prepossessing – far from it. Those old women squatting on the floor, with about five hairs, dyed a bright orange colour, are really disagreeable. They have harsh voices and they make an irritating noise. How thankful they ought to be for the veiling institution.

Isobel Burton, *The Inner Life of Syria, Palestine, and the Holy Land*, 1875, vol. I, pp. 145–6

The veil has perhaps two advantages for women. In a country where little notice is taken of them in general, it is certainly a sort of subtle coquetry, although it is rarely used since they hardly ever go out. However, by showing nothing, everything is left to be guessed at, and a lively imagination will go far beyond reality. The veil, therefore, excites the desires.

A more real advantage of the veil is that it completely covers the face. With us a girl who is ugly can try for a long time, and perhaps forever, to find a husband. The veil saves women from such disappointments but causes some for the husbands. Here you never know the face of the woman you are to marry, and the surprise of the husband when he sees for the first time the face of his wife after the wedding feast, if it is occasionally a pleasant one can often be very painful. It is true that he can seek consolation very quickly, either by taking another wife or by seeking an immediate divorce. But thanks to the veil, the woman has been married; at least she is sure that her ugliness will not force her to remain an old maid.

J. Barthélemy Saint-Hilaire, *Lettres sur l'Égypte*, 1857, pp. 147–8

In 1836, E. W. Lane published *The Manners and Customs of the Modern Egyptians*, which came to be regarded in the West as *the* account of how Egyptians lived – and influenced many later travellers. Lane felt quite free to analyse the form of 'Egyptian females', and what he called their rapid decline:

The general form and features of the women must now be described. From the age of about fourteen to that of eighteen or twenty, they are generally models of beauty in body and limbs; and in countenance most of them are pleasing, and many exceedingly lovely: but soon after they have attained their perfect growth, they rapidly decline; the bosom early loses all its beauty, acquiring, from the relaxing nature of the climate, an excessive length and flatness in its forms, even while the face retains its full charms; and though, in most other respects, time does not commonly so soon nor so much deform them, at the age of forty it renders many, who in earlier years possessed considerable attractions, absolutely ugly. (p. 36)

Lucie Duff Gordon tried to give a more balanced picture in one of her letters:

Of all the falsehoods I have heard about the East, that about women being old hags at thirty is the biggest. Among the poor fellah women it may be true enough, but not nearly as much as in Germany; and I have now seen a considerable number of Levantine ladies looking very handsome, or at least comely, till fifty. (*Letters from Egypt*, 1986 (1st edn 1865), p. 20)

Nevertheless, it became a platitude bandied around by travellers that Eastern women all became withered hags at thirty. The following pieces show little sympathy, or awareness that poverty, anywhere in the world, was not the best recipe for staying young and beautiful. The last piece, written in a 'humorous' book by James Cleugh in 1955, continues to present this idea.

After this long description, the reader will perceive with pleasure that we are approaching an interesting theme, the first question of mankind to the wanderer – 'What are the women like?' Truth compels me to state that the women of the Hijazi Badawin are by no means comely. Although the Benu Amur boast of some pretty girls, yet they are far inferior to the high-bosomed beauties of Nijd. And I warn all men that if they run to Al-Hijaz in search of the charming face which appears in my sketch-book as 'a Badawi girl', they will be bitterly disappointed: the dress was Arab, but it was worn by a fairy of the West. The Hijazi woman's eyes are fierce, her features harsh, and her face haggard; like all people of the South, she soon fades, and in old age her appearance is truly witchlike. Withered crones abound in the camps, where old men are seldom seen.

Sir Richard F. Burton, *Personal Narrative of a Pilgrimage to al-Madinah and Meccah*, 1907 (1st edn 1855), vol. II, p. 85

King Cophetuas, prone to love beggar-maids, are not of everyday occurrence; and I have rarely found people to sympathise with me in my admiration of these dirty Venuses. For it must be confessed that they are as dirty as their occupations make them. Not that they have any special fondness for filth; for they wash their persons daily, and their clothes as often as might be expected, considering that they rarely possess a change. But, in spite of their efforts, they are always begrimed more or less; and the odour of the dye used in their garments is so repulsive, that only travellers possessed of cosmopolitan nostrils can venture to approach them.

It is worthy of remark, that nothing is more rare than respectable-looking old age among fellaha women. They all shrivel early into hags. Neither is there any beautiful childhood of either sex; and it is really wonderful that the miserable pot-bellied creatures, covered with dirt, and sores, and flies, which crawl about the dunghills of the villages, should grow up into fine hearty young men and charming maidens.

Bayle St John, *Village Life in Egypt*, 1852, vol. I, pp. 49–51

But of the woman of this region. It is an obvious result of the aridity of the air, its almost constant heat, and of the floods of light with which everything is ceaselessly bathed, and stimulated, that she is, in comparison with the woman of Europe, forced into precocious development, and maturity, and consequently, which is the main point, and, indeed, the governing element in the matter, into premature decline and decay. To signalize one particular that is external and visible, this climate appears to expand, to dry, to wither, to wrinkle the skin with a rapidity, and to a degree, unknown in our more humid and temperate regions. A woman, under these trying influences, is soon old. Between nine and ten is the age of womanhood. Marriage even often takes place at this age, or soon after. She is quite at her best at fifteen; decay is visible at twenty; there are signs of age at twenty-five. . . .

That 'age cannot wither her' is, then, precisely the opposite of being a characteristic of the Arab, or with them, polygamy would never have been the practice over this large portion of the earth's surface.

In our cold, humid, dull climate opposite conditions have produced opposite effects. Here the woman arrives slowly at maturity; and, which is the great point, fights a good fight against the inroads of age. Man has no advantage over her in this respect. And when she is marriageable, she is, not a child of ten years of age, but a woman of twenty, with sufficient knowledge, and firmness of character to secure her own rights. The consequence, therefore, here is that men have felt no necessity for maintaining a plurality of wives; and if they had wished for it, the women would not have allowed them to have it. *Voilà tout.*

Nature it is that has made us monogamists. No religion that has ever been accepted in Europe has legislated in favour of the opposite practice, because it was obvious, and all men were agreed on the point, that monogamy was most suitable to, and the best arrangement for us. The exceptional existence of the Arabic custom in European Turkey is one of those exceptions which prove a rule.

F. Barham Zincke, *Egypt of the Pharaohs and of the Khedive*, 1873, pp. 377, 379

Physically the fellahin – with the distinction noted in favour of Lower as compared with Upper Egypt – are a fine muscular race, the average height of the men being from five feet eight to five feet nine inches, and that of the women in proportion. Under nine or ten years of age, most of the children have very spare limbs and distended abdomens, but as they grow up their forms rapidly improve, and in full age the majority, as a rule, become remarkably well-proportioned – with fine oval faces, bright deep-set black eyes, straight thick noses, large but well-formed mouths, full lips, beautiful teeth, broad shoulders, and well-shaped limbs. From twelve – the usual age of marriage – to eighteen or nineteen, nearly all the women are splendidly formed, and many of them are of real beauty; but once past their 'teens they rapidly wither, and as a rule are little better than wrinkled hags before thirty – a fact on which a recent writer is liberal and philosophical enough to base a strong apology for polygamy. . . .

J. C. McCoan, *Egypt As It Is*, n.d., p. 23

The women who from time to time descend to the river, to draw water also, but in their case in the vases of potters' clay which they carry – this fetching and carrying of the life-giving water is the one primordial occupation in this Egypt, which has no rain, nor any living spring, and subsists only by its river – these women walk and posture with an inimitable grace, draped in black veils, which even the poorest allow to trail behind them, like the train of a court dress. In this bright land, with its rose-coloured distances, it is strange to see them, all so sombrely clothed, spots of mourning, as it were, in the gay fields and the flaring desert. Machine-like creatures, all untaught, they yet possess by instinct, as did the daughters of Hellas, a sense of nobility in attitude and carriage. None of the women of Europe could wear these coarse black stuffs with such a majestic harmony, and none surely could so raise their bare arms to place on their heads the heavy jars filled with Nile water, and then, departing, carry themselves so proudly, so upright and resilient under their burden.

The muslin tunics which they wear are invariably black like the veils, set off perhaps with some red embroidery or silver spangles. They are unfastened across the chest, and, by a narrow opening which descends to the girdle, disclose the amber-coloured flesh, the median swell of bosoms of pale bronze, which, during their ephemeral youth at least, are of a perfect contour. The faces, it is true, when they are not hidden from you by a fold of the veil, are generally disappointing. The rude labours, the early maternity and lactations, soon age and wither them. But if by chance you see a young woman she is usually an apparition of beauty, at once vigorous and slender.

Pierre Loti, Egypt, n.d., pp. 121–2

I have seen two or three well-preserved women who were still beautiful at thirty, but they were quite the exception, and in generalizing the exceptions must be ignored. Poor, poor withered flowers! The only consolation they have for their early decay is, amongst the great ladies of the big tents, to hide its ravages by paint, and, amongst their poorer sisters, to meet their lot with resignation. But what is to make up to us foreigners for all the wrinkled faces and prematurely decrepit figures we see in the desert? This: the beauty of that desert is not all concentrated in its women; and the woman of the desert, to be in harmony with the spirit of its wide solitudes, has need of nothing but her own natural gestures, quite apart from what is strictly called beauty.

Mme Jean Pommerol, *Among the Women of the Sahara*, 1900, p. 40

Eastern women, even the young, are more often hideous than not, whatever legends may have been suggested by their seclusion and the dark eyes under the voluminous veil. And they tend to be old, in the European sense of wrinkles and flaccidity, at thirty.

James Cleugh, Ladies of the Harem, 1955, pp. 51–2

Vivant Denon, an artist with Napoleon's expedition to Egypt, declared, 'I will postpone the pleasure of drawing the Egyptian

women until such time as our influence on the morals of the
Orient will allow their veils to be lifted.' He then proceeded to
lift the veil and discuss their breasts:

As far as I have been able to see, the girls who are nubile, and for
whom such rigour does not yet apply, generally recall the lines of the
Egyptian statues of the goddess Isis. The ordinary women, who take
more care to hide the nose and the mouth than any other part of the
body, expose at every turn, not their charms but well-formed limbs
with a deportment that is more nimble than voluptuous. As soon as
their breasts stop growing they begin to drop, and the gravitational
pull is such that it would be difficult to be sure how far some might
fall. (*Voyage dans la basse et la haute Égypte*, 1802, vol. I, pp. 146–7)

The freedom which travellers allowed themselves to analyse
the bodies of 'native' women (not only in the Orient) came of
course from their general attitudes to colonial peoples. As a
painting of an Algerian woman was 'exotic' and a Parisienne in
the same pose was 'obscene', so it was perfectly acceptable to
describe and dissect the bodies of Oriental women. This was
the final act in the process of unveiling women. The pieces
from Suzanne Voilquin and Louis Pascal are typical of
hundreds. C. S. Sonnini, who wrote on courtesans earlier in
this chapter, was fascinated by sexual perversions and women's
bodies. In the extract here he described the process of
depilation, using a rather bland language to disguise the
salaciousness of his report.

The abuse of very hot baths generally deforms women's breasts. It is
only among girls of ten to sixteen years of age that this important
detail of the beauty of our sex could endure comparison with
Western women. The defect is so pronounced among many wet-
nurses that they have the appearance of absolute freaks. In the streets
I often stop in front of these tableaux, each time in genuine surprise
. . . this young child sitting astride the mother and leaning down to
beg for nourishment; and the mother offers the child high up on her
shoulders the source from where her baby must draw life. When the
children can walk, it is even easier – they stand in front of their
crouching mother and hold in their small hands the natural feeding
bottle which carries the milk from the mother to the little mouth.

Veiled half-truths

Knowing all this, you can imagine how overstretched the organ has become in these hot regions among women of twenty to thirty years.

Suzanne Voilquin in Rouchdi Fakkar, *Aspects de la vie quotidienne en Égypte*, 1975, pp. 62–3

The women do not cover their faces and far from shunning glances, they seem to encourage them and are delighted to be scrutinized. Their only clothing is a pair of floating white linen trousers. Their breasts are quite naked and, free from the terrible corsets which deform them in Europe, stand up confidently and firmly.

Louis Pascal, *La Cange*, 1861, p. 199

The women – and I am speaking only of those who are married, for the girls keep themselves as they are until the day of their wedding, when they have the veil provided by nature pulled pitilessly away – who are anxious to keep their body sleek in every part, do not use a razor or a *nouret* which they say leave those rough marks that they take such care to avoid. They will do everything necessary to appear perfectly beautiful. They submit to a painful operation, a violent and complete stripping which is done by applying cooked honey, turpentine or some gum. When the substance has dried it is pulled off with everything that is sticking to it. Fortunately, it is not often necessary to repeat this rather hard method. If a new production of hair appears it is only a light down, as soft as the finest wool and easy to get rid of. After some years this type of growth has stopped completely. If there is a mistake of nature and a woman gets a beard on her face, they use the same recipe to get rid of it.

C. S. Sonnini, *Voyage dans la haute et basse Égypte*, 1798, vol. I, pp. 306–7

The last two extracts in this chapter have something in common – the authors were both working as doctors and drew on this experience in their books. C. B. Klunzinger worked in Upper Egypt and in this piece he used a visit to a female patient as a pretext to describe the clothing of Egyptian women, slowly stripping her down until her whole body profile was alluded to. The Duke of Pirajno was sent as a doctor to Libya later, in 1924. When his book was reprinted in 1985, Dervla Murphy wrote in a preface:

[the Duke] frankly enjoyed describing the bodies of naked tribeswomen, paying special tribute to their breasts. These descriptions are neither scientific nor salacious. The Duke appreciated beauty: beautiful carpets, beautiful landscapes, beautiful buildings, beautiful women.

He may very well have done, but he was a doctor. If he had been 'frankly describing the bodies' of his Italian patients, would that have been equally acceptable?

The court is filled with a great crowd of women who have come out of sympathy to check and shorten with the gift of eloquence the patient's attack of fever. All that we see, however, is a lot of bundles of clothes lying together, and resembling a bird's-eye view of a crowd of people holding up umbrellas. We march on to our examination, and find the patient, who is veiled, lying in an open apartment, next to the court. Her hand has to be almost forcibly drawn forward to let us feel her pulse, and it is only after our repeated request, which is supported by the master of the house, that a very foul tongue is protruded through a slit in the robe enveloping her, which is otherwise quite close. The slit is shifted when the cheek, the eye, the forehead, the other half of the face, has to be examined, in order that the whole countenance may not be shown. When we ask the patient how she feels, the answer sounds like the oracle of a sibyl from the recesses of a closed temple.

REVELATIONS

At last one of the cloths in the heap opens out wider and wider; a frightful face, above whose brow there projects a tuft of hair dyed with henna of a bright fox-red, but showing also in parts its natural silver-gray colour, looks boldly round, and thereupon the old woman begins in a shrill screeching voice the endless story of her sufferings. Soon the younger generation also acquire sufficient courage to uncover here a hand, there an eye or a foot, only to withdraw them, however, with the slightest movement on our part. But gradually we inspire more confidence; our medical utterances afford consolation and hope; the figures uncover themselves more completely, and for a longer period; two coal-black eyes are fastened upon us each encircled with antinomy, the eyes themselves large and fiery, but with a somewhat squinting look on account of a spot on the pupil. The large eye is the strong point with Egyptian women, but also the weak point, as it is commonly affected with some disease or marked by some defect. The blackening of the eyelids was a general custom among the ancient Egyptians also, not only with the women, but even, as is still sometimes the case, with the men. The well-shaped and not too small mouth of the beauty now regarding us smiles upon us with innocent frankness. The covering for the head, made of a coloured woollen stuff of light texture, over which Egyptian women throw before going out the mantle which is in universal use, has meanwhile become loose, and has to be again tightly wrapped around the hair, ears, neck, and upper part of the breast, so that the oval countenance, the hair above the forehead, and the side-lock alone remain visible. During this process of rearrangement we catch a glimpse of that which oriental women keep concealed with the most sensitive delicacy, namely, the hair that crowns the head, with the numerous slender tresses, black as the plumage of the raven, that flow down on all sides. The coiffure of the women of ancient Egypt was exactly similar to this; even the side-lock was not wanting. The locks behind are allowed to hang freely down the back, and are tied at the extremities with long cords of red silk adorned with spangles and gold coins. Curiously shaped trinkets of gold, precious stones, or pearls depend from the ears; golden arrows and combs are stuck in the hair, which, where it meets the brow and sides of the face, is fringed with a row of ducats, sequins, little bells, and flakes of pure gold prettily wrought into the most singular forms. An oriental woman is thus somewhat expensive in her ornaments, for she disdains to wear sham trinkets. These ornaments are procured in times of prosperity before or after her marriage, and are worn all her life as unemployed capital yielding no interest. In seasons of misfortune, the woman may pawn them, but she never sells them unless reduced to the utmost need. As they last her whole life they are ultimately cheaper than the fashionable gewgaws of European cities that are destined to be cast aside at the end of a few months. The breasts are covered, but hardly concealed by a chemise of transparent gauze. Over this the women wear a narrow-sleeved garment, which fits tightly round the body, being fastened in front by a close series of silken knots reaching from beneath the breasts downwards, and which falls in folds straight from the hips to the feet. Oriental women are fortunately unacquainted with the confining instrument called a corset, and are still so backward in civilisation as to be unable to appreciate a waist of wasp-like tenuity. The legs are encased in a wide sort of drawers, which are fastened under the knee, but are continued down to below the edge of the frock, between which and the feet they move about in a rather picturesque manner. This style of drawers is not, however, in universal use. Instead of them a kind with legs gradually tapering towards the foot is often worn. In addition to the close-fitting dress above described, the women belonging to the towns of Upper Egypt wear a loose garment of light cotton of a blue colour, or with bright blue stripes and sometimes embroidered. This garment has no sleeves, but on each side there is a long slit extending from the shoulder nearly to the bottom of the robe, so that the arms can be uncovered any time. In the hot summer months the under garments are too tight for comfort, and this loose robe and the drawers are all that are worn in the house. Often, indeed, the drawers are forgotten, and the arm being carelessly lifted, the woman's whole profile from the shoulder to the ankles is disclosed to view.

C. B. Klunzinger, *Upper Egypt: Its People and Its Products*, 1878, pp. 50–2

In the low tent, which I had to enter almost on my hands and knees, Tahuk was sitting on the ground, wrapped in an outsize garment from which only her head emerged. She smiled at me displaying a wonderful set of teeth. Their sparkling whiteness contrasted sharply with her dark, full lips which were thickly plastered with a wine-coloured cosmetic.

The smile accentuated her prominent cheekbones and lit up a sea-blue reflection in her enormous, liquid eyes, edged with their darkened lids; the antimony extended the outline of the eyes towards the temples and faded into green where it blended with the ochre colour with which the whole face was covered. What really made this Tuareg woman astonishingly beautiful, however, was her auburn hair which was dressed in curled masses on each side of her head.

The disconcerting colour of the make-up on her Mongoloid features, combined with the mass of gold-copper hair, made her look like a bewitched oriental idol. The girl's face so fascinated me that I almost failed to notice the odour of her unwashed body.

My visit was not unexpected and Tahuk received me in a natural manner, using the traditional greetings in Arabic and addressing me as 'my lord' as she invited me to sit down beside her. She gravely accepted the first present I offered her, which was a mirror. Her

hands were beautiful and all her movements full of grace as she held
the mirror here and there to catch her reflection. When I produced a
bottle of hair lotion, however, she snatched it up with an exclamation
of pure joy and held the bottle to her nose, breathing the perfume
with eyes half-closed and biting her lip as though she were about to
swoon with ecstasy. With a sudden movement she seized and kissed
my hand, leaving a wine-coloured stain upon it. She turned back her
sleeves to the shoulders and spread the perfumed lotion on her arms,
holding them to her nose and murmuring ecstatic words. She passed
them under my nose also so that I too might enjoy the scent.

All at once she remembered that this was a doctor's visit and that I
had come to discover her sickness and – possibly – to cure her. She
hurriedly put aside the mirror and the bottle and began to tell me
how ill she was: she had pain here and pains there and a troublesome
cough that split her ribs. She carefully recited what she had obviously
been told to say, but when I questioned her she stumbled over her
replies and, becoming impatient, insisted that she had pains
everywhere.

Under her outer garment she wore a kind of Sudanese '*gandurra*',
a sleeveless garment slit up the sides as far as the hips. She removed
this with the rest because, she said, she wished me to hear how bad
her lungs were.

Her adolescent body – soft and supple as a cat's and stained all
over with indigo – did not seem to belong to the chrome-yellow face.
Her arms were slender but not thin; her breasts, stained with blue,
were like variegated marble, rose-tipped. Her waist was so small that
she could enclose it within her two hands, but her hips curved like
an amphora and her legs were long, slim and straight, right down to
the short feet with their rows of neat toes diminishing evenly in size
like tiny organ pipes.

After I had examined Tahuk from head to foot I came to the
conclusion that I had rarely found a human organism in such perfect
condition. When I told her so she was not at all pleased. For a
moment she began to sulk, but immediately her eyes lit up with a
mischievous smile. She lay on her back, completely naked, with her
head resting on my knee. She threw me an upward glance of
interrogation – but I was watching her wonderful hair, fearing that at
any moment a procession of lice might emerge from that gold and
copper jungle and begin to swarm all over me.

There was a long silence, in which I was quite at a loss for words.

Then the young Tuareg noblewoman spat skilfully against the side of the tent, and asked me in a low voice if I knew how to ride a colt . . . .[sic]

Duke of Pirajno, *A Cure for Serpents*, 1985 (1st edn 1955), pp. 136–7

Chapter 5

THE PILGRIM WAS IN ECSTASY

In 1798, C. de la Jonquière was in Egypt with Napoleon's expedition. Stuck outside Cairo, surrounded by sand and rubble, he and his army companions were hot and bored, only thinking of getting back to France. Suddenly things took a turn for the better: 'Two of our companions were able to get into a seraglio from where they brought negresses. This passed our time for a few days but we soon became tired of it' (Introduction to *Journal de l'expédition d'Égypte* by General Jean-Pierre Doguereau, 1904, p. 69). This brusque military report of an encounter with women in the Orient was unusual for, with the exception of writers like Flaubert – who recounted at length his adventures with the Egyptian courtesan Kuchuk Hanem – the typical male travel writer recoiled from overtly admitting to any sexual adventures. Even the Duke of Pirajno placed a few discreet dots after his account of being propositioned by a Tuareg woman. Knowing what their readers wanted, European writers provided much 'information' about the erotic life of Eastern women. While women visitors were taken on an organized tour to a harem, men often appear to have been taken to a brothel, or what they regarded as one. According to their accounts, however, they remained virtuous in the midst of temptation. No doubt some of the casual encounters with women were fictitious; some were written in highly romantic language in keeping with the 'spirit of the East' or, rather, the mood of the author; some were used to reinforce the prevailing idea of erotic, flirtatious women.

For various reasons, some travellers adopted a disguise on their journey, and played at being Arabs. Richard Burton is of course one of the most famous of these, and this piece was written on his pilgrimage to Medina and Mecca.

Close to us sat a party of fair Meccas, apparently belonging to the higher classes, and one of these I had already several times remarked. She was a tall girl, about eighteen years old, with regular features, a skin somewhat citrine-coloured, but soft and clear, symmetrical eyebrows, the most beautiful eyes, and a figure all grace. There was no head thrown back, no straightened neck, no flat shoulders, nor toes turned out – in fact, no 'elegant' barbarisms: the shape was that the Arabs love, soft, bending, and relaxed, as a woman's figure ought to be. Unhappily she wore, instead of the usual veil, a 'Yashmak' of transparent muslin, bound round the face: and the chaperone, mother, or duenna, by whose side she stood was apparently a very unsuspicious or complaisant old person. Flirtilla fixed a glance of admiration upon my cashmere. I directed a reply with interest at her eyes. She then by the usual coquettish gesture, threw back an inch or two of head-veil, disclosing broad bands of jetty hair, crowning a lovely oval. My palpable admiration of the new charm was rewarded by a partial removal of the Yashmak, when a dimpled mouth and a rounded chin stood out from the envious muslin. Seeing that my companions were safely employed, I entered upon the dangerous ground of raising hand to forehead. She smiled almost imperceptibly, and turned away. The pilgrim was in ecstasy.

> Sir Richard F. Burton, *Personal Narrative of a Pilgrimage to al-Madinah and Meccah*, 1907 (1st edn 1855), vol. II, pp. 197–8

John F. Keane spent six months in the Hejaz 'professing Mohammedanism' and here he described a chance encounter with two Bedouin girls.

It was now the heat of the day, the camp was sleeping to a man. The well was deserted, so, close up under the cold shade of its low wall I lay down with my birds and gun, to sleep or smoke away the rest of the afternoon well out of range of the insect pests and noxious exhalations of our dirty camp. Not far from the well was a solitary Bedawin hut, and I had just smoked enough to make me feel thirsty, when I saw come out of it two young girls with earthenware water-vessels under their arms. They were not veiled, and as they came towards me I could not help looking with more than common admiration at their lithe, slender figures and graceful movements. When they came nearer I saw that they had handsome, intelligent features, and were about sixteen and seventeen years of age, and evidently sisters. I must have been staring at them, for they both came up to me laughing, and said, 'Fortune, Shaykh.' (Among the Bedawi even the gentler sex will not wish you *peace*.) 'Upon you be peace,' said I, for I was a devout pilgrim. As they were drawing their water it occurred to me to help them; but that would not have been at all etiquette, so I sat and watched them at work. Their only dress was a dark-blue prettily embroidered 'cutty-sark', rather fascinating and very unembarrassed. All at once I thought, what a perfect 'Rebekah at the well' either of those girls would make in a picture, and the fancy took me to rehearse the scene with them. When she had filled her pitcher I said: 'Let me, I pray thee, drink a little water of thy pitcher.' And she said: 'Drink, Shaykh,' and when she had done giving me a drink, she said: 'Bakshish,' laughing wickedly at the solemn stranger's respectful manner. 'Oh, hang it!' I thought, 'Rebekah at the well! Why you wouldn't be fit to put behind a public refreshment bar.' I dropped my polite dignity; I may even admit I became rude. I sprinkled both the young ladies with a few drops remaining in the cup, and said: 'Yes, there is your bakshish.' Down went their pitchers, and into it they went, like pigs into porridges, with both hands baling out the contents of a large camel-trough over me, screaming and laughing like two young mad things. I emptied the contents of their own pitchers over them, and thoroughly drenched them; but I was nowhere, and got fearfully worsted. If it had not been for my wound I should have made a big splash; as it was, I was obliged to ask them to stop 'romping' because I was wounded. They would not believe me at first, but when they saw that I could not run away from them, but had to sit down, they stopped their fun and asked about the wound and soon grew quite sympathetic and interested. When they had refilled their vessels, I gave them the birds I had shot, and they went away with a merry laughing 'Fortune to you, Shaykh.' After they had gone I lay down in the sun of a sandy place to dry, and spent the rest of the day wiping the gun and smoking, until the evening meal.

John F. Keane, *Six Months in the Hejaz*, 1887, pp. 235–7

The next four pieces, all written by Frenchmen between 1855 and 1887, are graphic accounts of Western male hopes and fantasies.

The beautiful girl smiled and looked at me with a tenderness so passionate and gentle, which God seems to have reserved for Oriental girls. Night fell, but what could I do? Houris are not for the Christians and although the idea of embracing Islam came to me for a short while, I did nothing about it but went to sleep in the tent alongside my companions. . . .

Émile Gentil, *Souvenirs d'Orient*, 1855, p. 77

In a narrow street I stopped in front of a beautiful Oriental house whose open door revealed a large staircase, completely decorated with tiles and lit from top to bottom by an invisible light, a dying fire, a cloud of brightness which came down from some unknown source. Under this indescribable light each of the glazed steps was waiting for someone, maybe a portly old Muslim, but I think that they were calling out for a lover's footstep. Never in my life have I predicted, seen, understood or experienced such a feeling of anticipation as I did in front of this open door and this empty staircase watched over by an unseen light. Outside on the moonlit wall there was a large closed balcony called a *barmakli*, with two dark openings in the middle behind the opulent ironwork of the *mouchrabias*. Is she there inside, the one who lies awake, listening and hating us, the Arab Juliet whose heart is beating wildly? Perhaps, but her desire is only sensual, there is no soaring up to the stars as we would experience on a night such as this. In this warm and pliable land, so captivating that the legend of the Lotophages was born on the island of Djerba, the air is sweeter-smelling than anywhere else, the sun is warmer, the day is brighter – but the heart does not know how to love. These women are beautiful and ardent, but they know nothing of love as we know it. Their simple souls have never experienced romantic emotions and their kisses, it is said, are not the stuff of dreams.

Guy de Maupassant, *La Vie errante*, 1890, pp. 232–3

I advance near the gate, where a white-bearded patriarch and a group of children are gathered. Beautiful dark-haired girls pass by, with sunny eyes, supple gait, steady look, and each of their movements is full of indefinable grace. They wear white veils, tied round the forehead by a coloured band; a short tunic, fastened round the waist by a scarlet sash, falls down to the knee, leaving their slender, sinewy legs, of an admirable form, and their pretty, tiny, delicately arched feet, exposed to view. On their breast, above the tunic, slit at the sides, leaving the arms quite bare, silver clasps fasten the tucked-up sleeves of their *gandourah*; a short peplum descends just below the breasts, which heave gently beneath. Over it strings of massive silver amulets to ward off the evil *djinns*, give a slight tinkle as they flit along with a voluptuous undulating of their hips.

With an elegant gesture of their bare arms, encircled with twisted bracelets of antique design, they maintain on their shoulders their heavy *djourna*, and with the other they conceal the lower part of the face by drawing over their lips the fringe of their veils. And the ardent flame of their dark eyes gleams; and when they pass, smiling and curious, their white tunics grazing me, a sweet and penetrating odour of aloes and virgin freshness rises from their flowing robes.

G. Montbard, Among the Moors, 1894, pp. 106–7

It was a Bedouin camp. Some snarling guard dogs with long, dirty, white hair came towards me barking in a fearsome manner. Some horses were grazing here and there. It was evening and the camp presented a delightful picture. I wandered between the tents inside which I could see, in the light of the fire, groups of women and girls and then the Arabs who looked up towards me.

The wives and daughters of these men. I caught sight of one among them; oh, the pretty little savage. I hurried on so as not to see her any more, but two minutes later I found myself again in front of her tent.

Beside her an Arab was watching me, no doubt her father. He had two rows of beautiful white teeth. Did he want to bite me, or to smile?

'Bonjour,' he cried out.

'Well, you speak French?'

'Yes, we are Algerians from Biskra.'

I liked this Arab, he had a respectable air and I took to him.

'May I enter?'

'If you like.'

I held out my hand to him and offered him a cigarette, which he accepted. I sat down . . . beside *her*.

I was absolutely spell-bound and I answered in defiance of common sense to whatever the other said. I was looking for an excuse to talk to my neighbour and I found it in my pocket in the delicately carved figure of my pipe – a skull. Having set my heart on fire, the daughter of the desert – I like the sound of this word – lit up my briar root skull.

My God, her hands were quite black, but her eyes! They were very large and seemed to be veiled with a velvety glimmer, moist with very long black lashes! The fairest gazelle would have wept with shame seeing her eyes in those eyes.

So young, so sweet, with a mischievous little look which darkened the corner of her lips on and off.

Undoubtedly her costume was lightweight, a simple piece of blue material loosely fastened on the shoulder with a large fibula . . . but if there was little raiment, there were certainly many promises.

The conversation was languishing and I don't know what disastrous inspiration came to me to ask him: 'Is she your daughter?' He looked at me, then said, 'No, my *mouquière*'.

Yes, I *had* understood, my gazelle belonged to this jackal . . . she was his wife. Then I saw that I hadn't looked very closely at him at first, for now I found him hideous with his large teeth and dirty burnous, his . . . When I departed I shook his hand; oh! if only I could have crushed it!

Paul Fagault, *Tunis et Kairouan*, n.d., pp. 113–15

In his autobiography, Sir Henry Layard recounted an adventure he had had in Constantinople, when a Turkish woman invited him and a friend to visit her at home. Since she seemed to be 'surpassingly lovely' they determined to go, and this is his description of the visit.

We were in the habit of going on Friday afternoons to the 'Sweet Waters of Asia' to look at the gay and picturesque groups of Turkish women, who assembled there on that day in spring, and, seated on the grass with their children, enjoyed a kind of picnic, smoking their *narguiles*, drinking sherbet, and eating sweetmeats. We were returning from one of these excursions in Mr Alison's *caique*, which was rowed by three of the most stalwart and skilful *caiquijis* on the Bosphorous, when we perceived some ladies in very bright *ferijis*, evidently of high rank, standing on the marble steps of an imperial kiosk, built on the water's edge, and about to enter an eight-oared boat. We stopped for a time to observe them. One, who was the most richly dressed of the party, stepped into the *caique* followed by the others, who were evidently her attendants, and, seeing that we were looking at her, cautiously lowered her veil, and showed her face, which appeared to us, from the glimpse we obtained of it, surpassingly lovely, and made a sign which we interpreted as an invitation to follow her.

Accordingly, when her *caique* left the stairs of the kiosk, we directed our boatmen to keep as near to it as they prudently could. As it had a larger number of rowers than ours, we had some difficulty in keeping up with it, especially as our *caiquijis* were evidently unwilling to continue the pursuit, and did not row their best. When we came to the spot where the Golden Horn meets the two streams – one coming from the 'Sweet Waters', the other from the direction of the sacred suburb of Ayoub – the lady's *caique* turned into the latter. We were about to follow, when our *caique* struck against something, and a dead body rose to the surface of the water close to us.

Our boatmen now threw down their oars, and refused to go any further. The appearance of the corpse was an evil omen, warning them, they said, against taking any part in an adventure, which might have grave consequences both to us and to them. The ladies, they declared, belonged evidently to the harem of a person of high rank, and if we were caught by the police, or were seen following them, we might incur the greatest possible danger. As they could not be persuaded to continue the chase, we had to return home much disappointed.

The following morning a Turkish woman, closely veiled, called at Mr Alison's house, when I chanced to be there, and requested to speak with him. Having assured herself that no one except ourselves was present or could hear what she had to say, she told us that she had been sent by the lady, whom we had seen and followed on the previous day, to invite us to visit her. She refused to disclose the name of her mistress or to say who she was. If, she said, we would go to a garden wicket in a street in the Ayoub quarter which she described, at a certain hour on the following day, we would be admitted and the lady would receive us. She then left us.

Although the adventure was not without peril, and it was even possible that a trap might be laid for us, we determined to run the risk. The following day we accordingly went to Ayoub at the appointed hour. We had no difficulty in finding the wicket the messenger had described, in a narrow, solitary street in an out-of-the-way part of the quarter. The gate was at once opened by a woman, and we entered it, apparently unobserved. She led us across a garden to a large kiosk of old Turkish architecture, with broad, overhanging eaves. We were ushered into a large hall, the walls and ceilings of which were sumptuously and most exquisitely decorated with gilding and painted ornaments in the Oriental style, whilst the ceiling was inlaid with pieces of looking-glass, which produced a rich and lovely effect. Such in those days, before Turkish taste was corrupted by European influence, were the decorations seen in the palaces of the Ottoman nobles. On a very low divan at the further end of this hall was seated a lady, whom we recognised at once as the one we had seen at the 'Sweet Waters'. We had not been deceived by the glimpse she had allowed us to obtain of her face, when she furtively lowered her veil as she stepped into her boat. She was young and singularly beautiful, with the large almond-shaped eyes, the delicate and regular features, and the clear, brilliant complexion, somewhat too pale perhaps for perfect beauty, peculiar to Turkish women of mixed Circassian descent. She was splendidly clad in the dress then worn by wealthy Turkish ladies, before it was rendered vulgar and unbecoming by the introduction of French fashions. Round about her stood a number of girls, all richly clad, and for the most part exceedingly pretty, who were evidently her attendants.

She invited us to be seated on the divan beside her, and entered at once into conversation. She asked numerous questions upon all manner of subjects, politics included, said that she knew who we were, and that, seeing that she had observed us at the 'Sweet Waters', she had resolved to make our acquaintance, but that she had been imprudent in inviting us to follow her, and was glad that we turned back when we did. She then ordered *narquiles*, coffee and sweetmeats to be brought, which were handed to us by some of her damsels, she herself partaking of them with us.

We were soon engaged in a very lively discourse. The ladies were delighted with Alison, who spoke their language perfectly, and laughed uproariously at his jokes and anecdotes. No one knew better how to entertain and amuse Orientals than he did.

After we had talked for some time, the lady directed some of her attendants to play on the usual Turkish instruments, and others to dance, which they did very gracefully. But the dance soon degenerated into a kind of romp in which all the girls took part – pelting each other with comfits, and tumbling over each other on the floor and divans amidst shouts of laughter, to the great amusement of their mistress, who encouraged them in their somewhat boisterous play.

After we had passed nearly two hours very agreeably with our fascinating hostess and her ladies, we thought it time to withdraw. When we took leave of her, she made us promise that we would repeat our visit, telling us that she would send the same messenger as she had already employed to communicate with us, to let us know when she would receive us.

Sir Henry Layard, *Autobiography and Letters*, 1903, pp. 145–8

They never did return, having been told by an old Italian woman 'with a face pale with terror' that the lady belonged to the Palace and was probably the Sultan's sister.

Arminius Vambery, who later became Professor of Oriental Languages in Budapest, was employed as a tutor in an upper-class Turkish family in 1858. In this extract from his memoirs he narrated his efforts to make contact with the women of the house, without having anything much to say about them except that they were beautiful and appreciated his youthful ardour.

After the servants it was the harem, i.e. the Turkish female world, which caused me a good deal of trouble. Turkish women, the fair sex in general, are distinctly conservative, and they could not understand how the Pasha or Effendi could tolerate the presence of a Giaour in the Selamlik, i.e. in close proximity to the harem, and above all, how he could have come upon the idea of entrusting the education of his children to an infidel. Even now Turkish ladies are much more fanatical than the men; but at that time, the beginning of the reform period, they evinced an ungovernable hatred and aversion against everything Christian. They showed me their dislike in all sorts of teasing ways. Communication between the harem and the outer world is carried on by means of the Dolab, a round, revolving sort of cupboard. Everything intended for the Selamlik is placed in this Dolab, and when the women want to speak with any one outside they do so through the Dolab. When I heard the sound of a woman's voice, and shouted the customary 'Buyurun' ('At your service') into the Dolab, I either received no answer at all or else some rude rejoinder; and it was not till later, when I had trained myself to make exquisitely polite speeches and poetic compliments, that they vouchsafed to give me a short answer. After months of effort I succeeded at last in breaking the ice. My youthful fire could not fail to take effect, and the ladies, most of whom were very beautiful Circassians, who were much neglected by the old invalid master of the house, gradually began to praise my linguistic proficiency, and proofs of their favour were also forthcoming.

Arminius Vambery, *The Stories of my Struggles*, 1905, pp. 127–8

The next two pieces are by the same author. John Foster Fraser was a profuse travel writer who wrote books on many countries. The title of his book on North Africa, *The Land of Veiled Women*, indicates his main focus – and when he told his readers early on in the book that 'the women of the Sahara are all good-looking', we get a good idea of his state of mind. The passages below make it crystal clear.

Tum-tum, tim-tim-tum, tam, goes the drum. The flute player throws back his head, and the music wails.

Her name is Ramleya: the Daughter of the Sand.

She is the pure semitic type of Arab. She is tall and of alluring leanness, and her face is dark and long. Her eyes, kohl-smudged, are the shape of almonds. Her nose is beautifully aquiline, and has neat little protruding nostrils. Her lips are sensitive and sensuous, full, passionate. The eyes are closed as she glides, and her face is as impassive as that of a mummy.

Romance has laid hold of me tonight. For, as I sit and play with my cigarette, and watch the scene through the hanging fumes, I fancy some daughter of the ages has risen, and, whilst slumber still holds her, is dancing herself into life again. Her dark skin, the black of the kohl, the tattoo-marks of her tribe on the forehead, on her cheek, on

her chin, together with the graceful posturing, creates a feeling that
the thing is not quite earthly, that I have been reading Rider
Haggard, and all this is the figment of a dream. It is weird.

John Foster Fraser, *The Land of Veiled Women*, 1911, p. 16

I went to the bundle of white, which remained motionless. Ali
laughed, and exclaimed he had brought the *Roumi*.

The bundle half turned. The over-hood of white was thrown back.

I saw two large eyes, light brown like those of a young gazelle,
looking at me over the top of a veil. A long, thin hand, delicately
brown, with henna on the nails, and gold ornaments on the wrist,
was stretched forth. I took the proffered hand, and the palm was
warm and caressing.

Ali Mohammed was excited. Would I not sit down?

Here on a little table, no higher than a footstool, were sweet Arab
cakes, dishes of honey, fruits, amber-hued dates, mint tea, and water
chilled in porous flagons.

He was so sorry Lips of Pomegranate spoke no language but
Arabic, and she was sorry; but she was honoured I had come to her
brother's house. Never before in her life had she met a *Roumi*. She
was shy. She did not know the ways of the *Roumis*. *Roumis* and their
ladies, unveiled, met and talked and walked and were friends – so
different from the ways of the Moslem world....

I smiled at Lips of Pomegranate, and though the veil hid all but
her eyes I knew there was a smile in reply. Mysterious those
unblinking eyes, with the black arched eyebrows made blacker with
kohl, and a little streak of kohl joining the arches. Deep and
unfathomable eyes, steady in their gaze, that sent a pleasurable shiver
through an impressionable man.

I was thirsty, and I said so. Ali translated. Lips of Pomegranate
poured water into a goblet of copper and silver, and holding it in
both her little hands, held it toward me. Though seated on the floor,
I made a little bow and drank.

She offered cakes and Ali and I ate. But Lips of Pomegranate was
silent and ate not. So I protested. Ali said something. Lips of
Pomegranate hung her head. Ali spoke again. Then she raised her
delicate hands, and with a little movement loosed her veil, which fell
upon her lap.

She blushed. The hot blood showed through the soft olive skin.

Yes, she was beautiful. I felt Ali's gaze upon me, and I knew instinctively he was wondering whether I, the *Roumi*, was thinking his sister was beautiful.

It was beauty with something of the exotic loveliness of the orchid about it. The face was oval, the narrow nose was semitic; the lips were small and full and pouting and red and maddening. It was the face of a woman which a man's imagination conjures when it roams after reading Hafiz and Sadi and Omar Khayyam.

Hesitatingly, she raised her head until those soft eyes looked, with what I fondly thought was a lingering, searching look – looked straight at me as though in her little Oriental brain was the fever to fathom what was passing in the mind of the stranger – this big, awkward-limbed man from a far land.

Was the coquettishness of the woman triumphing over the shyness of the harem girl, and was she endeavouring to cast the spell of her eastern fascination over me? Maybe she interpreted the hot colour which came to my cheek. She dropped her eyes suddenly.

Turning to Ali, I said that if Lips of Pomegranate were the sister of an English friend, I would have no hesitation on congratulating him. Lips of Pomegranate intuitively, instinctively, knowing I was talking about her, questioned her brother. He told her what I said, for a deep glow suffused countenance and neck.

A lovely creature. I looked upon her and my senses became as if soaked in opium. I was filled with an ecstasy of emotion.

The sun began to dip. I realised that, and I murmured I had come to see the view. I jumped to my feet. Ali Mohammed rose and then offered cigarettes.

Lips of Pomegranate rose. How tall she was – as tall as myself. I asked if she would care for a Russian cigarette, and I produced my case. She bent, as she took the thin cardboard tube between her lips whilst I held a match. She smiled her thanks. It was a ravishing, provoking smile, tinged with sensuousness, and the minx knew it.

She lost her shyness. She threw aside her white cloak, which had umbrella'd her from the sun. Her dress was black and green edged with gold, a black zouave jacket, and the filmy gauze did nothing to hide the cadenced pulsations of her breasts. No corsets stiffened her waist. She was supple. Her frock clasped close, so that, when she walked, the sway of the slender hips was seen. As she moved across the roof to the parapet, with lithe, almost snake-like undulations, her wanton walk told of the lazy lasciviousness of her nature.

She knew. She was no woman if she did not know her charms.

Her glance was a caress. Those eyes, so timid at first, were capable of the reckless rapture of love. She was a sylph.

The sun sank in glory behind the golden desert, and pensiveness dreamed over the world. The air was thick with the odour of the gardens. The call of the muezzin sounded from the minaret. Spice-haunted dusk came quickly.

John Foster Fraser, *The Land of Veiled Women*, 1911, pp. 164–7

In 1910 Eustache de Lorey and Douglas Sladen published *The Moon of the Fourteenth Night*, allegedly based on the journal of a Frenchman, Édouard Valmont, who had been a colleague of de Lorey. Valmont had lived in Teheran for some time and fell into 'a liaison with a native woman' called Bibi Mah. Whether the journal really existed or not, the photograph in the book said to be of Bibi Mah was also used in the book *Queer Things About Persia*, by the same authors, and there it was said to represent 'a young dancer from Bokhara'. Nevertheless, the book provides some exquisite moments describing this relationship between the 'sensuous East' and the 'rational West'. In the first piece the Frenchman and the 'native woman' meet on the terraces at night.

Before such a prospect there was no room for hesitation. I arose. And, by an effect of telepathy to which the great Saadi was, perhaps, no stranger, there arose at the same moment on the other side of the wall, not a Peri of Space, not a transparent shade, but a lovely Persian woman of flesh and blood.

We remained for a moment mutually spellbound, and as if paralysed, gazing open-mouthed into each other's eyes.

She was the first to move, and was about to disappear when – not to give the lie to Saadi – I caught hold of her sleeve and held her back. She dared not cry out, for to attract the attention of the other inmates of the harem to her equivocal position would have been to court eternal disgrace and loss. So she contented herself with struggling – covering her face with the other arm.

'Wherefore plunge me in darkness by hiding from me the most beautiful of moons?' I asked, with truly Eastern rhetoric, and in very fair Persian. 'Another glimpse and you will have made roast meat of my heart!'

Her arm dropped slightly, revealing her eyes – great, startled eyes, black and profound. She was evidently astonished at hearing such speech in the mouth of a Frank.

This initial success encouraged me, and I recited to her all the exquisite things I had learnt from the poets of her own country. I must have been guilty of some barbarisms, for I could hear her laughing silently. The victory was with me.

Her arm offered no resistance; I loosened my hold, and she did not slip away. Then I whispered to her sweet things, such as can only be uttered in Persian, sweet in sense, and sweeter still in sound – a sweetness that lost nothing from my French accent. And she appeared to take a real delight in listening to them, these sweet things, which doubtless fell for the first time upon her ears, since the gentle art of flirtation is a grace unknown to the harem. She became oblivious of *les convenances*, and her arm falling aside unheeded, left her face disclosed to my admiring gaze.

Although a most naturally feminine thing thus to allow oneself to be admired and complimented by a young man, it was, none the less, a most serious offence in the eyes of a Mohammedan. Now that the thing was done, the wisest course seemed to enjoy to the full the stolen waters. When Mother Eve had once bitten into the apple we may be sure she finished it to the very core.

Nevertheless, my lovely neighbour remained passive and without response. Lovely she certainly was, strangely lovely, I might indeed say beautiful. Never had I seen such marvellous eyes. Large, melting, almond-shaped, they shone in their liquid orbits like stars upon a lake, and eclipsed every other feature in her face, the small, straight nose, the mouth, no bigger than one of themselves, the colourless complexion, like satin forgotten in the sun. The rounded oval of her face was framed in a white muslin *chargat*, which covered the whole of her head, fell back over her shoulders, and was gathered in folds beneath her chin by a gold fastening, giving her that likeness to a cloud-girt moon of which the poets sing. Two jet-black bands of hair were parted over her forehead, leaving only a tiny space visible above the long arched brows.

After a monologue in which I exhausted my supply of Persian, I stopped, and our two silences mingled, leaving speech to our eyes, or rather to our souls, if it be true that the one is but the mirror of the other.

What will be the outcome of this contact of the souls of Asia and

Europe? Will they be able to understand each other's language? Hardly! But these are big words to use of an innocent interview, a simple exchange of glances!

All the same it is exciting, and dangerous, and hopeless, utterly hopeless, for there is no fighting against the harem – one is defeated beforehand.

Eustache de Lorey and Douglas Sladen, *The Moon of the Fourteenth Night*, 1910, pp. 43–6

In the second piece he expresses some doubt about the wisdom of his move but not enough to prevent him from pursuing the 'adventure'.

I had been terribly to blame for not reflecting as to the possible consequences of my little flirtation. It had never occurred to me to resist what was at first mere curiosity and afterwards the powerful attraction of the mystery and danger of this Oriental adventure. And now that the wall of the harem had begun to fall I hesitated, naturally, to throw myself into the breach! What a pitiful hero of romance I should have made, to be sure!

Filled with distress, and with rage against myself – and above all against Islam the inexorable – I watched the poor child's slow tears.

They lingered, as if reluctant to leave the eyelids of Bibi Mah, these tears, pent in by the long lashes as by a dam of rushes. Then they dropped, one by one, and flowed over her cheek in different directions to lose themselves at last in the folds of her tulle *chargat*. One of them was so large and heavy that the lashes seemed to bend beneath its slowly moving weight. It fell on to her cheek, where it hung for a moment, as if irresolute, to slip down the next instant to the bewitching valley of a dimple at the corner of her mouth, then spreading, it reached her lips and hid in their rosy flower.

How I envied that tear!

Eustache de Lorey and Douglas Sladen, *The Moon of the Fourteenth Night*, 1910, p. 125

After much melodramatic action they finally come together.

She had greeted my entrance with a faint smile, which gladdened me, but she had no answer for me when I spoke to her. Her eyes searched mine, no longer with the pathetic charm of the beaten gazelle, but with a fixed impenetrable gaze, whose meaning I could not fathom. It was as if between us rose, invisible, the wall of the harem.

A soft light fell upon the amber oval of her cheek, with its spot of vivid scarlet, over which the long lashes traced a delicate shadow, and at the corner of her mouth, small and red as some ripe fruit, a dimple showed itself. I watched her with a sense of fascination, of strange emotion, my whole being passionately vibrant.

Her hair fell over the yellow gold of the cushions beneath her head in a myriad of strands, sweeping away on either side of her pale forehead like a raven's wings. Her delicate arched brows met above her nose, linked, as it were, by a tattooed star.

She pushed aside the coverlet with a quick gesture, and her bosom lay open to my view, with its exquisite lines, the throat rounded as an ivory column, whose swelling base gently lifted the transparent folds of its *pirhan* of shivered gauze. A subtle perfume of rose and ambergris accentuated the elusive sensuality, by whose voluptuousness I was bemused.

Bibi Mah's little hand lay white upon the flowers of the quilt; upon her shell-like finger-nails were henna-stained crescents. I kissed the shining crescents. I kissed the little hand of Bibi Mah.

She did not move. Her cheek rested where it had fallen against her shoulder, but her quickened breathing showed in the rising and falling of the gauze, the flash of its silver stars upon her breast. Her lips unclosed, moistly red as a pomegranate in the sun; and slowly, softly, gently, her eyelids lifted, hesitating, to fall again at once with a quiver of silky lashes.

Unconsciously I had bent lower, and my face was now quite close to hers, so close, indeed, that the end of my moustache brushed her cheek. She shivered, her head shifted, and her great dark eyes gazed into my own. This time their expression was different. I knew that glance, already caught sight of upon the terrace, that glance which had drawn my soul away; but it was glowing now with a strange new fire, a sparkle and a splendour hitherto unknown, whose irresistible magic opened before me a new Eden.

My brain swam, my ears sang with a sound of voluptuous music, and my lips grew faint at the burning touch of the lips of Bibi Mah!

Eustache de Lorey and Douglas Sladen, *The Moon of the Fourteenth Night*, 1910, pp. 207–8

Finally, of course, he realizes that East and West can never meet and refuses even to discuss the future with Bibi Mah. 'Why follow the lure of a dream that can never come true, when our reality is itself a dream?' he asks.

Ernest Griffin went to work as a doctor for the British Red Crescent Society in Tripolitania in 1912 – and discovered that, despite his sedate middle age, he was still susceptible to feminine charms.

As I was on the point of going, he [the rabbi] begged me to call and see a member of the community who was lying sick. I accompanied him through the town, and was finally shown into a house where a middle-aged Jew was lying on a palliasse. I was making a careful and impressive examination of his condition, when a shadow cut off the bright sunlight that was pouring through the door. Before I could look up, I heard the excited voice of Mustapha saying, '*Mon docteur, regardez donc la jolie juive!*' I glanced at the figure in the doorway, and, ignorant as I am in these matters, I at once saw that during his stay in Paris my interpreter had by no means neglected the most important of all studies, for the young Jewess was indeed beautiful. A mass of black, glossy hair crowned a head poised proudly on a slender, graceful neck. Dark eyes, veiled modestly under curving lashes, looked out from a delicately-chiselled face. Surprised at the sight of foreigners, whom she now beheld for the first time in her life, and who did not spare her an admiring scrutiny, a rich blush drove the pallor from her cheeks. The colour sped in a wave down her neck, fired the whiteness of her bosom, and tinged the rounded arms that escaped from her scanty robe. Her half-parted red lips revealed a perfect row of teeth, and her eyes falling gently to the ground invited a glance to her arched feet and slender ankles.

Sometimes one is apt to forget that sedate middle age has chilled the blood of youth, and I must confess that, for the moment, my attention was singularly diverted from the woes of my patient.

Ernest H. Griffin, *Adventures in Tripoli*, 1924, pp. 134–5

The women always looked impoverished and ill-nourished. While their men-folk were away fighting they lived on a miserable pittance of flour, allowed them by the Government. I remember one day, on returning to the tents after a good gallop on Darkey, I saw a large bundle of firewood lying on the ground, and beside it the curled-up figure of an Arab girl; apparently she was weeping bitterly. I asked Mohammed what the matter was. He shrugged his shoulders and told me to take no notice, suggested cynically that the crying was put on for my benefit. As he, however, was inclined to be harsh with visitors of the fair sex, I told him not to interfere, but to get back to his pots and pans; for what indeed can a greasy cook know about drying a woman's tears?

'What is it, Fatima?' I asked gently, and she shyly lifted two glistening eyes to mine. (Untruthful Mohammed! This was no make-believe; these were real tears that glittered in her eyes and hung like jewels on her fringing lashes.) Then her veil flashed across her face again.

'Speak, Fatima!' I urged.

Slowly she lifted herself from the ground and sobbed out her story: her father had been killed in the war; she was terribly hungry; she had spent all day gathering firewood, and now – a heart-breaking sob – Mohammed had refused to buy it.

I exclaimed with horror at this brutality and was rewarded by a dropping of the veil and a little, wan smile. The stones of the desert had hurt her feet too, and an arched foot was held up for my inspection; a foot fresh from Nature's mould, with dainty toes, uncramped and unconfined; so different from the tortured, distorted feet the sight of which makes the most hardened of us shudder when a civilized woman takes off her stocking. But Fatima had still another confidence to make – if only the Doctor Bey knew how heavy the load had been, how it had hurt her shoulders. Then a furtive glance round to make sure that Mohammed was far away and none but professional eyes could see, and a discreet area of smooth skin was exposed with an ugly scratch across it. I grew indignant.

'Mohammed!' I called sharply. '*Mais, mon Dieu*, what is this? What are we here for? Have we not come to help the poor and unfortunate? This young lady's father has been killed in the war, and yet you refused to buy her wood!'

Mohammed muttered some libellous remark to the effect that he did not wish to encourage bad characters about the camp, thrust a coin into the girl's hand and marched off.

Fatima clutched the coin in a tiny hand but showed no signs of departing. She looked at me appealingly with her veil caught coquettishly between little white teeth and an arm displayed effectively against the tent pole.

I asked her what more she wanted. Alas! food was so dear – a sob – Mohammed had given her so little; but, praise God! – eyes lifted to Heaven – the Doctor Bey had a kind heart.

I took a hasty glance to see that Mohammed was not a witness of my weakness and then put a piece of money into her hand. She glanced at it, gasped with pleasure and seized my hand to kiss it. I snatched it away as etiquette demands, and calling up my best Arabic I said: 'What a pretty girl you are, Fatima!'

An illuminating and satisfied smile crossed her face, and conquering woman went on her way rejoicing.

Ernest H. Griffin, *Adventures in Tripoli*, 1924, pp. 232–4

To end, a piece by Isobel Burton in which she talked about the seductive voice of Eastern men, and a moment of romance expressed by Gertrude Bell.

There is something in an Eastern man's voice peculiarly seductive. The women's are shrill, discordant, and nasal, they put your teeth on an edge, and *vous agacent les nerfs*. The commonest Moslem, Druze, Kurd, Afghan, or Bedawi, has a soft, yet guttural accent, that comes from the chest, in which there is passion and repose – it is rich and strong, but restrained; it becomes music when reciting, and tells upon the ear like the soughing of the distant wind, or like the gondolier serenades of Venice as they come floating along the water, under the shimmer of the harvest moon. I have heard that rare voice but once or twice in Europeans, and that was because they had lived in the East, or had Tuscan mothers; and there is a laziness and yet a virility in the Spanish voice that reminds me slenderly of the Oriental.

Isobel Burton, *The Inner Life of Syria, Palestine, and the Holy Land*, 1875, p. 366

The Sheikh and all the swells came to call and took me into the village to look around. Dear, nice people! I am sorry to leave them. I haven't left them yet, however, for the Sheikh, Ibrahim, is still in my tent door as I write. He makes well, I must say, being singularly beautiful. It is a hot, hot night.

The Letters of Gertrude Bell, 1947, p. 90

Chapter 6

THE VOICE OF SEX CRYING IN THE WILDERNESS

Dancing produced strong reactions from travellers and the subject falls well between the last chapter and the next. European tradition led them to expect a romantic and voluptuous performance; European prudery led them to damn it; Eurocentrism led them to ridicule it. Douglas Sladen, who often produced lurid prose when writing about women, poured forth a string of invective against Jewish dancers in Tunis – and provided the title of this chapter.

I was rather disgusted that, whenever you asked what you ought to see in Tunis, people took it for granted that you would want to begin with the Arab *café-chantant* and hip-dancing. I think these performances amongst the dullest and most revolting which the thirst for sight-seeing has ever persuaded me to sit out. There is no fun and no music in them, and I soon tire of the novelty of seeing Oriental musicians striking an earthenware drum with the edges of their hands, and whining with their voices a monotonous chant without words.

Nor is the music improved if the band is increased by twangers on one-string fiddles and screamers upon bamboo flutes, though the latter have the antiquarian interest of appearing on Egyptian monuments. One often sits listening to this sort of thing for an hour before the hip-dancing begins. The Arabs do not mind, because they feast their eyes all the time on the elephantine charms of the Jewish dancers.

The whole thing was disgusting to me, commencing with the Arabs themselves, who sat about the hall, transgressing the Koran by drinking alcoholic liquors, and leering at the Jewesses.

The Arab, when he sails down from the Kasbah in a fluttering white burnous, is often beautiful and romantic enough to turn the head of almost any woman; but the Arab at a *café-chantant*, lolling back on his chair with glazed eyes and a bock of beer in front of him, is a beast – but not such a beast as the women who dance before him.

The hall is not seated like an English music-hall, but more like a café on the boulevard, the chairs being arranged round little tables, for every one is supposed to order drinks, as well as pay the entrance money. Sometimes a party of friends go together to one of these cafés, but their principal patrons are apt to go along – in itself a bad feature. The Arab dresses himself to kill on most occasions, though he has nothing to kill, poor devil, except the Jewish women of pleasure. He goes to a *café-chantant* especially gorgeous, and lets the flower-seller – a man, not a beautiful girl – provide him with an armoury of the quaint tufts of tightly wired jessamine flowers in which he delights. He sits with them and his bock on the table in front of him, feasting his eyes on the row of female walruses who are going to dance.

There was a priest at Taormina who frightened his congregation into a religious revival by telling them that hell would be full of Germans. The sight of these women might cure a subaltern of his taste for music-halls. They are horrible, horrible, horrible! They are human sows, whose faces are daubed with vermilion and whose bodies are decked with tawdry chiffons which would disgrace a Guy Fawkes – as far as they are decked at all, for they show an expanse of bosom and bare arm – and shoddy white silk breeches, stretched over the legs of hippopotami. I can find no comparison in the brute creation for their leer, for in the abuse of love He made man a little lower than the animals. One might call it bestial, for want of a better word; but no beast would look like that, unless he were a baboon, man's fallen brother. An amorous boa-constrictor would look refined and romantic beside these 'strange women' of the Bible.

Their eyelashes are blackened and their eyes brightened with kohl till they stare like a house to let. Their fingers are reddened with henna – I think even the gums of their large, open, man-hunting mouths are picked out with something to make their teeth gape at you. You want to get away from them, as you want to get away from a red-eyed bull, seeking what he may destroy. They are like huge, hideous, wicked, terrifying images of Moloch, waiting for men to be roasted alive in the brazen arms of their lust. You long to put a stone wall between you and those snakes' heads, with their glaring eyes and ravening jaws, before the entertainment begins.

It takes some time beginning. You sit there for an hour or more in front of these *grosses juives*, white elephants to anything but an Arab. While the musicians drone their chant and bump their drums, you are supposed to be taking in their points. You see various messages passing up to them from voluptuaries seated by themselves. At length the foreigners show signs of moving, in despair of there being anything like a performance. If the proprietor estimates that the movement is genuine, he tells the first dancer to begin. She advances to the footlights with a grin of triumph. She has no doubt that she is perfectly lovely and love-compelling, though she looks like a balloon with legs, as she towers above the footlights.

Doubtless the hip-dancing, which means the swaying of a mountainously fat body, might suggest all manner of passionate declarations if you were able to give it a fair examination; but the rolling about of this uncontrolled mass of obesity is too ungraceful. The whole figure of the woman is so revolting to European ideas of feminine charm, that you soon transfer your attention from the dancer to the audience. Even the interest of the audience is disgusting.

It seems like a recollection of a nightmare to recall even the slightest and the least ill-looking of the dancers, as she stood on the stage above us in her ridiculous little muslin dressing-jacket and enormous tight-fitting breeches of white satin, revealing a monstrous area of bosom and arms covered with sham jewellery, and with what coarse beauty there was in her face inflamed with splashes of red and black and white pigments – the voice of sex crying in the wilderness.

Douglas Sladen, *Carthage and Tunis*, 1906, vol. II, pp. 480–4

In 1798, on a voyage to Syria, C.-F. Volney wrote about Arab dancing. Claiming that a detailed description would be too much for the delicate ears of the readers, he went on to feed them titbits about the 'lewd representations' which comprised the dance. In fact, most of the authors included in this chapter represented dance in the same way – and the charge of lewdness should more appropriately be levelled at them. Niebuhr's account also reveals much about his general attitude to women.

It is by no means the case that dance, which with us is as esteemed as music, holds the same position in the opinion of the Arabs. They believe this art is stigmatized with a kind of shame; a man could not indulge in it without dishonour, and it is only tolerated among women. This seems a very strict judgement but before condemning it, it must be realized that in the Orient dance is not an imitation of war, as with the Greeks, or a combination of pleasing attitudes and movements, as in our country, but a lewd representation of the most audacious love. It is the type of dance which, taken from Carthage to Rome, heralded the decline of the republican morality there. Later revived in Spain by the Arabs, it remains there called the *fandango*. Despite our liberal ideas, it would be difficult to describe this dance without shocking the reader. It is enough to say that the dancer, arms outstretched, with a passionate air, singing and accompanying herself with castanets, stands in one place and performs movements of the body that even passion takes care to hide in the shadow of the night.

C.-F. Volney, *Voyage en Égypt et en Syrie*, 1959 (1st edn 1787), p. 392

A respectable Mahometan, who should indulge in dancing, would disgrace himself in the estimation of his countrymen. The women, however, value themselves upon excellence in this exercise, and practise it without scruple, reckoning it their duty to contribute to the pleasures of their husbands, by every little art in their power. When by themselves, too, in an assembly consisting only of women, on occasion of a marriage, or any other solemnity, they vie no less than before their husbands, in dancing.

A person from Tripoli related to me in what manner the women of that city amuse themselves upon festive occasions, and I have good reason to believe, that the same customs prevail also in Turkey and Arabia; however, I do not pretend to be absolutely certain; for it is impossible to meet with an eye-witness of those amusements. My Tripoli acquaintance had his information from his wife, who ingenuously told him whatever he asked.

No woman would presume to appear in an assembly, if she were not handsome and magnificently dressed. If the entertainment happens to be in the house of a family of rank, fifty of the greatest beauties in the city assemble, all dressed out in great splendour. In their train, they bring out their handsomest slaves, who attend in a separate room, to take care of the coffers containing their mistresses' clothes. After the ladies have been seated for some time, and have been served with refreshments, young girls are called in, to divert the company with vocal and instrumental music. The most distinguished lady in the company then rises, dances for a few minutes, and passes into the next apartment, where her slaves are in waiting to change her dress. She lays all aside, even her slippers embroidered with gold and silver, and retains only her headdress and bracelets, which are richly ornamented with jewels. In the mean time, the rest dance, and in their turns leave the room to change their dress; and this is successively repeated, so long, that a lady will sometimes change her dress ten times in one night; and put on so many different suits, every one richer than another. They strive all to command admiration; and their endeavours end, as among us, in jealousies and grudges.

The Greek women have so fully adopted this piece of Eastern luxury, that they change their dress on the slightest occasions. An European settled at Constantinople, told me, that he had seen a Greek lady, the wife of one of his friends, whom he visited, put on five different dresses, in the space of two hours. These instances prove the power of instinct, and the uniformity of the character of the sex, all over the world.

The men disdain to practise this exercise, but amuse themselves sometimes with seeing dancing girls exhibit, who go about, and dance for hire, either in places of public resort, or in private houses upon festive occasions. Those dancers are called, at Constantinople, *Tschingane* or gypsies, and at Cairo, *Ghasie*. They are young married, or unmarried women, belonging to a separate and despised class of the lower people, who intermarry only among themselves. Their parents are commonly farriers by trade. They are attended only by one man, who plays on the *semenge*, and sometimes by an old woman, who plays on the tambourine, and appears to watch over their conduct; they are said, however, not to be of the most demure and rigid virtue. Yet no married Mahometan incurs any obloquy by carrying them to dance in his house; and they go wherever they are well paid. But an unmarried Mahometan dares not invite them to his house; and we never met with any of them in the houses of any of the French merchants, who, by a regulation of their sovereign, are all restricted to celibacy.

At first, we never saw them but by accident, and in a public house without the city; but towards the conclusion of our stay in Egypt, we had better opportunities of gratifying our curiosity. A great part of the houses in which the Europeans live, stand along the great canal which passes through Cairo: and those *Ghasie* accordingly derive their best profits from dancing opposite to these houses in the canal, when it is dry, before the opening of the dyke. At that period, we made sometimes one troop, sometimes another dance before us. We needed such amusements to divert the gloomy ideas which the prospect of our departure raised in our minds. Yet, however much disposed to receive entertainment, they did not please us at first; their vocal and instrumental music we thought horrible, and their persons appeared disgustingly ugly, with their yellow hands, spotted faces, absurd ornaments, and hair larded with stinking pomatum. But, by degrees, we learned to endure them, and for want of better, began to fancy some of them pretty, to imagine their voices agreeable, their movements graceful, though indecent, and their music not absolutely intolerable.

M. Niebuhr, *Travels Through Arabia*, 1792, vol. I, pp. 137–41

Vivant Denon and Bayle St John continued the allegations of indecency, as did the Hon. Lewis Wingfield, who went on to dissect the anatomy of an Ouled Nayl performer. The next two authors dismissed the dancers as being of little interest to a European, while Captain Fred Burnaby, who was travelling on horseback through Turkey, told his hosts just what the Lord Chamberlain would have made of the performance.

They had brought two musical instruments, an accordion and a drum made of terracotta, which they beat with their hands. They were seven; two began to dance and the others sang and accompanied them with castanets in the shape of small cymbals the size of a 6 pound piece. The movement with which they clicked one against the other gave infinite grace to their fingers and wrists. Their dance was at first voluptuous, but then it became lewd, no more than a coarse and indecent expression of sensual passion. What made these scenes even more distasteful was that at the times when they still had a minimum of discretion, one of the musicians would come forward, with the inane air of one of the clowns in our own entertainments, to disturb with a loud laugh the scene of ecstasy which would end the dance. . . .

Despite their licentious life, the *almes* are taken into the harems to teach the young girls everything that will make them more pleasing to their husbands; they give them lessons in dancing, singing, charm, and all sorts of voluptuous pursuits. It is not surprising in a society whose morals place voluptuousness as the main duty of women, that those who make a profession of pleasing should be the teachers of the fair sex. They are invited to all the great feasts and when a husband wants to gladden the life of his harem he also calls them there.

Vivant Denon, *Voyage dans la basse et la haute Égypte*, 1802, vol. I, pp. 154–6

A colony of Ghawazees, or dancing-girls, was here established, not exactly for the purpose of attracting strangers. They had chosen this secluded spot as a kind of academy, where the young and ignorant might learn the graceful arts and allurements peculiar to their strange community.

A fat, frowsy dame – accustomed, no doubt, of old, herself to exhibit with the light fantastic hip – was at once mistress of the coffee-house and superintendent of the chaste education of the infant Ghawazee. Two pupils, probably first of the first form, were shown to us, and ordered to repeat some of their lessons. They were quite a credit to the establishment, and, though barely ten years old, had little to learn, except passion. Like two lovely automata, they went through every manoeuvre of their elder sisters; but whilst the Arabs assembled swore with admiration and grunted out lascivious sighs, we could not help feeling saddened by beholding childhood thus profaned. The frowsy dame, who counted on being handsomely rewarded, watched our faces anxiously, and asked if we were displeased. New in the country, we made some objections, and were comically misunderstood. Had this accommodating lady been acquainted with Shakespeare, she would have compressed her answer into one phrase, –

'Younger than they are happy mothers made';

but, not being so learned, she entered into a variety of details, physiological and other, with which we could well have dispensed. Changing the subject, we inquired the origin of these charming children, and were told they had been bought from their fellah mothers. At the time I doubted the fact, and believed them to have been stolen; but sales of children are not uncommon in the villages, where extreme misery triumphs over the strength of maternal affection.

It seems impossible to obtain a distinct idea of the origin and history of the so-called tribe of Ghawazees. Of course the nature of their occupation precludes the possibility of any unity of blood; but there are certain traces of a distinct type, which reappears here and there in remarkable purity. Forms and faces cannot surpass in beauty those of the complete Ghawazee; and, wonderful to say, in spite of the life of debauchery these women lead, they *keep* far better than their more virtuous sisters. Does labour destroy beauty more effectually than vice? Or is it that the Ghawazee, leading a life of leisure from her youth upward; surrounded ever by some of the accidents of wealth – garments of fine tissue, ornaments of gold and silver, – feeding on stimulating food and drinking something more generous than the cold water of the Nile; her ears soothed by music, and her imagination spurred by amatory songs, and by communion with men rendered intelligent for a while by passion – under all these influences does the Ghawazee acquire a mental superiority, which acts outwardly, and successfully combats the fatal progress of decay? The hetairae of ancient Greece retained their charms when those who, perhaps, eclipsed them as maidens had settled down into demure matrons, not lovely but respectable; and the same observation has been repeated on their modern descendants – 'for instance, Ninon de l'Enclos'. These are not satisfactory speculations. It might be possible, however, to explain the mystery to the honour of virtue, and to the advancement of our notions on female education.

The facts which have suggested these remarks are well known to all Egyptian residents; and it is scarcely necessary to allude to the celebrated Kutchuk Hanem, who, for I know not how many seasons, has withstood the admiration of a whole procession of pilgrims to Gizeh. No doubt she will one of these days be pushed from her stool by some more youthful competitor, and compelled to become a Magdalen in spite of herself; but in those unrigid countries the daughters of the castanet are not driven to fall back on philosophy, piety, scandal-mongering, or the hospital. A new career opens when the old one has closed; and Safia, who has lately become a decent gentlewoman of Cairo, after twenty years of public life, is by no means an extraordinary instance. Most probably her wealth had something to do with finding her a respectable husband; but I venture to say that many an Arab, who might be fascinated by her talents for society or her glory, would turn away with contempt from a quiet widow-lady of equal age and fortune. We have seen similar things in Europe, where public opinion is more meddling and censorious, and where the excuse scarcely exists that virtuous women are mewed up in ignorance and inexperience.

The tribe, or rather corporation of dancing-girls, seem to have existed from the earliest times. They preserve traces of a distinct language, unless the few uncouth words peculiar to them ought not rather to be regarded as mere slang. I am inclined to think there is some affinity between them and the gypsies, – the men who profess to be their parents often following precisely the same occupations as these vagabonds, being tinkers, smiths, makers of ornaments, especially of supposed magic rings.

Bayle St John, Village Life in Egypt, 1852, vol. I, pp. 23–7

The Oulad Nayls are *the* institution of the desert *par excellence*, and will hold a place in my memory long after the other details of this journey shall have passed away. They are the 'dames légères' of the Sahara, and come generally from one special tribe in the vicinity of Laghouat. In this strange country, where the woman is not the equal of the man, we find a still stranger subject for marvel. The Oulad Nayls are far from being looked down upon for their little peccadilloes; on the contrary, they are a much-honoured race. No wedding is complete without their presence, and no women marry so well as these fair but frail daughters of the plains. Having made market of their beauty for a certain time, they return to their tribe, buy a few fields and some palm-trees, and set up as respectable proprietors – a fit mark for heiress-hunting spendthrifts.

Their costume while pursuing their craft is very wonderful indeed. They are so wrapped up, and overloaded with clothes, that it is difficult to get any idea of their figures, as one sees nothing but a tangled mass of long draperies and handkerchiefs and chains, which don't seem to belong anywhere in particular. I will nevertheless endeavour to dissect one of these extraordinary anatomies, piece by piece, as far as I am capable of so difficult a task.

The body is draped, in the first place, in a long gown, that trails far behind, made usually of Manchester cotton print or some flimsy native stuff, which is joined at the shoulder by large silver pins, and doubled under the arms, so as to leave the sides bare to the waist. To one of the silver pins is attached a loose banana handkerchief, used sometimes in the dance, and sometimes to mop the perspiring face of beauty. Round the waist is an immense length of silken belt, wound round and round the body, and hanging in tassels to the feet. Their feet are encased in little embroidered slippers, or red morocco boots, over which fall the monstrous silver anklets, whose clanking gives notice of the approach of the fair one, and reminds the traveller of a prison yard. From the shoulders falls a cloak, dark and thick, and over that again is hung a white-striped cotton and silk sort of burnous, which sometimes trails in the mud, and is occasionally drawn over the head. The head is the most remarkable thing of all, and gives its *cachet* to the figure, more especially when seen from behind, as it is a great deal wider than the body (about three-quarters of a yard across altogether) and quite without form. The hair is plaited into four times its ordinary bulk by the addition of horse-hair and wool; and over this is built up an edifice of chains, sequins, and gold handkerchiefs, such as would supply half-a-dozen ordinary women. The fabric is only taken down once in three or four months, and forms, with its profusion of adornment and glittering scarfs, a comfortable nest for every description of unclean insect, such as must, I should imagine, have been nursed in the heads of our great-grandmothers. Under the chin is often tied a gauze veil of red or green, which is knotted about the neck, and covers the whole construction. They steep their hair in henna as well as their hands, and this renders them even more filthy than they would otherwise be. Their silken burnouses and gowns are almost hidden under the weight of ornament with which they are encumbered – yards of silver chains about their necks and waists, on which are strung daggers and looking-glasses, and great boxes of talismans, all of solid silver; while the wealthier damsels have, in addition to all this, magnificent necklaces of coral and silver beads. Their arms are loaded with immense bracelets, and their fingers concealed by multitudes of rings. All these costly gewgaws flap and rattle as the ladies walk, and produce a singular effect where many are about. Their faces would not be ugly were they not plastered with rouge, and painted in patterns. The eyebrows glisten with oil, and the whole physiognomy is a mass of grease, otherwise it would crack with the thickness of the repulsive unguents. From behind, as I have said, they present a very droll appearance – a mere bundle of clothes with a wide top, a tag, or a handkerchief, or a bit of gauze, sticking out generally of some inconceivable place, which gives a general impression of everything having been thrown at the figure, and stuck there by some magnetic power.

The Hon. Lewis Wingfield, *Under the Palms in Algeria and Tunis*,
1868, vol. II, pp. 42–6

I now suggested that the dancing should begin, and our Semitic M.C. hurried the ladies on by shouting *Hati jemalsin*, 'Bring a couple of camels'; for under this choice metaphor the fair sex is always addressed on such occasions. Presently 'the camel' appeared, and commenced what Burckhardt has described as 'graceful and delicate motions', but which reminded me forcibly of a top-heavy hollyhock, the dancer remaining on one spot, and merely swaying herself to and fro in a ridiculous and awkward manner.

E. H. Palmer, *The Desert of the Exodus*, 1871, vol. I, pp. 186–7

Some of the principal inhabitants were present to meet us, and the entertainment of the evening consisted of coffee and pipes, with minstrels and dancing girls. The performances of the latter were more curious than edifying, and to see them once is sufficient.

Sir W. G. Armstrong, *A Visit to Egypt in 1872*, 1874, p. 141

Some gipsy men now entered, and, squatting down on the carpet, began to tune their lutes. One of their party carried a fearful instrument. It was rather like the bagpipes. He at once commenced a wild and discordant blast. The musicians were followed by the dancers.

The chief of the gipsy women was provided with a tambourine. She was attired in a blue jacket, underneath this was a purple waistcoat, slashed with gold embroidery, a pair of very loose, yellow trousers covered her extremities. Massive gold earrings had stretched the lobes of her ears, they reached nearly to her shoulders, and by way of making herself thoroughly beautiful, and doing fit honour to the occasion, she had stained her teeth and finger-nails with some red dye. Her eyebrows had been made to meet by a line drawn with a piece of charcoal. Gold spangles were fastened to her black locks. Massive brass rings encircled her ankles, the metal jingling as she waddled around the room.

The two girls who accompanied her were in similar costumes, but without the gold spangles for their hair, which hung in long tresses below their waists. The girls, advancing, took the hand of Vankovitch's wife, and placed it on their heads as a sort of deferential salute. The Pole poured out a glass of raki for the fat woman, who, though a Mohammedan, was not adverse to alcohol. She smacked her lips loudly; the man with the bagpipes gave vent to his feelings in a more awful sound than before; the lutes struck up in different keys, and the ball began.

The two girls whirled round each other, first slowly, and then increased their pace till their long black tresses stood out at right angles from their bodies. The perspiration poured down their cheeks. The old lady, who was seated on a divan, now uncrossed her legs, beating her brass ankle-rings the one against the other, she added yet another noise to the din which prevailed. The girls snapped their castanets, and commenced wriggling their bodies around each other with such velocity that it was impossible to recognise the one from the other. All of a sudden, the music stopped. The panting dancers threw themselves down on the laps of the musicians.

'What do you think of the performance?' said Vankovitch to me, as he poured out another glass of raki for the dancers. 'It is real hard work, is it not?' Then, without waiting for an answer, he continued, 'The Mohammedans who read of European balls, and who have never been out of Turkey, cannot understand people taking any pleasure in dancing. "What is the good of it when I can hire someone else to dance for me?" is the remark.'

'They are not very wrong,' I here observed; 'that is, if they form an idea of European dances from their own. Our Lord Chamberlain would soon put a stop to these sort of performances in England.'

'The Lord Chamberlain, who is he?' inquired an Armenian who was present, and who spoke French.

'He is an official who looks after public morals.'

'And do you mean to say that he would object to this sort of dance?'

'Yes.'

'But this is nothing,' said Vankovitch. 'When there is a marriage festival in a harem, the women arrange their costumes so that one article of attire may fall off after another during the dance. The performers are finally left in very much the same garb as our first parents before the fall. We shall be spared this spectacle, for my wife

is here. The gipsies will respect her presence because they know that
she is a European.'

Fred Burnaby, *On Horseback Through Asia Minor*, 1877, vol. I,
pp. 220–3

The next piece from the novel *Askaros Kassis the Copt* by
Edwin de Leon, describes the disgust of the American ladies
when they witness dancing in the house of a princess.

She clapped her hands thrice sharply together, when a curtain was
suddenly pushed aside at one corner of the apartment, and three
Ghawazee, or dancing girls, bounded into the room, and commenced the
wildest dancing; unseen musicians, behind the curtain, accompanying
their movements with the wailing music of the fife, and of the *darabouka*
drum. To describe their dance would be next to impossible, for it had in it
more of St. Vitus or of St. Anthony than of Terpsichore.

Their movement was at first slow and measured, like the opening
of the Tarantula; but soon the music grew faster and more furious,
and, with the rising din, faster and furious grew the posturings and
contortions of the *Ghawazee*. They writhed and twisted their lithe
bodies and sinuous limbs in strange muscular contortions – into
almost impossible positions – keeping time to the music with every
motion. They advanced and retreated; one personating a man,
another a woman, in every attitude of timid supplication – audacious
wooing, rejection, despair, angry violence, consent, successful love,
rapture, agony! and closed the strange performance with grossness
too revolting for description.

The visitors, fascinated at first by the wild novelty of the
performance, were soon disgusted by its coarseness; especially in the
great feat which was the crowning performance, the 'Nakle a ho', or
'bee-dance'; for the conception and execution of this dance
surpassed any indecency of the French or American ballet corps –
very far exceeding the bounds of the most lax propriety.

The young girls and the ancient maiden averted their eyes, and
fixed them upon their pipe-bowls, while this more than Bacchanal
frenzy was gone through with, to the infinite amusement as well as
the unutterable scorn of the princess, who regarded their behaviour
as hypocritical prudery. She herself applauded warmly the strongest
and most indelicate parts of the performance, stimulating the dancers
to yet more frantic indecencies; and when, panting, exhausted, and

in sheer breathlessness, they ceased – divested almost entirely of the voluminous wrappings with which they had begun the dance – dusky models of the Eastern Venus, whose priestesses they were! – Nezle flung to each of them a purse of gold, as her parting benison.

Edwin de Leon, *Askaros Kassis the Copt*, 1870, pp. 104–5

In his book on Cairo, H. de Vaujany gave a report on the current position of the dancers in Egypt. As with many other writers, the introduction of a subject concerning women was the signal for a switch in linguistic style – from staid prose to purple passage.

Compared to what they were in the past, it must be acknowledged that today the almehs have fallen from their earlier position; they have come down to the rank of the most vulgar courtesans. Wanting to preserve the morals of the people of the Delta, and particularly in the capital, Abbas Pasha exiled the almehs to Upper Egypt. The public singers at Qeneh, Luxor and especially Esneh certainly do not merit the title of almehs. Mingling with ghawazi (dancers) you will see by turn the same women singing and dancing one after the other or in groups of two or four. Their song is monotonous, slow, singularly primitive and absolutely foreign to musical ideas in our countries, yet it has an indefinable charm. Indeed, its monotony is its strength; in the course of time it submerges the soul in a kind of ecstasy and lulls it into a deep reverie. . . .

The small number of almehs still in Cairo are much more reserved than those of Upper Egypt; they live in areas which are rarely frequented by foreigners. It is only by chance that foreigners will see them at parties given by rich Egyptians. The dancers (ghawazi) are as rare in Cairo as are the almehs; they can be met beyond Siout at Qeneh. But, under European influence, they have lost their unique style; they no longer execute their dances with all the necessary accessories; in the presence of women they show much more restraint in their movements.

Egyptian dance has no resemblance at all to dance as we know it in Europe; it consists of a succession of poses, contortions, gestures, which have only one aim – to express or provoke voluptuous feelings. The dancers usually wear silk robes of gaudy colours, where reds and yellows harmonize with bright greens and sky blue; their arms and legs are bare, with large bangles; a light band of gauze half covers the breasts. Their eyes are lively and bordered with kohl, and stand out sharply against their mat complexion. A diadem of gold pieces circles the forehead and in the black hair which falls around their shoulders there are numerous little pieces of the same metal threaded in. The generosity of the spectators is always adding to this dazzling jewellery. The dances and some of the costumes are identical to those in the paintings of the ancient hypogeums, and no doubt they have been kept up by tradition.

When the dancers are called to a private house they never appear before men and women together. For the men, the dance usually takes place in the *mandarah* (a room on the ground floor). A small orchestra composed of string instruments, the *tar* and the *darabouk*, which are used to mark the rhythm, is placed in a corner. The dancers occupy the part of the salon called the *dourqah*, and the spectators silently sit on the divans and enjoy the pleasure of the show which is taking place. The artists, who are generally young and pretty women, begin their choreographic exercises by moving around the room with slow and measured steps and graceful arm movements. They accompany themselves with copper castanets (*sagat*) fixed to the thumb and middle finger of each hand, which they play with marvellous dexterity. The clinking of the *sagat* responds to a jerky movement of the hips. After going around two or three times undulating the body in all directions, and assuming more provocative poses, their legs stop moving, as well as the upper part of the body, except the arms which they move following the lewd feelings which seem to animate them. Agitated by the incessant trembling which they accelerate with audacious energy or slow down languidly, their bodies develop a suppleness beyond belief, trembling like a leaf, caused by an unambiguous nervous impulse. It is impossible to imagine a more lively and realistic pantomime, more voluptuous and stirring movements, or contortions expressing with less discretion all the physical sensations; the quivering hips, falling down and lifting up again with unimagineable speed, give the impression of an indescribable amorous frenzy. . . .

There are several varieties of dances which are basically very similar; they are all executed with grace, lightness and extraordinary passion. One of the most popular is the dance of the bee (el-nahleh). The *ghawazi* pretend to have been stung by a bee which they search for inside their costume, uttering little cries, trying to catch hold of the imaginary insect. Without stopping the dance, they quickly remove a first piece of their clothing and throw it down; then they throw aside a second piece, calling 'nahleh, nahleh', with gestures which express by turn the fear of being stung and the hope of soon getting rid of the enemy. After much fruitless searching, they end up with only one very light veil which they leave to float at the mercy of their movements. Little by little the dance becomes more lively, the figures animated and then, 'quite unintentionally', the last piece of the costume joins the others. Now the dancers draw near to each other, separate, cross over and turn back towards each other as though to incite each other to amorous encounters. They take pleasure in the most lewd poses; supple as reeds, they twirl around, then come back into position face to face; motionless, their body thrown backwards, arms stretched out, hands clenched, flesh quivering, they abandon themselves to the impressions which the paroxysms of passion produce on them; at this moment the music becomes gentler, it is no louder than the panting breath of the actresses and the tinkling of the gold pieces in their hair. Suddenly noticing their state with 'surprise', they pick up their veil with a gesture of modesty and wrap it around their waist, and the dance stops for a moment while small glasses of arak are passed around. The *ghawazi*, who are far from being over modest, come and begin talking familiarly with the guests whose favour they want to win or whose generosity they want to sting.

Then the dance begins again with new vigour; the flimsy scarf which is resting around their hips is removed and flutters in the air; the poses become more and more wanton; you would think that it was the ancient Bacchanalia celebrating an orgy. After some time they slowly put back their clothes without pausing in the dance.

When the show is finished, the artists come to sit among the spectators or on the knees of those whom they favour with their cajolery. The happy mortals who are the object of this distinction must, according to the rules of good form, moisten some small golden pieces and place them delicately on the forehead, the neck and bosom or the arms of those who have favoured them.

H. de Vaujany, Le Caire et ses environs, 1883, pp. 88–93

When the Reverend Charles Bell was in Cairo in the 1880s, he regarded the dancers with pity and compassion. However, he did not see them perform, for he was told by a fellow traveller that 'the exhibition was indecorous to a degree, and that he was glad when it was over' (*A Winter on the Nile*, 1888, pp. 255–6). The Marchioness of Dufferin and Ava was invited to a performance and found it 'very peculiar'. She sat through a few dances and then left, 'knowing that we should see nothing new' (*My Russian and Turkish Journals*, 1916, p. 284).

Mme Jean Pommerol spent some time in the Sahara, where she found the women to be very childish. After relating how they spent time dancing in front of each other, she went on to explain the reason for this. It was only a rehearsal for the real thing – the time when they would perform for men. It was apparently inconceivable to her that women might just have enjoyed dancing for its own sake. Countess Malmignati, however, set out searching for romance and was entranced by everything about the desert life. The dances she witnessed by torchlight outside the 'Sultan's' tent were like a stage spectacle, a wonderful setting for the romance she sought.

In a word, the ways of the women of the Sahara are full of contradictions; contradictions of feeling, of sentiment, but everything is more or less childish with them, even their dancing, of which they are insatiably fond. I have already spoken of the dancing of the women of Wargla, but the love of this amusement is general in the Sahara, and women dance before each other in a manner not a bit more modest than that of the fassedett, though it is decidedly less graceful. Between their cups of tea they give themselves up to posing in all manner of attitudes, twisting their bodies about in a manner often anything but pleasing, holding themselves rigid, whilst the spectators stare at them, and assuming indifferent, passionate, polite, or disdainful expressions, according to the mood of their audience. They seem to like to practise what will please the opposite sex when no representatives of that sex are present. Although they are not aware of it themselves, there is, in fact, something voluptuous about them, an unconscious struggling after an erotic ideal in their dancing, the ornaments they wear, and the perfumes they use.

To please! To please! That is their one desire, and they have so very few opportunities of pleasing the opposite sex. For all that, in this country where those who wish to be attractive have not yet hit upon the idea of low-necked bodices, they accumulate fine clothes, piling them up one on top of the other, with a view to the delectation of husbands and lovers. Brocaded silks, spangled tulle, tissues of gold and silver, some real, some imitation, falling in straight folds, gleaming disguises, mysterious covering, suggesting the hidden charms. And all this glittering metallic lustre, this raiment of gold, is the very condensation of the dreams of many races, the synthesis of all the confused mirages emanating from the sultry sands of the Desert. No idea has yet been conceived of any other luxury than that of sensuous form. Genii, angels, phantoms – whether infernal or divine – have no other; Paradise itself promises nothing more as a reward to the faithful.

Sacred draperies, these, such as were worn by matrons in the movable and venerated tents of the patriarchal family in times long gone by. Unchanging forms, immutable lines, still everywhere in use except where tradition has been modified by the bad taste of the North. Immutable! How full of meaning is that word! For how many, many centuries have women aroused the love of men by the attractions of the same ornaments? Woman, eternally young, one generation rapidly succeeding another, blossom of the perfect flower that is to be, is ever there, even as one wave replaces another in the ocean, and the colour, the light, and the shade, appeal with the same force to the eyes of the men of to-day, as they did to those of past ages, and will appeal to others yet unborn!

Mme Jean Pommerol, *Among the Women of the Sahara*, 1900,
pp. 340–3

When the meal was over, the Sultan arranged some dancing. Torches were lit around the tent. Two men with huge drums went into the circle, calling the women to get ready for the dance. Six men with a kind of hornpipe accompanied them.

After a few minutes, the women came dancing in, slowly gliding, a big silver sword in one hand, in the other a burning torch. They were all fine, tall women, with classical features, dressed in long, flowing red gowns, covered with a purple shawl. Round their head they wore a golden ornament with many gold and silver coins falling down on their foreheads.

This dance was a slow, rhythmical gliding, swinging the swords and torches in time. It was like a dance in a trance! The men with the drums danced too, while playing. They jumped between the women, pursued them, teased them, their faces changing into all sorts of funny grimaces. They were grotesque and humorous to a degree, and would have made their fortune in any European music hall. They leaped about like devils or evil spirits, and made a strange contrast with the calm dignity of the dancers.

The dance lasted for more than three hours; when the women tired, others came gliding in to relieve them. It was a beautiful sight, with the flaming torches, and the graceful, slow movements of the women and their silver swords and golden coins glittering in the light. When the dance was at last finished, we all threw some silver into the circle, and the Sultan invited the dancers to have a meal in our tent. They had some more boiled wheat with pieces of lamb, and we all drank *arrack* with water. It was long after three o'clock when we at last reached our tents.

Four days we spent with our tents pitched near to the Roallas' encampment. Four days of friendship with the Sultan Al Tayar, days of romance and beauty!

Countess Malmignati, *Through Inner Deserts to Medina*, 1925,
pp. 81–3

Chapter 7

CONVERSATIONS OF PROFANE LOVE

For centuries Western travellers have talked about the depravity of Oriental women. The notion of women being 'locked up together' in the harem and bathing together naked clearly made many men feel both insecure and deprived of the sexual pleasure which was their right. Apparently, if women spent much time together in groups it was evident that they would become immoral and, in any case, this was a 'fact' well documented in the West. George Sandys began his travels in the Turkish empire in 1610 and informed his readers of the 'unnatural and filthy lust' which he had been told was practised daily in the public baths.

The men take them [the baths] up in the morning: and in the afternoon the women. . . . But the women doe anoint their bodies with an ointment made of the earth of *Chios*; which maketh the skin soft, white, and shining, extending that on the face, and freeing it from wrinkles. Much unnaturall and filthy lust is said to be committed daily in the remote closets of these darksome *Bannias*: yea women with women; a thing incredible, if former times had not given thereunto both detection, and punishment. They have generally the sweetest children that ever I saw; partly proceeding from their frequent bathings, and affected cleanlinesse.

George Sandys, *Sandys Travailes*, 1652, p. 54

Monsieur de Thevenot, who published his travel record in 1665, believed that since the women were naturally idle and maltreated by their husbands, depravity was inevitable.

When they go through the streets their head is wrapped in a piece of linen which also covers their forehead as far down as the eyes. Just below the eyes another piece covers the nose and mouth and is tied behind the head, leaving nothing but the eyes uncovered. Even if they show their hands they are taken to be women of no honour, and for this reason the sleeves of their clothes are left hanging to cover their hands. Despite this, on occasions when they find themselves in a corner of a street where they think they will not be seen, they lift their veil to allow themselves to be seen by a friend or a young man who pleases them – but by doing so they risk both their honour and a beating.

Now, these women are extremely haughty and nearly all of them want to be dressed in brocade even though their husband has scarcely any bread. Yet they are extremely lazy, spending all the day sitting on a divan with nothing to do, except perhaps to embroider some flowers on a handkerchief. And as soon as the husband has a penny he must use it to acquire a slave. This great idleness results in depravity and they put all their thought into ways of amusing themselves. The Turks do not believe that women go to paradise and barely recognise them as rational animals. They take women simply to serve them as they would a horse. But since they have many women, and often give their love to their own sex, these poor women see themselves abandoned and therefore try their best to find elsewhere what they cannot get from their husband.

> Monsieur de Thevenot, *Relation d'un voyage fait au Levant*, 1665,
> pp. 106–7

In Elias Habesci's book *The Present State of the Ottoman Empire* (1784) he also spoke of 'unnatural lasciviousness' as well as stating that it was not difficult to have a romantic intrigue with a Turkish woman. Here there was some oneupmanship between Habesci, a Greek resident in Constantinople, and Sir James Porter, the British Ambassador there, who had apparently asserted that such liaisons were almost impossible. 'Probably this British minister had no such inclination for such intrigues,' Habesci retorted. Later in the book he informs future travellers where to go to arrange a liaison.

The most infamous lasciviousness is likewise common in the chambers of the girls. Nor is it at all astonishing that handsome girls, well fed, undergoing neither fatigue nor vexation; girls that have nothing to do but to prepare themselves for sensual pleasures, and who think of nothing but Venus and her son, should give way to unnatural lasciviousness, for want of the proper means of gratifying their amorous inclinations. Notwithstanding the consciousness of the fatal doom that awaits them, if they are discovered, the violence of their passions makes them rush precipitately upon their ruin. Alas! how many of these unhappy girls are thrown, tied together in guilty couples, into the sea, from that part of the Seraglio which faces Kadi-Roa (Calcedonia).

Elias Habesci, *The Present State of the Ottoman Empire*, 1784, p. 177

As the Turks have several wives, and those who are rich and noble have a *Harem* full of women, it naturally follows, that their wives are not satisfied with such husbands, and that they wish to supply their deficiency. Besides, a Turk of high rank, whose house is at Constantinople, is sometimes sent upon the service of his sovereign to a remote province of the empire. In this case he takes along with him only one or two of his best beloved wives, or mistresses, and leaves the rest in this harem, to expect his return in a few years or perhaps never. These women then, whose desires have been raised to the highest pitch by their voluptuous mode of life, study every means of gratifying them, and make use of many successful stratagems for that purpose. An affair of gallantry with a Turkish women is, indeed, attended with very great danger, and a variety of difficulties for the Christian lover; but he must be a stranger to the human heart, or to the powers of the tender passion, who does not believe that every risk is sometimes run, and every difficulty surmounted, by the votaries of Venus, in this as well as other countries.

Elias Habesci, *The Present State of the Ottoman Empire*, 1784, p. 385

C. S. Sonnini has been quoted earlier. His account of his journey for the *ancien* French Government dropped to extraordinary levels of abuse against the population of Egypt. In the first extract he explained in great detail how the women were abused by their men, and in the next breath remarked that the subject was too disgusting to continue. He then revealed that the women resorted to lesbianism and masturbation in order to quench their sexual desires. In the second extract he was able reliably to inform his readers that 'the women of Upper Egypt' were in the daily habit of murdering their husbands.

If the inhabitants of Rosetta are less barbarous than those of other parts of Egypt, they are no less ignorant, less superstitious or less intolerant. Among them we find, although slightly toned down, the same hard character, the same implacable hatred towards the nations of Europe, the same inclination towards vengeance, the same treachery; and they indulge in the same shameful vices. That love against nature which the women of Thrace punished when they killed Orpheus who was guilty of it, that unthinkable taste which dishonoured the Greeks and the Persians of antiquity, is the delight or rather the disgrace of the Egyptians. It is not for women that love songs are composed, nor on women that they lavish their tender caresses; other objects excite them. Sensual pleasure for them has nothing to do with love and their rapture is nothing more than the convulsions of brutality. The same depravity which, to the shame of the civilized nations, is not unknown to them, is widespread in Egypt among rich and poor. In milder climates it is an exclusive inclination, but here it is combined with one for women. After satisfying his favourite, and criminal, passion, the man of these countries returns to his harem and burns some incense in honour of the nature that he has just outraged. He is an uncivilized sacrificer who knows nothing about the sweet feelings, the outpourings of the heart, the delicious abandon, the wonderful glowing outbursts of two souls who understand and come close to each other. There are no delicate moves, no different approaches, no gracious details; everything is rough and appears lifeless – merely a disgusting physical act.

The outrages which the Egyptians commit against nature do not stop here. Other beings receive their horrible favours, and their wives must also compete with the animals which they enjoy. The crime of bestiality is well known to those perverse men who flaunt it with shameless effrontery. In Rosetta we have seen wretches indulging in the side streets in broad daylight.

Let us now draw a curtain over these revolting scenes, and enter into the places where beauty languishes, where, like a flower that has been abandoned by the caresses of the warm breeze and left to the

withering blast of the south wind, deprived of sensitive consideration, she fades and wastes away under the yoke of a jealous barbarian
who torments her with his suspicions and defiles her with his
profanity. . . .

These women visit each other frequently. Their conversations are
not always noted for their decency and modesty. The total lack of
any education or morals; the laziness and the wealth in which they
spend their days; the relentless constraint under which they are held
by men so far removed from any delicate actions or feelings; the
certain knowledge they have that the men keep their love for other
objects; the intensity of their affections; a climate that sets on fire
hearts which are disposed to tenderness, but to no avail; the nature
whose powerful voice – too often disregarded by those whom she
calls to share her pleasures – arouses her senses; all of this helps to
direct their fiery imagination, their desires, their conversation
towards one end which they are not free to attain.

They enjoy themselves when they get together by exchanging
clothes with each other. These disguises are only the prelude to and
the pretext for less innocent games which Sappho is said to have
taught and practised the details. Experienced in the art of deception
but not knowing how to quench the ardour which consumes them,
they are just as licentious when they are alone. They resort to sad
means, poor compensation for a deprivation which, in a climate both
hot and dry and for souls burning with desire, is hard to bear.

    C. S. Sonnini, *Voyage dans la haute et basse Égypte*, 1798, vol. I,
                                        pp. 277–9, 284–6

It is not usual to come across jealousy where there is no love.
However, the women of Upper Egypt who neither love nor are
loved, are sometimes seized by a jealous fury when they see their
husbands having a fancy for other women – a desire which is quite
common and purely physical, where the heart is nothing. Offended
pride wreaks havoc in passionate souls who know nothing of true
love. Dissimulating rather than cruel, they put a slow and deadly
poison into the blood of an unfaithful husband. Each day you see
examples of a vengeance which cannot be excused by the ecstasy of
passion. Their deeds are planned in silence and they savour coolly
and in long draughts the horrible pleasure of slowly squeezing the
life out of the unfortunate one. I have not witnessed what I am now
going to recount, but they are facts which have been unanimously

attested and are accepted in the country as established and incontrovertible.

Evil-minded women do not choose to inflict a quick death, for their terrible jealousy would not then be satisfied. They procure a slow wasting away which is worse than death itself. They find within themselves the poison which suits their needs. The periodic discharge which nature uses to preserve their life and their health becomes for them a means of making others perish. When mixed with some food, a portion of this discharge makes a poison, and whoever swallows it soon becomes languid and wastes away. The women are careful to prepare these horrible meals during certain phases of the moon when, they believe, the results will be more certain. This poison has terrible effects, similar to those of scurvy. The body dries up; all the limbs become very weak; the gums become decayed and the teeth loose; the beard and hair disappear. Finally, after leading a life of languor and pain for a year, and sometimes more, the unhappy victim expires in the middle of his sufferings.

C. S. Sonnini, *Voyage dans la haute et basse Égypte*, 1798, vol. III, pp. 237–9

Such reports of licentiousness were so common in travellers' tales that it would be exceedingly boring to continue quoting them. As one author wrote:

Whenever I have spoken to you about the women of the Orient I have not spared you any details, because I am almost certain of arousing your curiosity. As far as morals, habits and life are concerned, the women of this country are so unlike those of Europe that the subject must always seem new to you. (M. Michaud and M. Poujoulat, *Correspondence d'Orient 1830–31*, 1835, p. 86)

Many Westerners were influenced by E. W. Lane's account of the obscene and licentious lifestyle of the 'women of Egypt' whose conversation, he claimed, was frequently so low that even a prostitute in Europe would not allow herself to discuss such subjects! This piece is included, therefore, because of the status of his book in the West. The next extract, by his sister, describes her visit to a public bath, where she found the

atmosphere unfit for the eyes and ears of an English woman –
because she would have to pass by naked women and children.

The most immodest freedom of conversation is indulged in by
persons of both sexes, and of every station in life, in Egypt; even by
the most virtuous and respectable women, with the exception of a
very few, who often make use of coarse language, but not unchaste.
From persons of the best education, expressions are often heard so
obscene as only to be fit for a low brothel; and things are named, and
subjects talked of, by the most genteel women, without any idea of
their being indecorous, in the hearing of men, that many prostitutes
in our country would probably abstain from mentioning.

The women of Egypt have the character of being the most
licentious in their feelings of all females who lay any claim to be
considered as members of a civilized nation; and this character is
freely bestowed upon them by their countrymen, even in conversation with foreigners. Numerous exceptions doubtless exist. . . . But
with respect to the majority of the Egyptian women, it must, I fear,
be allowed that they are very licentious. What liberty they have,
many of them, it is said, abuse; and most of them are not considered
safe, unless under lock and key; to which restraint few are subjected.
It is believed that they possess a degree of cunning in the
management of their intrigues which the most prudent and careful
husband cannot guard against, and consequently that their plots are
seldom frustrated, however great may be the apparent risk of the
undertakings in which they engage. Sometimes, the husband himself
is made the unconscious means of gratifying his wife's criminal
propensities. Some of the stories of the intrigues of women in 'The
Thousand and One Nights' present faithful pictures of occurrences
not unfrequent in the modern metropolis of Egypt. Many of the men
of this city are of the opinion that almost all the women would
intrigue if they could do so without danger; and that the greater
proportion of them do. I should be sorry to think that the former
opinion was just; and I am almost persuaded that it is over-severe,
because it appears, from the custom with regard to women generally
prevailing here, that the latter must be false. The difficulty of
carrying on an intrigue with a female in this place can hardly be
conceived by a person who is not moderately well acquainted with
eastern customs and habits. It is not only difficult for a woman of the
middle or higher classes to admit her paramour into the house in

which she resides, but it is almost impossible for her to have a private interview with a man who has a hareem, in his own house; or to enter the house of a man who is neither married nor has a concubine slave, without attracting the notice of the neighbours, and causing their immediate interference. But as it cannot be denied that many of the women of Egypt engage in intrigues notwithstanding such risks, it may perhaps be true that the difficulties which lie in the way are the chief bar to most others. Among the females of the lower orders, intrigues are more easily accomplished, and frequent.

The libidinous character of the generality of the women of Egypt, and the licentious conduct of a great number of them, may be attributed to many causes; partly, to the climate, and partly, to their want of proper instruction, and of innocent pastimes and employments: but it is more to be attributed to the conduct of the husbands themselves; and to conduct far more disgraceful to them than the utmost severity that any of them is known to exercise in the regulations of his hareem. The generality of husbands in Egypt endeavour to increase the libidinous feelings of their wives by every means in their power; though, at the same time, they assiduously study to prevent their indulging those feelings unlawfully. The women are permitted to listen, screened behind their windows of wooden lattice-work, to immoral songs and tales sung or related in the streets by men whom they pay for this entertainment; and to view the voluptuous dances of the ghawazee, and of the effeminate khawals. The ghawazee, who are professed prostitutes, are not unfrequently introduced into the hareems of the wealthy, not merely to entertain the ladies with their dances, but to teach them their voluptuous arts; and even indecent puppets are sometimes brought into such hareems for the amusement of the inmates. – Innumerable stories of the artifices and intrigues of the women of Egypt have been related to me.

Edward William Lane, *The Manners and Customs of the Modern Egyptians*, 1860 (1st edn 1836), pp. 303–5

On entering this chamber a scene presented itself which beggars description. My companions had prepared me for seeing many persons undressed; but imagine my astonishment on finding at least thirty women of all ages, and many young girls and children, perfectly unclothed. You will scarcely think it possible that no one but ourselves had a vestige of clothing. Persons of all colours, from the black and glossy shade of the negro to the fairest possible hue of complexion, were formed in groups, conversing as though full dressed, with perfect *nonchalance*, while others were strolling about, or sitting round the fountain. I cannot describe the bath as altogether a beautiful scene; in truth, in some respects it is disgusting; and I regret that I can never reach a private room in any bath without passing through the large public apartment. . . .

The first operation is a gentle kneading of the flesh, or champooing. Next the attendant cracks the joints of those who desire to submit to this process. I confess I did not suffer such an affliction. Some of the native women after this are rubbed with a rasp, or rather with two rasps of different kinds, a coarse one for the feet, and a fine one for the body; but neither of these rasps do I approve. A small coarse woollen bag into which the operator's hand is inserted, is in my opinion preferable. Next the head and face are covered with a thick lather, which is produced by rubbing soap on a handful of fibres of the palm-tree, which are called leef, and which form a very agreeable and delicate-looking rubber. It is truly ridiculous to see another under this operation. When her head and face have been well lathered, and the soap has been thoroughly washed off by abundance of hot water, a novice would suppose that at least *they* were sufficiently purified; but this is not the case – two or three of such latherings, and as many washings, are necessary before the attendant thinks her duty to the head and face accomplished. Then follows the more agreeable part of the affair, – the general lathering and rubbing, which is performed by the attendant so gently, and in so pleasant a manner, that it is quite a luxury; and I am persuaded that the Eastern manner of bathing is highly salubrious, from its powerful effect upon the skin. . . .

I wish I could say that there are no drawbacks to the enjoyment of the luxury I have described; but the eyes and ears of an Englishwoman must be closed in the public bath in Egypt before she can fairly enjoy the satisfaction it affords; for besides the very foreign scenes which cannot fail to shock her feelings of propriety, the cries of the children are deafening and incessant. The perfection of Eastern bathing is therefore rather to be enjoyed in a private bath, with the attendance of a practised vellaneh.

The Englishwoman in Egypt: Letters from Cairo with E. W. Lane, Esq., By his Sister, 1844, vol. II, pp. 171–5

Emmeline Lott, 'shut out from all rational society' in the
hareem of Ismael Pacha, found herself confronted every day
with 'the manners most repugnant, nay, revolting, to the
delicacy of a European female'. She was forced to witness:

A lady of the Harem, not more forward than all the rest,
Well versed in Syren's arts, it must be confessed,
Shuffle off her garments, and let her figure stand revealed
Like that of Venus with no charms concealed.
(*Harem Life in Egypt and Constantinople*, 1865, vol. I, p. 211)

Furthermore, 'the odalisques' indulged in impure talk and
wicked actions – the seeds of which lay in woman's nature, she
claimed. Lucie Duff Gordon tried to correct the impression
given in 'Mrs Lott's most extraordinary book'. She found the
atmosphere of a Turkish hareem rather like a tea-party at
Hampton Court, but more dull.

Possibly the most vicious passage in this anthology came
from the pen of the Hon. Lewis Wingfield, who recommended
rape as the best way of pleasing an Arab (as opposed to a
'Moorish') woman!

The Arab wife has, as a natural result of her degraded position, very
little delicacy, and no modesty whatever. She admires only that
which is violent and energetic. Thus the best way to please her would
be to penetrate, by stratagem or otherwise, under her tent awning,
and make love to her by the side of her sleeping husband. But were
the husband to wake and kill his rival, she would not be sorry – her
admiration would only be turned into another channel.

The Hon. Lewis Wingfield, *Under the Palms in Algeria and Tunis*,
1868, vol. I, p. 227

In the following extract from his novel, *Askaros Kassis*, Edwin
de Leon was prodigal in his generalizations about Eastern
women.

The face of the princess glowed with gratified vanity at these
impassioned words, poured out with burning ardor – either felt or

feigned – by the lips she loved best. With all the *abandon* and recklessness of an Eastern woman – who flings all modesty and all reserve to the winds, and whose sense of shame seems utterly to disappear with the veil that has concealed her face – she threw herself on the divan beside her lover, and lavished upon him all those terms of endearment of which the Eastern tongue is so profuse. She removed the fez cap that he wore, and toyed with the short, clustering curls of his hair; and, reposing her head upon his breast, looked up into his face with a soft glow on her features, and a tenderness in her eye, that transformed her into another woman from the eagle-eyed and imperious Nezle Khanum of every day. She seemed to renew her own youth with proximity to this young lover, the beauty of whose face and form were well calculated to inspire admiration in the heart of woman.

Edwin de Leon, Askaros Kassis the Copt, 1870, pp. 136–7

Another character in the same novel is described here:

But had Askaros seen the cruel, sinister smile that writhed the thin lips, and the evil glare in the downcast eye, veiled by its long feminine lashes, he would have better understood the equivocal promise that had just been made him. . . . an expression of subtle malignity crept over the face, and blent with the ferocity that covered it like a veil. (pp. 92–3, 94)

The language chosen to describe this sinister person is interesting, for the character is a man.

The West had always known that the origin of all this voluptuousness and depravity was Islam. 'Islam cannot foster purity or chastity,' pronounced the Reverend Charles Bell in 1888 (*A Winter on the Nile*, p. 270). W. M. Thomson, an American missionary, spent some months in 1852 with the Metawelies near Sidon. The women were not only depraved, he said, but barbarous and hypocritical – and their religion was the cause. The Duc d'Harcourt attacked Egyptian women for the usual reasons, arguing on the one hand that the hot-house atmosphere in which they lived was the cause of their wickedness, on the other hand that Muslim men were right to keep them strictly confined *because* they were so depraved.

The law which obliged persons affected with loathsome diseases to dwell without the camp is still in force, not merely among tent-dwelling Arabs, but also with these people. We spent the hot summer months of 1852 in a village above Sidon. The inhabitants are nearly all Metawelies, and very fanatical. On a rocky hill south of our house, a poor woman was thus separated, living in a booth of green branches. She was not allowed to leave her solitary shelter, and no one was permitted to visit her but the person who carried her daily allowance of food. There she passed her wretched days and nights until death delivered her from this dismal solitude. We remonstrated with the people against this barbarity, and the *men* consented to have her brought into a room hired for the purpose, where we could provide suitable food, and Dr. Van Dyck prescribe for her disease. But the *women* rose in furious clamour and rebellion against the proposal, and we were obliged to abandon it. We did this more willingly when we ascertained that the dying wretch herself would neither take the medicines nor taste our food; and yet she was being devoured by that horrid disease generated by vice and pollution. I was amazed at the barbarity and hypocrisy of the women. Sternly they passed her by, day after day, until she died; but then they assembled in troops, and screamed, and tossed their arms, and tore their hair in boisterous grief. There is a sad callousness in the composition of this people; at least they lack those beautiful traits of kindness and sympathy with the diseased and wretched which so adorn Christian countries, and fill them with hospitals, societies, and committees, to shelter, aid, and cure them. Religion makes the difference; not that the Metawelies are without religion, and plenty of it too. While the above tragedy was slowly enacting before our eyes, the feast of Ramadan was kept in its utmost stringency, though it was blazing midsummer, and the people nearly perished with thirst. They neither ate, drank nor smoked for more than fourteen hours of fierce sunshine, and even young children were forced to go through this long fast. There was public prayer, too, in abundance, a sort of Metawely protracted meeting.

Even the women assembled daily at the fountains, performing their ablutions, and going through their genuflections and prostrations beneath the noble walnut-trees which adorn the hill sides of beautiful Jebaah. Nowhere else have I seen Moslem women thus pray in public, and the whole performance is immodest and disgusting. They are a sallow, forlorn and ill-conditioned generation, every way inferior to the Christian women who dwell by their side. It is religion that makes the difference, even though the Christianity known there is little better than a caricature of the religion of Jesus.

W. M. Thomson, *The Land and the Book*, 1890, pp. 191–2

It must be remembered that before marriage the girls have no relationship whatever with the man they must marry; the marriage is a business which is arranged without them and on which they are barely consulted. In any case, what could they have a personal view on from behind their enclosure? Once married in this way, living in the house of a husband who is perhaps not very pleasant and forced to share not only with the other legitimate wives but also all the women who, as servants, form part of the harem and have been brought up to think of no other pleasures than those of the senses – what could possibly persuade them to remain faithful, except the constraint, the many restrictions which custom places on their freedom.

It is perhaps not out of place here to recall the tales of the 1001 nights, which are famous throughout the Orient; their fundamental idea is to present a singularly unfavourable opinion of women's virtue. A sovereign, who had suffered many conjugal misfortunes, realized in his great wisdom that the only reliable way of not being deceived by his wife was to have her put to death the day after the marriage. And this was what he did until the day he married a girl who related such a wonderful story, which she always stopped at dawn, that every morning she obtained a reprieve until the next morning.

Contemporary acts witnessed by Muslim men in Egypt justify their apprehensions. Among the women of rich families who have received some education, European ideas (or so-called ones) have only brought depravity – or so people say. Frankly, it is not surprising. In particular, the study of language enables them to read the worst novels, and to throw themselves into a kind of literature which can be imagined. They see the liberty which our women enjoy, and this has no value in their eyes except for the sexual liaisons which it could facilitate. As long as the rules of confinement are strictly observed and the guardians keep good watch, everything is kept in order; but as soon as the cage is opened, the bird will fly away. . . .

Those women who think themselves civilized because they understand a few bad French novels and wear Parisian dresses at

home, are not therefore any better for it. There is no reason to be
surprised by this, and if the Egyptians are distrustful of it they are
quite right. These women are difficult to keep in order. You may
wonder how women find the opportunity for depravity, given the
profusion of precautions with which they are surrounded, the
enclosures which no man can pass, the veils with which they are
always covered, the eunuchs who never leave them. It is these, in the
last analysis, that everything hangs on; when they are paid enough
they will fall in with all the wishes of the woman – and she is free to
dispose of her fortune as she wishes.

If one reflects in depth on all the circumstances in which women
are placed, one would agree that Muslim men are quite right to
increase the obstacles around them and to mistrust the new customs
which tend to appear: the liberty which European women enjoy
would, among Muslims, lead to shocking profligacy.

Duc d'Harcourt, *L'Égypte et les Égyptiens*, 1893, pp. 116–19

Strolling through the streets of Algiers, Guy de Maupassant
'happened upon' an area of prostitution – 'joyful prostitution'
which revealed immediately 'the profound difference between
European modesty and Oriental carelessness'. Reading such
words it would be easy to forget that prostitution was
widespread in Europe at this time, although the stories of Guy
de Maupassant would be a sufficient reminder.

The next two authors were women. Mme Jean Pommerol
claimed to have struggled with her conscience before putting
in print her view that women in the Sahara were *not* depraved.
Rather, they had no code of morals at all. The second writer,
M. E. Hume-Griffith, went to Persia with her husband, a
missionary doctor, in 1900. Expressing sisterly concern for the
situation of Persian ladies, she then repeated a story she had
been told about their cruelty.

my earnest desire to hurt nobody's feelings, above all not to wound
those who have welcomed and helped me, is very hampering. I
hesitate. Shall I or shall I not express my opinion? In the end I reply
to my own question: 'Truth is one and indivisible, to hold my peace
would be treason to her.'

I feel bound, in fact, if I am to give any true picture of the life of the Saharian women, to touch on the delicate question of their code of morals. People know only too well what that of the men is, whether they be Arabs or Berbers. But how about the women? – I mean the wives or future wives, ignoring those who omit the ceremony of marriage altogether.

Now, it seems to me, though it is a hard thing to say, that the women have no code of morals properly so called, for they are more like the gazelles and the cats to which I likened them above, than to responsible human beings. No one would talk of the morals of a pet gazelle or cat, shut up from all possible communion with its fellow-creatures, and that is really what the Arab and Berber women are supposed to be by the men to whom they belong. They cannot get out, so where is the merit of their stopping in? But it so happens that, in spite of all the locks and keys, they do get out sometimes, purely, be it explained, for the fun of the thing, rather than for any evil purpose. And, alas that it should be said! there is always some evil-minded go-between, generally an old woman, ready to turn indiscretion into real mischief. The husband makes fast the outer door with heavy bolts and strews sand outside it, that any trespassing footprints may remain as witness against intruders, but it is quite easy to get out by the terrace at the back, which is connected with the low wall above the narrow street. The go-between gets admission on some pretext, such as having fresh sweetmeats to sell, or she comes to beg alms, and when the master is safely away at the Moorish café, listening to the local gossip, or amusing himself in a less innocent way, the whole thing is easily enough arranged. The next morning, the master of the house will examine the sand on the threshold and say to himself: 'There is old Bielle the negro's footprint, and that was left by the nurse, and there is my own, but, Allah be praised, little Zorah's is not there!' Poor deluded fellow! his little Zorah jumped down like a cat from the wall at the back into the street as soon as her gaoler's back was turned, and you saw nothing, heard nothing, knew nothing, or if you had any suspicions you kept them to yourself, for fear of ridicule or from an unacknowledged dread of some malignant *jinn* or evil spirit having been at work.

In the dawar of the nomad tribes intrigues are alike more easily arranged and more romantic than in the towns. They are carried on between children of the same soil and of the same race, and there is about them something of the fierce passion characteristic of primitive manners. When the shades of night are just beginning to yield to the sweet influences of the tremulous dawn, at that witching moment when a glamour is thrown over everything, a corner of the tent is stealthily raised, and the lover, with bated breath and hushed foot-steps, glides into the very arms of the adored one. But beware, ye foolish ones! Be not too sure that the jealous husband is not on the watch; for if he is he may kill you both, or if he does not go so far as that he will certainly accuse him who has 'robbed his tent' before the Cadi, and try to salve the wound to his honour by extorting a good many dollars from the offender, so that the hour which began with kisses may very possibly end in tears.

This kind of thing goes on in the town, the kasr, or beneath the burning open sky, with a simplicity, a *naïveté*, which is almost innocent, it is so utterly natural and unsophisticated. The fact is, it is not fair to judge these children of the desert by our own European standard, they are of a type so utterly different to any with which we are familiar. The sensuality is physical only, it does not affect the soul in the least. Highly nervous, impulsive and passionate, with but little intellect, the women of the Sahara are not depraved and their lapses from the straight path do not leave any real stain upon them. Old women quite forget the slips of their youth; they were to them so natural, so entirely a matter of course, that they do not see any inconsistency in preaching to young girls on the subject of modesty, and over their own past a kind of delicate veil is thrown, which takes the place of the chastity on which they never set any real value.

Of course, I did not find all this out at first. The remarks I have just made are the result of long study on the spot, and I need not dwell more on a painful subject, only I want my readers to bear what I have said in mind and to remember the significant native proverb:

'Virtue will flourish amongst us when salt germinates and coal puts forth sprouts.'

Mme Jean Pommerol, *Among the Women of the Sahara*, 1900, pp. 42–6

The Persian lady has very little in her life to elevate or refine her mind, and so we cannot wonder if at times we see in her many revolting characteristics. When we think of all she has to endure, and how little happiness comes to her lot, our wonder is that she retains even a semblance of womanhood. Should we be any better under like circumstances?

If a woman is treated continually as if she was nothing but a beast of burden, is it to be wondered at that in some cases her nature becomes almost as the beasts of the field? Weird stories are told of the extremities to which women have been driven, and the cruelties which they have perpetrated.

The following is one which I heard in Persia. It was in the days when famine was rampant throughout the land. There was a certain man of high position who collected and stored all the corn he could gather, and then refused to sell at anything but famine prices; finally he was arrested and sent to Teheran, where he was tried and condemned to death. The Shah could not determine on the manner of death to be ordered for this rascal, but at last decided to hand the unfortunate man over to the mercies of the royal anderoon to be put to death by them. The ladies and women servants consulted together, and decided to keep the wretch in their quarters and kill him by inches, day by day. The method they chose was to cut him to pieces with scissors till he died!

I cannot vouch for the truth of this story, and I trust it is not true, but I give it to you as I heard it. But one thing I know to be true, and that is, when a Persian woman is once roused to anger, jealousy, and passion, there is hardly anything too dreadful for her to contemplate doing, in her longing for revenge.

M. E. Hume-Griffith, *Behind the Veil in Persia and Turkish Arabia*,
1909, p. 105

To end this chapter on the moral judgements made by Europeans, the same author tells how she tried to clean up the language of the women in Mosul!

Swearing is very largely indulged in by men and women alike; it seems to come as naturally to them as swimming to a duck. Originally the words 'wallah', 'yallah', 'billah', were used as swear expressions; but are now looked upon more as ejaculations equivalent to our 'good gracious!', 'goodness' etc. Some of the women cannot keep the expression *wallah* out of their conversation, though I try hard to persuade them to do so. . . . We started an anti-swearing society amongst a few of the women; it was quite funny to see how they endeavoured to keep back the old familiar words which had been on their lips since childhood.

M. E. Hume-Griffith, *Behind the Veil in Persia and Turkish Arabia*, 1909, p. 240

'How can lives be beautiful,' asked the author, how can 'the innocency of childhood so dear to the hearts of English parents' be maintained by women who are beautiful, but whose beauty is 'tainted with the blackness of sin'?

Chapter 8

SLAVES TO PREJUDICE

The assumption that women are more ignorant, more 'traditional' than men has a long history and, when the women are non-European and the writer European, accusations of prejudice and superstition are common. The only remarkable thing about this first extract, written in the 1790s, is the long list of skills attributed to rural women. We might well ask, who was the slave to prejudice?

The women of the towns, we were told, for we hardly ever saw them except in Baghdad, have all the delicate spirit, the kindness, the grace of their sex, and perhaps as much education as the men to whom they belong. As for the rural women, whom the doctor gave us the opportunity to see or hear, they seemed to us to be very uncivilized, very ignorant, and much more slaves to prejudice than their husbands. They veil themselves as carefully as in the towns and live in an even more secluded way. They do all the work in the house, they care for their children, do the cooking, milk the cows, the goats and the sheep; prepare the milk products, make the yoghurt and butter which the men sell in the town. They spin cotton and wool on a small spinning wheel in their free time. They use animal dung and cut up straw to make cakes which are dried in the sun and used as fuel, for wood is very scarce. They do no work in the fields, this work is all done by the men.

G. A. Olivier, *Voyage dans l'Empire Othoman*, 1800, vol. III, pp. 68–9

The Princess of Belgiojoso claimed to be better placed than most travellers to understand Syrian society, for she could enter the harem, which was 'hermetically closed to all men'. In the following piece, written in 1861, she related an incident in which she was involved in a village; in the second piece she revealed much about her general attitude to women and men. The Princess herself was a strong woman, an Italian patriot and an important figure in Parisian intellectual circles in the mid-nineteenth century, where her afternoon receptions were celebrated.

One of these incidents took place in a village called Kupru. I had the opportunity in this village, where I had to change my escort, of playing the role of doctor for a young girl who had been ill for a year. Her father, overcoming his aversion to Christians, begged me to visit her. My travelling companions moved some distance away and the young girl, accompanied by her mother, appeared before me. She was a magnificent creature, large and strong, but completely in proportion: a beautiful oval face, large almond-shaped eyes, velvety black, a nose which was more aquiline than Greek, a complexion which must have been glorious – and still was except that ill health had replaced the freshness by a fever. This beautiful being appeared profoundly sad, and it was impossible to look at her without becoming interested. Her mother, who had the same type of beauty as her daughter and was still beautiful, seemed to be extremely anxious and suffering because of her daughter's condition. These two women spoke to me with a confidence and warmth which was in contrast to the surly reserve of the master of the house.

It was not difficult to ascertain that the young girl was suffering from a complaint of the heart and, although I am little inclined towards romance, I could not stop myself from suspecting that this illness came from the mind. The privileges of a doctor are almost unlimited in this country where doctors are so few, and I did not think I was being indiscreet to find out whether some unhappiness, some mental shock, had occurred before the symptoms appeared.

'Alas, yes,' replied the mother. 'In eight days' time it will be exactly a year since my poor daughter had a terrible shock and since then she has been in this state.'

'Could I know what was the cause of this shock?' The mother looked at her daughter who blushed and lowered her eyes; her chest rose up and down rapidly as though her breathing was becoming more and more difficult and restricted.

'Why are you so upset?' her mother asked. 'You know that you must tell everything to doctors.' Then she turned to me and said: 'The poor child cannot hear the slightest allusion to that fatal night without reliving it all. She will leave us for a few minutes, therefore, and I will tell you all about it.'

The girl then got up and went to the window while her mother leaned towards me to talk in confidence. I thought that I was now going to hear how her unnatural father had discovered a lover. 'Well, madame, that night my daughter was returning home after spending the day at her friend's house. She was coming up the steps in the darkness, followed by another woman. Suddenly, something came out of one of the upstairs rooms, came down the steps in front of my daughter and when it reached her it got caught in her clothes and made her fall. She cried out and picked herself up. At that moment the moon came out and my poor daughter thought she saw a black cat running away as fast as possible. Perhaps it wasn't, perhaps it was only a grey cat, which is what I have tried in vain to persuade her. But nothing will get the idea out of her head that it was a black cat that knocked her over.'

I was still waiting for the end of the story, but there was no more, the story was finished. I tried hard to discover, without displaying my ignorance of such matters, what was so frightening about this incident. All that I could find out was that black cats are evil spirits whose visits are bad omens. Nevertheless, however absurd the cause, the illness was no less real. I performed blood-letting, I suggested entertainment, exercise; but what distractions were there to be found within the confines of the harem, especially in the countryside? I decided that I would not pass through Kupra on my return for I could not bear to see the ravages which another few months of illness would inflict on this pretty daughter of my churlish host.

La Princesse de Belgiojoso, *Asie Mineure et Syrie*, 1861, pp. 44–7

The tradition of female weakness is not confined to the realm of story-telling in the Orient, and the stronger part of the population shows great consideration towards the weaker. Since women are considered to be weak, everything – or almost everything – is permitted to them. To fly in a temper without reason, to have no common sense, to chatter without rhyme or reason, to do the exact opposite to what she is asked, and especially what she is ordered to do, to work only as much as she feels inclined, to spend wildly the money which her husband has earned, to decide she is ill, to complain about everything and nothing – all these are her privileges. By virtue of which law, which institution, by the effect, direct or indirect, of which custom or principle does she enjoy this privilege? The law leaves her defenceless, at the whim of her lord and master, while customs condemn her. It is, therefore, only the kindness of heart, tenderness or natural generosity of man which ensures woman this almost absolute impunity.

La Princesse de Belgiojoso, *Asia Mineure et Syrie*, 1861, p. 96

The Reverend Joseph Wolff travelled widely throughout Persia and Russia distributing copies of the Bible and trying to convert the population. At Acre he met an Englishman called Carne who was looking for a wife, and successfully converted him to the idea that Eastern women were stupid. (The strange style of the book came from the fact that he dictated it to friends when he was old.)

This Levantine tried to make Carne marry a beautiful woman of Damascus; for Carne's chief object in his journey to the East was to marry a lady as beautiful as those described in the Arabian Nights. Wolff, however, dissuaded him from doing so, by telling Carne, 'You may, perhaps, easily succeed in finding a lady with amiable lips, and with her eyebrows painted with yellow colours; yet she may be as stupid as a cow, and with hind quarters like an elephant, and so she will come home to you!' Thus Wolff succeeded in disgusting Carne to such a degree with the Eastern ladies, that he abandoned the idea of marrying any of them; and he said, 'Now I shall go home, and as I have not succeeded in marrying an Eastern lady for beauty's sake, I shall marry an English one for the sake of her money.'

Joseph Wolff, *Travels and Adventures of the Rev. Joseph Wolff*, 1861, p. 140

Although travellers were intensely curious about the details of women's dress, they found it childishness on the part of Eastern women to be interested in European dress. In the next two extracts by Isobel Burton and Mme de Voisins, the authors related the same story in order to demonstrate the naïveté of the women they had visited.

The moment we arrive and are announced, the whole family will run to meet us, at the boundary gate, which separates them from the world. They will kiss us, and take our hands, and with all the delight of children, lead us to the divan, and sit around us. One will fly for sherbet, another for sweets; this for coffee, that for narghilehs. They are so pleased with a trifle; for example, today, that we are delighted because we are dressed like them, and they consider that we have adopted their fashions out of compliment to them. They find everything charming, and are saying how sweet we look in their clothes. If we were habited in our own clothes they would be equally happy, because they would examine every article, would want to know where it was bought, what it cost, how it was put on, and if they could find it in the 'Suk'. Their greatest happiness is to pull your hair down to see how it is done, and to play with your hat. If you come in riding habit, they think you are dressed like a man. A lady's cloth riding under-garments are an awful mystery to them, and they think how happy we are to dress like men, and follow our husbands like comrades, whilst nobody says anything against us on that account. They envy us our knowledge and independence, and they deplore the way they are kept, and their not being able to know or do anything.

This feeling, of course, exists only among town harims, who receive enough visits to know there is another sort of woman's world than the one they enjoy. . . .

Do you see that old woman? She is a sort of faithful dependant in this harim. Do you hear what she is saying? You have by mistake put on your black-kid gloves, and she is asking why your face is so white and your hands so dark. She probably thinks the human race in our part of the world has piebald specimens. Pull off your glove and throw it on the ground. There! She has run away shrieking. She is one of the old school, and is quite innocent of anything European. Your glove, being of a thin kid, stands out open like a hand upon the ground, and she confidently believes you have torn your skin off for the pleasure of astonishing her. She will not touch it for the world.

Isobel Burton, *The Inner Life of Syria, Palestine, and the Holy Land,*
1875, vol. I, pp. 148–9

I have just, quite unintentionally, committed an imprudent act, an extraordinary blunder. My hat fell off, pulling it behind the hood of my burnous, and I wanted to put it back on with my black-gloved hand.

'Oh! oh!' says a Khoumir woman, 'who is this woman? White face, the hands of a negress, she is not a believer.'

The women surround me. Some of them are very young, well built and pretty, their features quite elegant; but what colour! A patina of bronze! They are dressed like the Arabs of the other tribes of the East; a cotton shirt with large sleeves hangs down to the knees and is held by a red woollen sash; a long piece of white woollen material is wrapped around them, well draped, with one end wound around the head and held in place by a camel-hair rope.

'Who are you?' an old woman asks me.

'I am French and a Christian.'

'What are you doing here?'

'I want to become informed and see if the Khoumir women are as hospitable as it is said.'

They laugh and are clearly flattered.

'Why is your face so white – actually my face has always been brown – and you have the hands of a negress?'

I obligingly remove one of my gloves.

'Wonderful,' they cry, 'the Christian is removing her skin.'

Mme de Voisins, *Excursions d'une Française dans la régence de Tunis*, 1884, pp. 67–8

As Lucie Duff Gordon, who came from a radical background in England, frequently complained in her letters, most travellers never stopped to consider the background to the life of the people about whom they were so quick to make generalizations. Europeans were usually totally ignorant about the current economic and political situation in the countries they visited, and as unconcerned about the poverty in the Orient as about that in Europe. They were more interested in finding links with the past to demonstrate that Oriental society had not changed for thousands of years – or proving that Islam was the cause of all the misery around. The next two authors, for example, were quite indifferent to the state of medical provision in Tunisia or Egypt when they accused women doctors and midwives of ignorance and immorality.

As for the qabela or midwive, she is nothing but a '*Faiseuse d'anges*', to use the expression established by our courts of assizes. It is hard to believe what bizarre and often odious means she uses in order to bring about a delivery. Among the strange prescriptions used by these wretches to facilitate a birth, the most original is certainly this. . . . The midwife prepares a potion of anything filthy and evil-smelling: the most stinking water mixed with the most disgusting refuse is the base of this powerful philtre which the invalid must drink to the last drop. It is unusual if disgust does not bring about a violent contraction of the diaphragm, and this convulsion will lead to the delivery. At other times the midwife puts on to the belly of the woman in labour a handmill, like those which every native household uses to grind corn. She turns the two stones and thus produces a terrible commotion throughout the patient's body. The shock, the shaking and jolts, the weight of the appliance all produce the desired effect.

The baby often dies after all these terrible exertions, or is still-born. What does it matter? Abortion is not a crime in Muslim countries; it is even tolerated, and it is the midwives who are responsible for this terrible act. Now, just as the midwife is allowed to kill the cursed seed in the womb which is the beginning of life, so no one will feel the slightest remorse in exposing the frail creature to the painful experiences which we have described. As a result, the native midwives are much better at murdering than giving birth.

One becomes very indignant seeing this most noble and important function of womanhood abandoned to ignorance, charlatanism and crime. But how could it be otherwise in a country where polygamy and divorce extinguish the pure sentiments of paternal affection and married love? Remembering what we have said about the condition of Muslim women, it is easy to understand why these wretched creatures would not be attracted by maternity.

G. des Godins de Souhesmes, *Tunis*, 1875, pp. 159–61

In Egypt, women doctors are principally consulted when there is illness in the hareem, that is, amongst the women and children, and these women it is needless to remark are ignorant old wives who know nothing about medicine or the internal conformation of human beings. They are passable midwives from the practical experience they are compelled to gain during many years' attendance upon helpless females, but as far as cause and effect in disease are concerned they know nothing beyond the use of a few charms and prayer gymnastics, assisted by simples such as the following –

For fever: shoot a hawk, open its stomach and rub the contents upon the forehead and palms of the patient. For headache: blister the nape of the neck with a hot iron, then suck the place, at the same time tying a handkerchief tightly round the forehead of the patient; and so on. . . .

The female doctors are a great evil in Egypt, as they frequently, I am led to believe, attempt operations upon women, the perpetration of which in England if found out, means penal servitude for life, and in some cases the 'Woodie!'

Warm Corners of Egypt, by 'One who was in them' 1886,
pp. 196, 198

Lady Anne Blunt, an English aristocrat, was what the blurb to the 1985 reprint of her book *A Pilgrimage to Nejd* called 'only the second woman to penetrate the interior of Arabia'. Apart, that is, from those living there, presumably. In her introduction to the new edition, Dervla Murphy compares the Blunts to the majority of nineteenth-century explorers. Unlike the others, they were very interested in the details of ordinary life. This was no doubt true, but the following description of her conversation with some women at Hail tells us more about Lady Anne Blunt than about the women she visited.

About three days later I paid a visit to the harim of Mamud's uncle. This gentleman, Suleyman, we were already acquainted with, from seeing him at Court on several occasions. He had sent me an invitation to visit his family, and two black slaves came to escort me to their house, one of the dependencies of the palace. In a kahwah opening out of a small yard, I found the old man waiting to receive me. He dyes his beard red, and loves books, amidst a pile of which he was sitting. I was in hopes that his conversation would be instructive, and we had just begun to talk when, alas, his wife came in with a rush, followed by a crowd of other women, upon which he hastily gathered up all his books and some manuscripts which were lying about, and putting some of them away in a cupboard, carried off the rest and made his escape.

Ghut, his wife, was the stupidest person I had seen at Hail, but very talkative, and hospitable with dates, fresh butter floating in its own butter-milk, and sugar-plums. The many-coloured crowd of white, brown, and black attendants, slaves, and children, were not in much awe of her, and chattered away without a check to their heart's content. All were, however, respectful and attentive to me. Ghut's daughter, another Zehowa, presently arrived with a slave carrying her son, Abderrahman, a child about a year old. This Zehowa was good-looking, but nearly as stupid and tiresome as her mother. She was very much taken up with showing me her box of trinkets, which she sent for on purpose to display before me its contents. These were of the usual sort, gold ornaments for head and arms and ankles, set with turquoises and strings of pearls. The furniture of the room, which she and her mother specially pointed out for my admiration, was also like what I had already seen – presses or boxes on legs, and ornamented with rude silver plaques.

The conversation was dull. Here is a sample: *I.* 'What do you do all day long?' *Zeh.* 'We live in the kasr.' *I.* 'Don't you go out at all?' *Zeh.* 'No; we always stay in the kasr.' *I.* 'Then you never ride' (I always ask if they ride, to see the effect) 'as we do?' *Zeh.* 'No, we have no mares to ride.' *I.* 'What a pity! and don't you ever go into the country outside Hail, the Desert?' *Zeh.* 'Oh, no, of course not.' *I.* 'But, to pass the time, what do you do?' *Zeh.* 'We do nothing.' Here a sharp black boy interrupted us, 'O, khatun, these are daughters of sheykhs, they have no work – no work *at all* to do, don't you understand?' *I.* 'Of course, I understand perfectly; but they might amuse themselves without doing work,' and turning to Zehowa I added, 'Don't you even look at the horses?' *Zeh.* 'No, we do nothing.' *I.* 'I should die if I did nothing. When I am at home I always walk around the first thing in the morning to look at my horses. How do you manage to spend your lives?' *Zeh.* 'We sit.' Thus supreme contentment in the harim here is to sit in absolute idleness. It seems odd, where the men are so active and adventurous, that the women should be satisfied to be bored; but such, I suppose, is the tyranny of fashion.

Lady Anne Blunt, *A Pilgrimage to Nejd*, 1985 (1st edn 1881), pp. 246–8

The next four extracts, also by women, again tell us little about the women they were writing about. Identifying more with their race than their gender, these women all adopted a condescending tone and compared the women they were visiting to children and animals. Mme Pommerol likened the women of the Sahara to children, cats and gazelles; Edith Wharton and the Countess Malmignati used images of the aviary and birds. Gertrude Bell's arrogance is typical of much of her writing about women. Distinctly unsympathetic to their problems – whether in England or the Middle East – she preferred to have conversations with Arab men.

WHO ARE THEY?

To the question with which I have headed this first chapter of my account of my sojourn amongst the women of the Sahara, the fact that I am of their sex enables me to give a very true reply; for as a woman I have been able to learn to know them well, to understand their unformed characters, breathing the same air as they do, camping upon the same sands, and honoured by their intense and perhaps too demonstrative friendship.

In every great tribe, in every small sedentary community, the women have their own special costume, their own peculiar amulets, their own manners and customs, setting them apart from every other group. Their dispositions, too, are modified by circumstances; some gaining courage from their surroundings, whilst others grow more timid. Their figures, always supple, become thinner or plumper as the case may be. Their complexions are either sallow, tanned, or pink; but, in spite of these superficial differences of form or feature, their characters are radically the same, bearing the unmistakable impress of the terrible climate, the restricted conditions of their life, and of the stern Mussulman faith, professed for some nine centuries at the least, by all the races of the Desert.

Frivolous, childish and cunning, these women have no scruples, for they themselves believe the doctrine of Mohammed, that they have scarcely so much as half a soul apiece. Their natures are, in fact, as I have just remarked in other words, quite undeveloped; and although they are remarkably plastic, they are incomplete, in the same sense as is a statue roughly outlined in the block. Greedy, voluptuous, spiteful and untruthful though they be, they are yet morally superior to the Arab and Berber women of the Tell, or Algerian Sahara. They have the proud, free carriage, so unlike that of their sisters of the North, of women accustomed to live in the open air. When young, there is something alike of the cat, the gazelle and the antelope about them. They are indeed infinitely interesting, but much in the same way as are the animals to which I have compared them.

Their black or greenish eyes, enlarged with *kohl* from the very day of their birth, full of combined fascination, reticence and mystery, have never looked upon any other scene than the vast and gloomy stretch of white sand of their native land, broken only here and there by a few rocks or the declivities known as dunes, dotted with tufts of the grasses called *diss* and *drinn*, which are green for a short time in spring, but dry and grey for the rest of the year, and grow in considerable quantities at wide intervals, the sand collecting behind them. The only tree, and that of very rare occurrence, is the palm, decorative enough, no doubt, but somewhat melancholy. No variety anywhere, except the scattered bones of dead camels, and over all the fierce sun, rising and setting in a furnace of a sky implacably blue.

The eyes of these women have scarcely seen any shade but that thrown by the scattered tents or the yet more melancholy mud houses of their tribe; and there are actually women of the towns – and oh, what towns those are! – who have never entered a tent, and other women of the desert who have never been inside a house. As a matter of course their range of ideas is restricted, and their vocabulary is as limited as are their thoughts.

They know, for instance, that their fingers spin the fleece of the sheep and the coarse hair of the camels; they know, too, who dyes the wool, who weaves it, and who knots it into fringes; for it is their own industrious hands which prepare the colours, wring out the dye, and, in a word, get the raw material into shape for the market. But their knowledge stops there; they do not know who makes the cotton stuffs and silk handkerchiefs brought to the desert by caravans. Understand well what I mean; they don't know whether it is a man, an angel, a demon, or what they call a *jinn*, who produces these things. Of course, however, I am only speaking of those whom our effete civilization has not yet touched, or given a smattering either of its science or its vice; and these include the greater number, in fact, the mass, of the true women of the true Sahara.

The dreary expanse of their native land does not, however, suppress their gaiety. Their laugh still rings out high and clear. The narrow limits of the tent or of the clay hut do not shackle the freedom of their movements; the poverty of their language does not prevent them from instinctively recognizing the innate poetry of the songs they transmit from generation to generation. And about them there is a something – I know not what, so difficult is it to define – irresistibly attractive to us Europeans, which is better than intelligence, and better than physical beauty. It is, maybe, that perfect resignation (after more than one crisis of furious revolt) to their fate, as fixed by the angel-writer, the scribe of Allah himself, combined with the absolute harmony of their voices, their smiles, their gestures, their costumes and their ornaments. . . .

Mme Jean Pommerol, *Among the Women of the Sahara*, 1900, pp. 1–5

The Sultan had sent word to Mme. Lyautey that the ladies of the Imperial harem would entertain her and her guests while His Majesty received the Resident-General, and we had to hasten back in order not to miss the next act of the spectacle.

We walked across a long court lined with the Black Guard, passed under a gateway, and were met by a shabbily dressed negress. Traversing a hot dazzle of polychrome tiles we reached another archway guarded by the chief eunuch, a towering black with the enamelled eyes of a basalt bust. The eunuch delivered us to other negresses, and we entered a labyrinth of inner patios and passages, all murmuring and dripping with water. Passing down long corridors where slaves in dim greyish garments flattened themselves against the walls, we caught glimpses of great dark rooms, laundries, pantries, bakeries, kitchens, where savoury things were brewing and stewing, and where more negresses, abandoning their pots and pans, came to peep at us from the threshold. In one corner, on a bench against a wall hung with matting, grey parrots in tall cages were being fed by a slave.

A narrow staircase mounted to a landing where a princess out of an Arab fairy-tale awaited us. Stepping softly on her embroidered slippers she led us to the next landing, where another golden-slippered being smiled out on us, a little girl this one, blushing and dimpling under a jewelled diadem and pearl-woven braids. On a third landing a third damsel appeared, and encircled by the three graces we mounted to the tall *mirador* in the central tower from which we were to look down at the coming ceremony. One by one, our little guides, kicking off their golden shoes, which a slave laid neatly outside the door, led us on soft bare feet into the upper chamber of the harem.

It was a large room, enclosed on all sides by a balcony glazed with panes of brightly-coloured glass. On a gaudy modern Rabat carpet stood gilt arm-chairs of florid design and a table bearing a commercial bronze of the 'art goods' variety. Divans with muslin-covered cushions were ranged against the walls and down an adjoining gallery-like apartment which was otherwise furnished only with clocks. The passion for clocks and other mechanical contrivances is common to all unmechanical races, and every chief's palace in North Africa contains a collection of timepieces which might be called striking if so many had not ceased to go. . . . But for the enchanting glimpses of sea and plain through the lattices of the gallery, the apartment of the Sultan's ladies falls far short of Occidental ideas of elegance. But there was hardly time to think of this, for the door of the *mirador* was always opening to let in another fairy-tale figure, till at last we were surrounded by a dozen houris, laughing, babbling, taking us by the hand, and putting shy questions while they looked at us with caressing eyes. They were all (our interpretess whispered) the Sultan's favourites, round-faced apricot-tinted girls in their teens, with high cheek-bones, full red lips, surprised brown eyes between curved-up Asiatic lids, and little brown hands fluttering out like birds from their brocaded sleeves.

In honour of the ceremony, and of Mme. Lyautey's visit, they had put on their finest clothes, and freedom of movement was somewhat hampered by their narrow sumptuous gowns, with over-draperies of gold and silver brocade and pale rosy gauze held in by corset-like sashes of gold tissue of Fez, and the heavy silken cords that looped their voluminous sleeves. Above their foreheads the hair was shaven like that of an Italian fourteenth-century beauty, and only a black line as narrow as a pencilled eyebrow showed through the twist of gauze fastened by a jewelled clasp above the real eyebrows. Over the forehead-jewel rose the complicated structure of the head-dress. Ropes of black wool were plaited through the hair, forming, at the back, a double loop that stood out above the nape like the twin handles of a vase, the upper veiled in airy shot gauzes and fastened with jewelled bands and ornaments. On each side of the red cheeks other braids were looped over the ears hung with broad earrings of filigree set with rough pearls and emeralds, or gold hoops and pendants of coral; and an unexpected tulle ruff, like that of a

Watteau shepherdess, framed the round chin above a torrent of
necklaces: necklaces of amber, coral, baroque pearls, hung with
mysterious barbaric amulets and fetishes. As the young things moved
about us on soft hennaed feet the light played on shifting gleams of
gold and silver, blue and violet and apple-green, all harmonized and
bemisted by clouds of pink and sky-blue; and through the changing
group capered a little black picaninny in a caftan of silver-shot
purple with a sash of raspberry-red.

But presently there was a flutter in the aviary. A fresh pair of
babouches clicked on the landing, and a young girl, less brilliantly
dressed and less brilliant of face than the others, came in on bare
painted feet. Her movements were shy and hesitating, her large lips
pale, her eyebrows less vividly dark, her head less jewelled. But all
the little humming-birds gathered about her with respectful rustlings
as she advanced towards us leaning on one of the young girls, and
holding out her ringed hand to Mme. Lyautey's curtsey. It was the
young Princess, the Sultan's legitimate daughter. She examined us
with sad eyes, spoke a few compliments through the interpretess, and
seated herself in silence letting the others sparkle and chatter.

Conversation with the shy Princess was flagging when one of the
favourites beckoned us to the balcony. We were told we might push
open the painted panes a few inches, but as we did so the butterfly
group drew back lest they should be seen looking out on the
forbidden world. . . . At this point one of the favourites called us in
from the *mirador*. The door had just opened to admit an elderly
woman preceded by a respectful group of girls. From the new-
comer's round ruddy face, her short round body, the round hands
emerging from her round wrists, an inexplicable majesty emanated,
and though she too was less richly arrayed than the favourites she
carried her head-dress of striped gauze like a crown.

This impressive old lady was the Sultan's mother. As she held out
her plump wrinkled hand to Mme. Lyautey and spoke a few words
through the interpretess one felt that at last a painted window of the
mirador had been broken, and a thought let into the vacuum of the
harem. What thought, it would have taken deep insight into the
processes of the Arab mind to discover; but its honesty was manifest
in the old Empress's voice and smile. Here at last was a woman
beyond the trivial dissimulations, the childish cunning, the idle
cruelties of the harem. It was not a surprise to be told that she was
her son's most trusted adviser, and the chief authority in the palace.

If such a woman deceived and intrigued it would be for great purposes and for ends she believed in: the depth of her soul had air and daylight in it, and she would never willingly shut them out.

Edith Wharton, *In Morocco*, 1984 (1st edn 1920), pp. 135–42

The visitors were all grouped on the low divans on the *estrade*, men and women separately, and a chair was arranged for me in the centre. They were all sitting around me and hanging on my words as if I were the Delphic Oracle. They expected me to say something marvellously clever or extraordinarily interesting. They all kept obstinately silent. If I tried to enter into conversation with someone who seemed a little less dull, the rest all cried out in alarm: 'No, you must talk to all of us at the same time!' I felt that this was impossible, and my speaking courage left me altogether, so that we remained silent, gazing at each other. I felt a kind of dull despair coming over me under the hypnotism of all those staring orbs! As a rule, when they are amongst themselves they chatter and talk all at the same time, and on hearing it one thinks a great quarrel is going on, or that something has happened in the parrot-house. But I should have preferred that torrent of tongues to this silence and those staring eyes around me.

I tried to persuade the young people to dance or sing, but in vain. 'They don't dance here, and to sing is considered improper for women in this country!' There were no theatres or books one could talk about; they had no intellectual interests whatever, only gossip, and again gossip. I told them that in Europe we go in very much for dancing, that quite young girls study it, and that it would give them grace and beauty. Whereupon the mother of two young elephants implored me to show her girls how to dance – perhaps it might improve their figures. Out of fun I promised to give them some lessons *à la* Isadora Duncan because the idea was too amusing, to imagine those clumsy masses of human flesh in Greek costume, trying Greek dances!

It is a pity that the women here all get so fat, because as a rule they are very pretty, and have most lovely complexions, their faces never being exposed to sun or wind. But to be fat here is considered beautiful! Often they tell me: '*Oh! madame, que vous êtes belle. Mais il faut grossir un peu!*' Their compliments are too funny. The way, for instance, someone is introduced to me. She at once says: '*Madame, que vous êtes belle.*' And nothing else! What am I to answer to such banality? They usually drown one in flatteries, their only form of conversation. I only wondered how it was possible to stay together and talk about nothing till two o'clock in the morning.

Countess Malmignati, *Through Inner Deserts to Medina*, 1925,
pp. 25–8

My Syrian girl is charming and talks very prettily but with a strong local accent. It adds enormously to one's difficulties that one has to learn a 'patois' and a purer Arabic at the same time. I took her out for a long walk on Friday afternoon and went photographing about Jerusalem. She was much entertained, though she was no good as a guide, for she had never been in the Jewish quarter though she has lived all her life here! That's typical of them. I knew my way, however, as every Englishwoman would – it's as simple as possible.

The Letters of Gertrude Bell, 1947, p. 58

Like many nineteenth- and twentieth-century men, Edmondo de Amicis had a strong dislike of 'intellectual' Western women – such as the foregoing writers. If he could have been present at any of these meetings, he would have found that none of the women fitted his idea of the perfect woman – neither the European 'blue-stocking' nor the Arab woman with an 'undeveloped soul'.

At all events – and it is no small praise – there are no dull blue-stockings among them, or wearisome pedagogues who can talk of nothing but language and style, or those spiritual creatures who dwell on a loftier plane than ordinary mortals. It is, however, perfectly true that in their narrow lives, cut off from all elevating association or occupation, with the instinctive desire of youth and beauty for love and admiration constantly thwarted and dissatisfied, their souls remain undeveloped.

Edmondo de Amicis, *Constantinople*, 1896, vol. I, p. 40

Coming from the pens of two Europeans the passage below is a wonderful piece of hypocrisy. Here women were condemned as childish because they enjoyed the stories of the *Arabian Nights*!

The women of the harem are childish and easily amused. Marvellous stories, more or less based on the *Arabian Nights*, in which the details relating to love are recounted with inconceivable crudity, the buffooneries of old women, their burlesque imitations, their clownings, ravish them. One of these has won in Teheran the reputation and vogue of an Yvette Guilbert with us. She tells stories and illustrates them herself, impersonating the characters of the romance. She imitates with as much fidelity the shy attitude of a blushing bride as the simpering of a middle-aged woman. And when a dragon, a devil, or a djinn comes into the plot, she succeeds in pulling the skin of her face, turning up her nose with a string, turning her eyelids out, and so on, assuming the most terrible and monstrous aspects imaginable. A story told by her is as much appreciated in Teheran, and as highly paid, as a monologue by Chevalier in London.

Eustache de Lorey and Douglas Sladen, *Queer Things About Persia*,
1907, p. 163

Finally, Guy de Maupassant has the last word on women's 'limited minds'. Unlike men in North Africa, women were only able to understand the tangible, he declared. As a result they not only required men to see them through their daily life, but also to intercede with God on their behalf. Presumably he understood all this from the Europeans who went to the mosque to arrange liaisons with these 'creatures'.

Having removed my shoes I entered the koubba. In a narrow room a Muslim scholar is sitting on his heels reading a manuscript which he holds in both hands at eye level. Books and parchments are scattered around him on the mats. He does not turn to look when I enter.

Further on I hear a rustling, a whispering. As I approach all the women crouching around the tomb quickly cover their faces. They look like large flakes of white linen with eyes shining out. In the middle of this froth of flannel, silk, wool and linen children are sleeping and wriggling around, dressed in red, blue and green. The scene is charming and naïve. They are at home here with their saint, for whom they have decorated the room – because God is too distant for their limited minds and too great for their humility.

The women do not turn towards Mecca but towards the body of

the marabout, and they place themselves under his direct protection, which means that they are still, as always, under the protection of man. For their women's eyes, so gentle and sad, accentuated by two wide bands, are not able to see the immaterial, can only understand the tangible. It is the male who feeds them, defends them, supports them in life, and after his death it is the male who speaks to God on their behalf. They are all there around the tomb which they have decorated and painted in gaudy colours until it rather resembles a Breton bed that has been coloured and covered with materials, with silken fabrics, with flags, with presents.

They whisper and chatter among themselves, and tell the marabout all their concerns, their worries, their disputes, their grievances against their husband. It is a very intimate and domestic reunion of gossiping women around a relic.

The whole chapel is full of their strange gifts; clocks of all sizes which tick away the seconds and strike the hours, votive banners, copper and crystal chandeliers – so many that you can't see the ceiling – of all sizes, hanging side by side just like in a light shop. The walls are covered with stylishly decorated tiles, whose dominant colours are green and red. The ground is covered with carpets and the light pours in from the cupola through three arched windows, one dominating the other two.

This is no longer a severe, stark, mosque where there is only God; it has become a boudoir decked out for prayer by the childish taste of these wild women. Often gentlemen come here to arrange a rendez-vous or to exchange a few words in secret. Europeans who can speak Arabic sometimes come here to establish relations with these shrouded, slow-moving creatures, of whom one can see nothing except their gaze.

Guy de Maupassant, *La Vie errante*, 1890, pp. 137–9

Chapter 9

AS TO THE POSITION OF WOMEN

When discussing the position of women in Oriental society, writers were concerned to emphasize the superior position held by women in Christian countries and the effects of intelligent motherhood in those same countries. Many authors conceded that Muslim women were tender and affectionate mothers, but argued that this affection was not accompanied by intelligence. The result, they complained, was millions of bad mothers producing a future generation which would further debilitate an already feeble society.

In a book entitled *L'Islam et la psychologie du musulman* (1923) André Servier generalized about 'Muslim woman' and her ability as a mother.

The result is that in Islam today women are treated just as their forebears were treated in the time of the Prophet. But what was then progress is today a regression.

A Muslim woman thinks and acts just as the wives of Mohammed thought and acted. Cut off from eternal life, they remain in the barbarity of ancestral customs. Compared to the condition of women of other religions, she is a slave. A luxurious animal, a beast of pleasure to the rich; a beast of burden to the poor; she is nothing more than a poor creature sacrificed to the pleasure of the male. Condemned to ignorance by the egoism of man, she cannot even hope in the future. She is perpetually cloistered, an eternal slave. Her ignorance and barbarity weigh heavily on the children whom she raises and to whom she passes on her prejudices and antiquated ideas. Ignorant herself, she creates ignorance; barbarous herself, she spreads barbarity around her; a slave herself, she gives her children the souls of slaves, with all the deficiencies of servile beings: the dissimulation, the deceit and the falsehood.

André Servier, *L'Islam et la psychologie du musulman*, 1923, p. 305

The next few extracts are a small sample of different opinions on motherhood in the Orient, written over a period of more than 100 years. Here we encounter some of the same complaints made about working-class mothers in Europe, and little awareness of economic and political conditions and change in the countries the authors were visiting. The last extract by Edith Wharton, the famous American novelist, describes a visit to a household of women. Given the number of novels she wrote with women characters caught up in arid marriages and confined by strict social codes, the lack of sympathy she displayed in her accounts of visits such as this is quite remarkable – particularly since she spoke no Arabic and was aware that no real communication could take place through an interpreter.

Women in the Orient have not yet realized that the way of keeping their youth for as long as possible and enjoying without interruption the delightful pleasures of social life, is to withdraw from the most sacred of duties by placing the precious fruit of their marriage in the hands of a mercenary. They find the caresses of the child whom they feed at the breast much sweeter, much more pleasant, than the smile of a perfidious and corrupt world. If their way of life is simpler and less tumultuous, if their pleasures are less lively, less stimulating, there is compensation in the calm of the senses, the peace of the spirit, the health which they keep, the life which they pass on to their children. In the Orient there is very little incidence of that multitude of illnesses caused by milk pouring out, the swellings of the breast and milky deposits which afflict so many European women and may take them away in the prime of life.

If by some extraordinary chance a woman loses her milk and has to use a wet-nurse, she will bring her into the house and have her treated with the same regard and the same attention that she receives herself. Whether Muslim or Christian this foster mother must never abandon the child whom she has fed with her milk and must continue to provide it with maternal care. For as long as she lives she will receive from the child or its parents tokens of lasting gratitude. In fact, she will be incorporated into the family where she will be considered and respected as a second mother.

G. A. Olivier, *Voyage dans l'Empire Othoman*, 1800, vol. I, pp. 102–3

If, in addition to this, you consider that the population of Turkey diminishes every year, as is always the case in all ill-governed countries; and here it is positively alarming, partly from polygamy, and partly from infanticide – (for women in the Harems who have had one or two confinements, and have grown tired of child-bearing, as they soon do, especially if they have been daughters, think it no sin to destroy their unborn offspring), for I have known even Princesses to leave their only sons when they were dying to the care of Moslem nurses for a whole week together, while they went out visiting; – if you consider this, I say, does it not become natural to ask, How is it possible for future hopes to knit themselves to young branches, to fresh roots, when the pith of the tree has lost all its vital powers?

Emmeline Lott, *Harem Life in Egypt and Constantinople*, 1865, vol. II, pp. 310–11

All Turkish mothers and many Armenians of the lower orders administer strong sleeping draughts, generally of opium, poppy-head or theriac, to their infants; some carry the abuse of these to such an extent that the children appear always in a drowsy state, the countenance pale, the eyelids half closed, the pupils of the eyes contracted, the lips parched and dry, and a peculiar hazy expression fixed upon the face; all the movements are lethargic, in marked contrast to the sprightly motion of a healthy European child.

A Consul's Daughter and Wife, *People of Turkey*, 1878, p. 10

Both at home and at school the Moslem learns almost nothing that will serve him in good stead in after life. Worse than this; in those early years spent at home, when the child ought to have instilled into him some germ of those principles of conduct by which men must walk in the world if they are to hold up their heads among civilized nations, the Turkish child is only taught the first steps towards the vicious habits of mind and body which have made his race what it is. The root of the evil is partly found in the harem system. So long as that system keeps Turkish women in their present degraded state, so long will Turkish boys and girls be vicious and ignorant.

Turkish mothers have not the slightest control over their children. They are left to do very much as they like, become wayward, disobedient, and unbearably tyrannical. I have often noticed young children, especially boys, strike, abuse, and even curse their mothers, who, helpless to restrain them, either respond by a torrent of foul invective, or, in their maternal weakness, indulgently put up with it, saying, *'Jahil chojuk, ne belir?'* (Innocent child! what does it know?')

A Consul's Daughter and Wife, *People of Turkey*, 1878, pp. 153–4

At this season of the year the fields are alive with labourers, who sing as they work. Eye and ear alike are charmed with the gay and lively scene. Among the men we see many heads full of character, and many pretty faces among the women and girls, who often go unveiled; but the prettiest sight in all the Nile valley is that of the young boys and girls here, who up to the age of about five generally run about perfectly naked – the sweetest little brown pets. The babies in arms are less pleasing; their mothers generally carry them about on their shoulders, and they are rarely kept clean. Many women when they go out to their work leave the babies behind to take care of themselves, and the traveller who wanders through the streets of a fellah village in harvest-time, deserted by the inhabitants and guarded only by the shabby dogs, may come across more than one cradle and nurse as that transferred to his portfolio by Herr Gentz, and here set before the reader. I myself once came on an infant lying on a scrap of carpet by a heap of durrah in the middle of a field, kicking its little legs, and minded only by a dog. Not a fellah mother would have passed by it without offering it the breast, and its own mother would no doubt come and fetch the little screaming thing in due time.

G. Ebers, *Egypt, Descriptive, Historical and Picturesque*, 1898, vol. II, p. 191

In spite of their febrile activity and tropical bird-shrieks, we waited in vain for tea; and after a while our host suggested to his son that I might like to visit the ladies of the household. As I had expected the young man led me across the *patio*, lifted the cotton hanging and introduced me into an apartment exactly like the one we had just left. Divans covered with striped mattress-ticking stood against the white walls, and on them sat seven or eight passive-looking women over whom a number of pale children scrambled.

The eldest of the group, and evidently the mistress of the house, was an Algerian lady, probably of about fifty, with a sad and delicately-modelled face; the others were daughters, daughters-in-law and concubines. The latter word evokes to Occidental ears images of sensual seduction which the Moroccan harem seldom realizes. All the ladies of this dignified household wore the same look of somewhat melancholy respectability. In their stuffy curtained apartment they were like cellar-grown flowers, pale, heavy, fuller, but frailer than the garden sort. Their dresses, rich but sober, the veils and diadems put on in honour of my visit, had a dignified dowdiness in odd contrast to the frivolity of the Imperial harem. But what chiefly struck me was the apathy of the younger women. I asked them if they had a garden, and they shook their heads wistfully, saying that there were no gardens in Old Fez. The roof was therefore their only escape: a roof overlooking acres and acres of other roofs, and closed in by the naked fortified mountains which stand about Fez like prison-walls.

After a brief exchange of compliments silence fell. Conversing through interpreters is a benumbing process, and there are few points of contact between the open-air Occidental mind and beings imprisoned in a conception of sexual and domestic life based on slave-service and incessant espionage. These languid women on their muslin cushions toil not, neither do they spin. The Moroccan lady knows little of cooking, needlework, or any household arts. When her child is ill she can only hang it with amulets and wail over it; the great lady of the Fazi palace is as ignorant of hygiene as the peasant-woman of the *bled*. And all these colourless eventless lives depend on the favour of one fat tyrannical man, bloated with good living and authority, himself almost as inert and sedentary as his women, and accustomed to impose his whims on them ever since he ran about the same *patio* as a little short-smocked boy.

The redeeming point in this stagnant domesticity is the tenderness of the parents for their children, and Western writers have laid so much stress on this that one would suppose children could be loved only by inert and ignorant parents. It is in fact charming to see the heavy eyes of the Moroccan father light up when a brown grasshopper baby jumps on his knee, and the unfeigned tenderness with which the childless women of the harem caress the babies of their happpier rivals. But the sentimentalist moved by this display of family feeling would do well to consider the lives of these much-petted children. Ignorance, unhealthiness and a precocious sexual initiation prevail in all classes. Education consists in learning by heart endless passages of the Koran, and amusement in assisting in spectacles that would be unintelligible to Western children, but that the pleasantries of the harem make perfectly comprehensible to Moroccan infancy. At eight or nine the little girls are married, at twelve the son of the house is 'given his first negress'; and thereafter, in the rich and leisured class, both sexes live till old age in an atmosphere of sensuality without seduction.

Edith Wharton, *In Morocco*, 1984 (1st edn 1920), pp. 151–3

In his book on the religious, civil and military organization of the Ottoman Empire published in 1825, M. Grassi had this to say on the position of women in Turkey and Europe.

In Turkey the women have two advantages which those of Europe generally do not have. The latter often work as much as and more than their husbands, either on the land or in different branches of industry, in order to provide for their family. In Turkey and in all the Muslim states, it is the husband alone who is concerned with the means of keeping his wife and children. If he does not provide reasonably for her needs according to her rank she has the right to end the marriage. The other advantage granted to women is that instead of bringing a dowry to the husband it is the men instead who must bring money to the woman and give presents to the family of the bride, according to their rank and wealth.

These two advantages are not unimportant. The opposite is true for our women who, in the countryside generally, are weighed down by hard work in the fields and harvesting. Our daughters, young pretty and interesting in all respects, often do not find a husband because there is no dowry or because of the prejudices adopted towards the inequality of the conditions.

M. Grassi, *Charte Turque*, 1825, vol. II, pp. 23–4

While he was right that European women worked hard in

agriculture, Grassi was quite wrong that no Muslim women did so, and his opinions on the relative merits of the position of women in Muslim and Christian countries are obviously a male view on the matter.

In 1822 the Vicomte de Ségur published his three-volume work on women, their condition, and their influence in the social order – among all peoples and throughout history! His book is a plea for increased rights for women so that they may become better wives and mothers. I have included this small piece because of his reply to arguments by Montesquieu that if women in Muslim countries were not secluded, they would be raped.

Any country where women do not hold that position in the social order to which nature has called them is even farther from the state of civilization than are the savages. For, if they do not respect their women at least they do not shut them away.

It is surprising that Monsieur de Montesquieu should justify this Muslim practice by saying that in countries where women are secluded the influence of the climate on the passions is so great that, should they be granted their liberty, attacks against their chastity would be inevitable and their resistance non-existent.

Would it not be more just to lock up the aggressors?

Le Vicomte J.-A. de Ségur, *Les Femmes*, 1822, vol. I, pp. 168–9

Much of the remaining part of this chapter consists of eulogies on the position held by women in the West. The first author, writing in 1854, was quite clear that only Christianity could lift 'Mohammedan, Jewish and heathen daughters' to their rightful position in society, and encouraged 'Christian females' to promote their religion worldwide.

Among all nations, and in all ages, there have been found both contemners, and advocates, of the weaker sex. But Christianity alone has given to the woman that prominent position, to which she is lawfully entitled.

There is a passage extant in the literature of an ancient and civilised nation to the following import: 'It is as little possible that wisdom should be found amongst women, as for an ass to ascend a ladder.' Of Socrates it is also said, that he compared women to the brute creation. The laws of Scythia forbade women's testimony to be taken, in consideration of their 'levity, their prejudice, and malice'. Such was the degraded state of her, who was made equal in rank, dignity, and station, with the other sex; and such is her state to this day, in those countries where the light of the Gospel has not yet penetrated. How then ought Christian females to exert themselves to promote that religion, amongst all nations, which has taken them out of that degraded condition, and restored them to the original position, assigned to them by the Lord of the creation! The Mohammedan, the Jewish, and heathen daughters, call especially for their aid.

How different is the language of the Christian, with reference to the daughters of Adam to that of Pagan philosophers, Rabbinic and Mohammedan divines. 'Woman,' says Dr Cross, in his admirable publication, entitled *Physiology of Human Nature*, 'is, under God, the true creator of personal character, and, in the aggregate, of national character also; for the destiny of a nation, so far as human instrumentality goes is really the charge of each succeeding female generation. Senators may make the nation's laws, – statesmen may wield the national resources, – universities may perpetuate its learning; but the women of the country develop its moral characteristics:– and, like as the mind, and the physical being, constitutes the man, so the moral features of a people, and not their geographical situation nor political relations, constitutes a nation in the eyes of Him who rules and will judge all the world.

'How greatly, then, does man err, and how superficially does he estimate woman's position in the world, in conceiving that aught is needed to make it co-equal with his own! Those, indeed, who do not perceive in them the very head and front of moral instrumentality, most clearly undervalue and mistake her character and office. Man and the schools may finish the structure; *but woman it is who lays the corner-stone, which truly remains ever the head of the building.*

In a country where the woman is neither taught reading nor writing; where the cultivation of her mind is entirely neglected; where her faculties are only fixed upon ornaments, dress, and food; where, in short, she is on a level with the brute creation, – considered as "a useful and necessary animal" – it is no wonder that superstition has its sway over her mind.'

Reverend N. Davis, *Evenings in My Tent*, 1854, vol. 2, pp. 18–20

At the same period Florence Nightingale was visiting Egypt. In this letter, she had nothing to report in favour of the country except its past! And, as for women, they *were* nothing and *had* nothing, she claimed.

Without the past, I conceive Egypt to be utterly uninhabitable. Oh, if you were to see the people! No ideas that I had of polygamy come near the fact; and my wonder is now, not that Sarah and Rachel were so bad, but that they were not a great deal worse. Polygamy strikes at the root of everything in woman – she is not a wife – she is not a mother; – and in these Oriental countries, what is a woman, if she is not that? In all other countries she has something to fall back upon. The Roman Catholic woman has a religion – the Protestant has an intellect; in the early Christian, in the old Egyptian time, women had a vocation, a profession, provided for them in their religion, independent of their wifedom; here, she is nothing but the servant of a man. No, I do assure you, the female elephant, the female eagle, has a higher idea of what she was put into the world to do, than the human female has here. I never knew of a religion, ancient or modern, that I could not have some points of sympathy with, – but with the Mahometan, how few.

Florence Nightingale, *Letters from Egypt*, 1987 (1st edn 1854),
p. 139

Mabel Sharman Crawford held similar views about Algerian women and in the first extract she based much of this opinion on the choice of a pronoun by a man who invited her to visit his family. In the next piece by the same author she recommended Christianity to Muslim women, quite ignoring the degraded position of many Christian women in the West as well as the East.

From her birth to her grave, the Moorish woman has no recognised existence in the world, beyond the circle of her home, and of her female friends. She lives and dies an ever-shrouded mystery. Her husband's dearest friend has never heard him mention her; and though the friend might chance to learn through his female relatives that she was dangerously ill, he could not say, 'How is your wife?' or

'I hope your wife is better,' without being guilty of a gross breach of decorum, which would not improbably be rebuked by the indignant answer, 'It is no business of yours to hope or care about my wife, or to concern yourself in any way about her existence.' Except under the comprehensive terms, How are your family? how is your house? how are your people? all enquiries relative to the health of the female inmates of any Moorish house are an insult to its proprietor.

The strictness of the code of etiquette in reference to this subject was strikingly exemplified to me one day by the mode in which a gentleman, proprietor of a native café, invited me to visit his wife, who lived in a neighbouring villa. Had he been alone, he would have said at once, 'My wife will be glad to see you, pray visit her'; but being in the café amidst a dozen of its frequenters, he merely said, '*They* will be very glad to see you in my house, should you pass that way.'

Mabel Sharman Crawford, *Through Algeria*, 1863, pp. 53–4

Short of Christianity, no teaching can elevate the character and position of Mohammedan women in any land; for, as long as she accepts the Koran as a rule of faith, she will unhesitatingly acquiesce in the mutilated life to which by it she is condemned; and if, in despite of this mighty influence, her mental faculties could be developed by education, she would probably purchase wisdom at a heavy price, galled by the bonds she is too weak to break, but whose weight she had learned to feel. Degraded by her religion into a toy or slave, a toy and slave she will continue, as long as the name of Mohammed is reverenced by her race. But prostrate as she lies, she yet takes ample vengeance for the injuries of which she is the victim; for, fatally sapping the native vigour of the Arab as well as of the Turkish race, she has doomed them both to stagnation and decay.

Mabel Sharman Crawford, *Through Algeria*, 1863, pp. 55–6

Mrs Albert Rogers was an extremely rigid Christian but very anti-Catholic. She was particularly incensed that the French in Algeria were not converting the Muslim population and while she was travelling around the country she distributed Bibles and religious tracts to anyone who would accept them. In this piece she lamented the life of 'these degraded ones'.

Met as usual today troops of Arab women, when in the Jardin Marengo. These poor veiled creatures – veiled alike in mind and body – bound in shackles which none but their own sex can loose, how one mourns over them, and longs to be able to reach them! But without a knowledge of Arabic, the hope is futile. The sight of them at almost every step, recalls Miss Whateley's 'Ragged Life in Egypt', with such added interest. I would we could employ an Arabic-speaking Bible-woman amongst them. The generality seem poor, miserable, stunted, frightened, and squalid; and I am sure, as far as I can glean from the mute language of looks, that they would gratefully welcome any such agency to their homes. It is seldom that they venture to extend their henna-dyed hands for alms, and when they do so, it is with such timid imploring accents.

Few positions in life, not even excepting American slavery, can be so utterly wretched as that of the very poor Arab woman. Amongst the richer Moslems the degradation of the women is mental and moral. Superadded to this, amongst the poorer classes the husband lays upon the shoulders of his wife, every conceivable burden. As far as possible he lives in the most perfect idleness, as one of the lords of creation. To the lot of the Arab woman it falls, to till the ground, to reap the harvest, to grind the corn, to knead the bread. If garments are wanted, it is she who must weave the cloth from the fibrous tissues of the aloe and the palm. Does her master condescend to expose Arab matting and baskets for sale, it is she who must fabricate the articles. If he be wealthy enough to own a half-starved quadruped, it is she who grooms, and feeds, and tends the animal, saddling him when her lord has need of him. Are purchases to be made, or heavy burdens from the town to be borne home, it is on her devoted head the weight must rest, while he does not so much as touch it with one of his fingers.

There is a baby, or small child, frequently appended to her person in addition, attached either to the shoulder or back, unless the arms happen to be empty. And though it is hers to prepare the meagre fare, it is not hers to share it with her husband, seasoned with the salt of love, which would make even a dry morsel savoury. No, she must stand aloof till his appetite is satisfied, when she may have the leavings. Nor has she any solace in maternal love. If her offspring are girls, they must be reared in all haste to share the mother's drudgery. If boys, ere they reach the age at which they might require a mother's tenderness, they become her superiors and masters, if not tyrants.

With them she may no longer eat, when their years permit them to share the father's meal. Oh, Christianity haste to tear the fetters, and rend the veil from these degraded ones: no meaner power can save them.

Mrs G. Albert Rogers, *Winter in Algeria, 1863–4*, 1865, pp. 58–9

Isobel Burton related to her readers a conversation with a group of Syrian women about the different lives led by Eastern and Western women. She presented a picture of Western marriage which was both idealized and contained an amazing list of wifely duties.

'You are all mistaken. Now listen to what I want to explain to you. Our lives and your lives are quite different. You are set apart to dwell amongst one another, mostly indoors, in a settled place; your lives would indeed be a failure without children. You are three or four, and your Lord and Master honours most who has the most sons; and why? Because your ancestor, in the old law, exactly as today, could not "meet his enemies in the gate" without being backed up by his stalwart sons and their sons, his brothers, and his uncles and their sons. In short, the family who could show the most fighting men were the most honoured, and carried the greatest weight in their town or tribe. So men chose wives who could bear them sons, and visited with their displeasure those who could not. The men of our races marry one wife, and a family will commonly be from six or eight to ten children. I have seen a woman nursing her twenty-fourth child. (Loud murmurs of applause, and Mashallahs.) Children are from Allah. If he sends them we bless Him, and if He does not we are contented, for we know that it is for some good purpose, some special mercy to ourselves. The English husband would not put his wife away for anything. I feel quite secure of my place. The Sidi Beg may marry another after my death, but not before. I never think about jealousy, and it is not in our customs that the "honour of the house" should notice his slaves, or any one but his wife. . . .

We all meet in society, men and women alike. In Franguestan girls are not veiled: they see young men in their fathers' houses. Men and women are all alike to us, except the one we mean to marry. Eventually a young man will say to himself, "I have to choose one woman with whom to live all my life, to love and respect her, and to trust everything to her prudence. I feel that such-and-such is the only one with whom I would willingly pass all my days." Then he goes to the girl, and he asks her to be his wife. If she says "No," there is an end of the matter, and nobody ever hears of it. If she says "Yes," they go to their fathers and mothers, and ask their blessing. The parents consent, and arrange the wedding. They are then betrothed, and have time before marriage to learn all each other's faults and good qualities, and to know exactly what they have taken upon themselves.'

'Mashallah! and how does it go on afterwards?'

'The woman must take as much pains to look pretty and dress well as she did before; and must love her husband, be very respectful to him, make his house bright and comfortable – even if it be poor, she must try not to make it look so to his friends; she must be constantly waiting upon him, and thinking what she can do to please him; she must also educate herself, that she may be able to be his companion, friend, adviser, and conᶜᵈante, that he may miss nothing at home; and finding all that he can desire in his wife, he has nothing to seek elsewhere; she must be a careful nurse when he is ailing, that he may never be anxious about his health; she must not unjustly or uselessly squander his money; she must take an interest in all his pursuits, and study them; she must not confide her domestic affairs to all her friends; she must observe the same refinement and delicacy in all her words and actions that she observed before her marriage; she must hide his faults from everyone, and always be at his side through every difficulty and trouble; she must never allow anyone to speak disrespectfully of him before her, nor permit any one to tell her anything of him or his doings; she must never hurt his feelings with a rude remark or jest, never answer when he finds fault, nor reproach him when he is in the wrong; never be inquisitive about anything he does not volunteer to tell her; never worry him with trifles, but rather keep the pleasant news for him when he comes home, and be looking her brightest and her best. Above all, she must see that all his creature comforts are ready. The wife who follows this recipe, O Leila, is never put away; she has no need of the "evil eye", nor love potions, nor papers written by the Shaykh. Her husband could not do without her; he loves her, and knows her as himself. He will listen to no voice but hers, and he would find a second wife very much in the way.'

Isobel Burton, *The Inner Life of Syria, Palestine, and the Holy Land*, 1875, vol. I, pp. 154–8

Edwin de Leon worked into his novel *Askaris Kassis the Copt* a conversation between an American visitor, Edith, and an Egyptian Copt, El Warda, which made clear that the different situations of Eastern and Western women arose from custom rather than religion.

During this careless talk, in which Edith asked questions and El Warda answered them, the young American first learned, to her surprise, how utterly different and repugnant were an Eastern and a Western woman's ideas both of propriety and of pleasure. For the native Christian of the East, though differing in faith from the Mussulman, yet carries into his life, manners and morals many of the peculiar customs and prejudices of the Turk, especially as regards his estimate and treatment of women.

With all of them the woman occupies a subordinate position – is not regarded as an equal or a companion, so much as a plaything, to be petted in the homes of the higher – a kind of upper servant in the households of the middle classes. The wife of the Copt, Armenian, Syrian, or Greek Christian, brings in with her own hands the tray of refreshments, and after meekly serving guest and husband, retires or remains quietly in a corner, without expecting to be addressed or to take part in the conversation. If spoken to, she glances at her husband to respond for her; and seems so fearfully embarrassed, no stranger repeats a second time the well-meant but painful politeness.

When these women go abroad, they also veil themselves, and it is considered a high compliment for a strange man, even in the house, to be permitted a sight of the face of an unmarried woman.

Edwin de Leon, *Askaros Kassis the Copt*, 1870, pp. 56–7

The Duc d'Harcourt made three trips to Egypt, the last in 1889, and he was very critical of what he saw. He argued that in Muslim societies 'the absence of surnames corresponds to the absence of family ties, in the extended sense of the word'. The fact that a wife's fortune remained hers during marriage and would be administered by her brother, rather than her husband or another male relative as usually happened in the West, indicated, he said, that 'the family as we know it cannot exist'. Having established this, he continued:

The absence of a family establishing itself with a separate existence means, *a priori*, that wealth is not stable; for in all countries, the only secure wealth is that which is the result of the successive efforts of many generations. But many other considerations have the same effect, mainly the empty role which custom gives to women.

An old Norman notary once told me that he had seen many families led to ruin by women as much as by men, but that he had never seen a family lifted out of ruin except by women. Whatever this wise observer may have noticed, it is certain that among us women play an important role in the household economy, and everybody knows that no amount of care by the husband can make up for a lack of order by the wife. In Egypt, on the other hand, no one supposes that a rich wife would occupy herself with the details of running a house; it would be considered servile and dishonour her. Then, in order to do the supervision, it would of course be necessary for her to leave the women's quarters, which would dishonour the husband.

Consequently, the wife stays inside the harem all day long, squatting or lying on a divan, smoking cigarettes or nibbling sweets. When you go into the selamlik, the only part of the house accessible to a male visitor, you are struck in the houses of the richest pashas by the appearance of disorder, or rather of an unimaginable negligence. A thick layer of dust covers the gilded chairs, which seem to have never been dusted since they left the shop; there are stains everywhere, the materials are torn, and this is a house which is considered to be rich, and does in fact have numerous servants. Everyone knows that to us disorder and negligence are signs of wasteful habits and extravagance. It is the same everywhere; because of the lack of order and economy in the running of their houses, the wealth of Egyptians is usually wasted.

It would be right to say that the personal fortune of the women does not escape this danger; they have the administration of their own property, but although this is enshrined in Islamic law, in their weak hands it becomes only a shadow of power. How could it be possible for a woman to do this administration from the depths of

the harem, speaking to no stranger, seeing nothing for herself, her
only intermediary being the inevitable eunuch?

Duc d'Harcourt, *L'Égypte et les Égyptiens*, 1893, pp. 40–2

Remarking that family background made little difference to the
way a woman was treated, the Duc d'Harcourt argued that far
from being a positive aspect of Islam, this was only a further
indication of the low respect accorded to women. However,
the different respect given to women in Europe according to
their class background as well as their sex, could hardly be
described as more egalitarian.

One result of this contempt for women on account of their sex, is
that the social and educational differences between them hardly
affect the way they are treated or the respect they are shown. It is to
the advantage of women of low extraction that, when they enjoy the
favour of their master, they are better treated by him than those who
do not please him, however good a family they may come from. It
has often been noted that in Muslim societies there is little disfavour
attached to having a slave as a mother; this is attributed to the
feelings of humanity with which Islam inspires all its teachings, and it
is praised for having developed egalitarian ideas in all its people.
However, I believe the explanation is much less lofty. I believe it is
the result of the low esteem in which Muslim men hold the whole
female sex, and the little importance given to where the woman
comes from. In his eyes, a woman counts for so little, her personal
qualities have so little value, that whether she is a slave or a princess
matters little. In point of fact, they have both received the same
moral and intellectual education; only their dress distinguishes them.
Therefore, no one would reproach the son of a slave with the servile
condition of his mother; his birth would be no obstacle to him
reaching the highest positions.

Duc d'Harcourt, *L'Égypte et les Égyptiens*, 1893, pp. 105–6

The Reverend Edwin Bliss and the Chevalier de Hesse-
Wartegg deplored the way the Turkish and Arab nomad men
in Tunisia treated their women – that is, they stated, as mere

receptacles for their lust. While no one would argue that all women in North Africa and the Middle East were well treated, any more than they were in Europe, we hear little about male violence and lust in Western countries from any authors, but many generalizations about Oriental men. In much the same way as Europe today is reluctant to admit that professional men batter their wives, so it was a very rare travel writer who mentioned that European men did so. In the third piece, Edmondo de Amicis began by saying that 'not infrequently' you would come across a family group sitting enjoying themselves; in the next breath he commented that it was an exceptional occurrence which proved that the institution of the family – mother, father, children – barely existed in Turkey.

So also in private life there are aspects of even the best of the Turkish people that can call forth only condemnation. Most noticeable, perhaps, is the condition of women, which is in the main thoroughly degraded. From her birth she is looked upon as a menial and an unfortunate. This is illustrated by the great amount of infanticide, especially if the child be a girl; by the haggard, ugly countenances of the old women, so different in that respect from the Armenians; the piercing shrillness of their voices, from which every tone of tenderness seems to have gone; the very general vulgarity of conversation and of thought, always attendant upon a condition of society where the woman must rely upon satisfying the passions rather than the heart of her husband. As already stated, there are exceptions, but in the main the condition of the Turkish women is very low. This condition reacts upon the men and makes them vulgar and sensual in the extreme. The everyday language of the average Turk would shock the lowest of the slum boys in our own cities. Under ordinary circumstances sensualism is kept measurably in check by the inevitable restraints of community life, but once let those be broken and lust reigns supreme, dominating everything. As a gentleman who knows them well and never hesitates to recognise their good qualities, has said, 'In a Turk's eye all that a woman has is sex, and for it he lusts with absolute brutality.'

Reverend Edwin M. Bliss, *Turkey and the Armenian Atrocities*, 1896, pp. 78–9

There are few nations on earth who concede to woman so low a position in proportion to man as the Arab nomads. The reason of this must not be looked for only in the low degree of their culture, but still more in their faith. Wherever Islamism penetrated, woman's position was lowered. It was so in Persia, in India, in Arabia, and Asia Minor. The Koran does not allow its followers to consider woman as a being equal to man, and this prejudice is so strong in all Mohammedan countries that all attempts at conversion and civilisation on the part of Christians will be in vain.

It can be safely assumed that the less woman is estimated amongst a people, the lower is the stage of their civilisation. The respect woman is held in is in proportion to the degree of culture, and rises with it; hence the equality of woman with man amongst the nations at the head of civilisation.

As long as religion does not enter into the matter, this humiliating relationship between the two sexes can be made to take a more favourable form with single races and tribes, but the Commandments of the Koran make this a matter of impossibility with the Arabs. They have adhered firmly to the laws of their religion for twelve hundred years, and for twelve hundred years the position of their women has remained the same. Even the fifty years of French rule could not obtain an amelioration of the sad fate of the Arab women subjected to it. The 'faithful' often humiliates himself: he will stoop to be your labourer, the servant of your servants; he will beg alms and execute your commands, but you cannot get him to show the least sign of respect or attention to his own wife, the mother of his children. He will caress his horse, stroke it and lead it gently, but he would not think of offering an arm to his wife. If an Arab lives in town, he has only one care, to hide her from everybody; if he lives in the country or in the desert, to make her work, for she is his slave.

To the Arab his wife is neither a companion nor a friend – not even a mistress. He scarcely believes that she has a soul like himself; she is an inferior being. In her youth she is the slave of his passions, and when she gets old and her charms begin to fade, she is put to the hardest labour. He beats her, does not give her sufficient food, and compels her to be servant of the young wife he has bought to take her place.

We can draw our own conclusion as to the character and disposition of these Bedouin women when we know the treatment they receive. If they know nothing of connubial faithfulness, and of domestic virtues, it is the fault of their religion and the fanaticism of their husbands. The Bedouin woman is possessed by only one feeling – abject fear and utter dependence on her lord and master.

The Chevalier de Hesse-Wartegg, *Tunis*, 1899, pp. 264–6

Not infrequently you may see in an out-of-the-way cemetery a father and mother, with their children gathered around them, seated near the grave of some relative, eating their luncheon, just like a laboring family in any other part of the world; and from the mere fact that it is uncommon, one finds himself strangely moved by this simple scene. You realize, as you watch them, how natural, how essential, and eternally and universally fitting is that junction of soul and body; that in that group, so complete in itself, there is no room for anyone else; that a single additional note and the harmony would be spoiled or destroyed outright; that, talk and argue as you may, the fact remains that the first condition, the elementary force, the cornerstone of an orderly and well-balanced society, is there before you; that every and any other combination of affections and interests violates a natural law; that this is a family, the other a herd; that this, and this only, corresponds to a home, the other to a wolf's den.

Edmondo de Amicis, *Constantinople*, 1896, vol. I, pp. 32–4

At the beginning of this century A. B. de Guerville tried to tell the readers of his book *New Egypt* about the position of women in the country. The only real Egyptian women, he said, were the peasant women but about them 'there is little to say, and she is so far removed from us and our civilization that the subject would lack all interest to the majority of readers'. What he really wanted to discuss was the position of women in the harem but this was impossible for two reasons: 'In the first place, the Egyptian's manner of seeing and of thinking is entirely different from ours, and, besides, woman and the harem are two subjects which he never cares to discuss with a stranger' (p. 145). So much for informed comment on women's lives.

In 1906 a conference of missionaries was held in Cairo 'on behalf of the Mohammedan world', and one of the sessions was on women's work for women. The women missionaries, in a subsequent book, sent out an appeal to all Christian women

on behalf of the women of Christian lands, firm in the
knowledge that 'the God of Christianity is a God of Love, the
God of Islam is an Oriental Despot'. Saving Muslim women
from their fate would be a heavy burden, but it would have to
be taken up they said, because 'No one else will do it.' In this
extract from the book we are given a picture of a Christian
woman's life in Egypt in contrast to the degraded, subservient,
passive life led by Muslim women.

It would be interesting to take a peep into some of the homes of
these representative Christian women and see for ourselves how a
Christian education has developed those wives and mothers into true
home-makers. First let us get acquainted with the dear old
grandmother who has just been on a visit to her son and his family
who live in our city. She and her son have come to make us a
farewell visit before she leaves for her native town. Her feeble voice,
her slow step, her dimmed sight, the appealing marks of old age
interest us in her. The good-bye kiss and an affectionate pat from her
withered old hand draw our hearts to her, the tender filial light in the
eyes of her son tells us that this gentle little old lady has been a
power for good. After they leave we learn in conversation with those
who know the story of her life that she is one of the faithful mothers
who has endured much persecution, separation from friends, leaving
a home of wealth and influence for one of poverty all for the sake of
Christ. The best commentary on her life is the beautiful Christian
home of this son, where his sweet ladylike little wife presides over
their family of clean, well-ordered children with all the gentle dignity
of a real home. Without any previous information it would be easy to
know that this home is a Bethel where Christ delights to dwell.

Annie van Sommer and Samuel M. Zwemer (eds), *Our Moslem
Sisters*, 1907, pp. 54–5

The next two pieces concern women in Algeria. Showing a
touching concern for the fate of desert people, Norman
Douglas concentrated his attention on the 'malign influence' of
the 'ignorant' middle- and upper-class women in towns, who
prevented their sons from being Europeanized. The next
extract is from a book which was read by nearly all travellers

before they set out for North Africa and was carried around with them on their travels. This highly emotive language and Eurocentric statement on the position of women in Algeria – 'despite the strictly equitable nature of the French rule' – comes from *Cook's Handbook for Algeria and Tunisia*, published in 1913.

The Arab woman is the repository of all the accumulated nonsense of the race, and her influence upon the young brood is retrogressive and malign. It matters little what happens in the desert where men and women are necessarily animals, but it does among the middle and upper native classes of the larger places. Here the French have established their so-called Arab–French schools, excellent institutions which are largely attended, and would produce far better results but for the halo of sanctity with which boys in every country – but particularly in half-civilized ones – are apt to invest the most flagrantly empty-headed of mothers. In Tunisia, as soon as the youngsters return home, these women quickly undo all the good work, by teaching them that what they have learnt at school is dangerous untruth, and that the Koran and native mode of life are the only sources of happiness. Then, to keep the son at home, the mother will hasten to catch a bride for him who shall be, if possible, more incompetent than herself, in order that she, the mother, may retain her ascendancy over him. The father, meanwhile, shrugs his shoulders: *Mektoub*! There is no fighting against such heroic perseverance on a woman's part; besides, was he not brought up on the same lines?

The mischief is done, for Arabs relapse easily; even native officers, who have served for years in the French army, will, on returning home, don the burnous, sit at street corners, and become more *arabized* than ever. So it comes about that, if the eyes of the former generation were entirely averse from French rule, the present one is Janus-faced – looking both ways. Some day, presumably, there will be a further adaptation, and their eyes, like those of certain flat-fish, will wander round and settle down definitely on the right side. . . .

Norman Douglas, *Fountains in the Sand*, 1986 (1st edn 1912), p. 31

The position of the Arab woman in Algeria is theoretically much preferable to that of her sex in Morocco or Turkey. The strictly equitable nature of the French rules forbids her being treated with harshness or sold into slavery; but practically she is not much better off than in other Oriental countries. She is the victim of a stupid and brutalising social code, founded on and bound up in a religion whose theory is pure, but whose practice is barbarous. She is either pampered or maltreated; a toy to the rich, a beast of burden to the poor. When a child is born to a Moorish woman, she considers it a blessing if a boy, and a curse if a daughter. Directly a girl comes into the world she is baptised in the name of Fathma, which is that of the mother of the Prophet. A week afterwards another name is given to her. The choice of appellatives lies between Nicha, Bedra, Djohar, Halima, Hasuria, Khadidja, Kheira, Zina, Zora, Krenfla, Messoudia, Kamra, etc.

If the Moorish girl's parents are poor, they will regard her only as an incubus. Her mother was probably married at ten or twelve years of age; she ages early, and each accession of maternal cares is to her only a renewed warning that she is no longer fair to look upon. As for the father, it is as much as he knows that he has a daughter till some one buys her off him in marriage. The rich girl is neglected by her mother, and is relegated to a corner of the harem and the care of an old negress. When she is old enough to be married – *i.e.* sold – the kind of life described by Mr. George Gaskell begins for her.

Beyond these characteristics there is nothing else to add to the social position of the Moorish women in Algiers. Their state of life is, no doubt, very pitiable. The Government can do very little to ameliorate it. They have guaranteed to the natives the possession of the civil law – which is the Koran – and the social code and the civil law are one. They might as well decree that the Arab women should go unveiled, or that the Arabs should leave off their burnouses, as interfere with the domestic arrangements of the Moorish gynaeceum.

Cook's Handbook for Algeria and Tunisia, 1913, pp. 21–2

Eleanor Calverley was an American medical missionary who went to Kuwait in 1912. In a similar manner to Isobel Burton earlier in this chapter, in this extract she tried to explain the difference between the position of women in the Occident and Orient through a conversation with some women. She showed more understanding than most writers of the life of Arab women, but was forced to ask herself whether she had been smug in her replies to questions.

'I saw you on the street, *Khatoon*, walking with your husband. When you came to a narrow place he stood back and let you go first. Can it be, that in your country, women are considered *better* than men?'

How, I wondered, could I make these friends understand an Occidental conception of chivalry? I had to make the attempt.

'No,' I began, 'it's not that women are considered better. But because a man, among Christians, loves and reveres his mother, he honors also all others of her sex.' This was not, I was aware, a very good answer. Muslims also, I knew, often loved and revered their mothers. And according to Muslim standards they might revere their wives. For this very reason it was considered better for a wife not to appear on the street with her husband. If it became necessary for them to go somewhere together, he walked first, and she, veiled beyond recognition, followed behind him, as though the two had no connection with each other. She would indeed have been dishonored by open acknowledgement on the street of being her husband's wife. As to the comparative superiority of the sexes, such a question never arose. The women themselves took it for granted that the male was the superior sex. Naturally boy babies were preferred to girls; but daughters were usually welcomed and loved.

It would take time for my guests to assimilate all they had heard from me that day, things so strange and unbelievable.

'You are very different from us,' one of them said as she held out her hand to say good-bye. 'But how we wish that *we* were like you!'

I thought of what this woman had said long after my callers had gone. Her response seemed to show that our difference was one of custom and privilege only. In our essential nature we were all women together, with natural longings that were not different, but alike.

On another occasion, I remember, it was a patient's husband who questioned me.

'Will you tell me how it is that your husband lets you go out on the street without a veil over your face?'

The man's question took me completely by surprise. Without premeditation I found myself answering:

'Such is the custom in my country. And I *do* wear a veil. Only, the veil is on the heart – not on the face.'

Afterward, I wondered whether I should have answered as I did. Had I sounded smug? Or had there been a hint of annoyance in my voice? Perhaps later, if asked that question again, I could think of a better answer.

Eleanor T. Calverley, My Arabian Days and Nights, 1958, pp. 72–3

The last extract in this chapter comes from the story for schoolgirls published in 1937 and quoted in Chapter 1.

'Oh, you'll get used to that sort of thing if you're here long enough,' said Mr Marsden. 'In Mahometan countries, you know, woman takes the second place. Some people deny her the possession of a soul at all; and in any case she's expected to look upon herself as very inferior to her husband. You see the master of the house riding the donkey while the wife trudges meekly in the dust, and it is the same all through family life.'

'How rotten!' Alison is what Miss Caroll at school calls a feminist. She believes in votes for women, and all that, and says she means to stand for Parliament when she's grown up. 'Why do the women stand for it? Haven't they got votes out here?'

'Oh dear, no.' Mr Marsden laughed. 'But I don't think they want them! The Eastern woman is quite content to play second fiddle to her menfolk.'

'Well, I'm glad I'm English,' declared Alison with much emphasis.

Kathlyn Rhodes, A Schoolgirl in Egypt, 1937, p. 37

Was this author of a book for English schoolgirls aware that as long as twenty years earlier Egyptian women had been on the streets joining in political demonstrations against the British?

Chapter 10

A COMPLETE STATE OF
CAPTIVITY?

William Rae Wilson, writing of his travels to Egypt in 1823, summed up the Western view of women's lives there.

Wives, in this corner of the globe, appear to be in a complete state of captivity. They are slaves to their husbands, and allowed to see no other persons at home than their families or relations, and when they do appear in the streets, their faces are completely veiled.

William Rae Wilson, *Travels in Egypt and the Holy Land*, 1823,
p. 119

Throughout the chapters of this book there has been a constant stream of words indicating that women in the Orient were ignorant and passive beings – either drudges and beasts of burden slaving away for their husband, or lying around all day in the harem enjoying the *dolce far niente*.

Occasionally, however, other aspects of women's lives were allowed to surface in travel books, even though they were often described as the exception. Sometimes it was almost accidental, a throwaway line here or there; sometimes it was because the writer was in a situation where she was able and willing to go beneath mere surface details. The next two extracts, written in the 1890s, give some idea of the outside leisure activities of women in different situations.

The inhabitants not only go forth into the country as represented in the New Testament, but they remain there and sleep in the open air, if occasion require, without the slightest inconvenience. Again the incidental mention of *women* and *children* in the great assemblies gathered around Jesus is true to Oriental life, strange as it may appear to those who read so much about *female seclusion in the East*. In the great gatherings of this day, at funerals, weddings, festas, and fairs, women and children often constitute the larger part of the assemblies.

W. M. Thomson, *The Land and the Book*, 1890, p. 405

The Turkish ladies go about with a freedom that ought to be sufficient for those of any nation. They shop in Pera and in the Mussulman quarters. They row about in caiques and visit their friends. On Tuesdays they assemble in the cemetery of Scutari. On other days they go to Therapia, the Islands, or to the Sweet Waters of Asia. They make their devotions in the mosques or at the tombs of the Sultans. They witness the exhibitions of the dervishes, and they do all these things with a will and an air of extreme enjoyment such as Christian women rarely show. Query, does it make one enthusiastic to live in a harem and see but one man? It would seem that freedom in the outside world has the effect of champagne on these otherwise cloistered women, and they have the merry air of children who have run away and quite believe that 'stolen fruit is the sweetest'.

Clara Erskine Clement, *Constantinople*, 1895, pp. 249–50

In his account of his journey in the Ottoman Empire, published in 1800, G. A. Olivier related how Turkish women managed to exercise an influence on public affairs. In the second piece Charles MacFarlane, who visited Constantinople in 1828, reported on a street demonstration by women protesting against an unpopular action by the Governor. This was not at all unusual, he said, although his view was that the women were sent out by their husbands to demonstrate. His account of the event, however, does not immediately bring to mind adjectives like 'passive' to describe the women.

The influence which Turkish women have on public affairs – in the nomination of agents of government, the distribution of favours and punishments – is much greater than we would imagine given that they live in seclusion. In the harems meetings take place which are not accessible to men, where the most interesting stories of the town and the provinces are related, where curious news is spread and plots and conspiracies are hatched. Women of all ages and all levels in society come to plead graces and favours for their husbands or relatives, or to make a complaint and demand protection against a husband who is over-jealous or too strict, or against a prominent individual. Frequently such a matter will be passed along a chain of several women before it arrives at its destination: a freed slave or a woman from the lowest class of the people may gain such prestige from their patroness that their protection is sought on all sides. Muslim women support each other and are always ready to make common cause. They are implacable in their resentment and rarely miss a chance to revenge themselves for any insult or offence, however mild.

G. A. Olivier, *Voyage dans l'Empire Othoman*, 1800, vol. I, p. 96

The necks of the softer sex are considered, even by the Turks, as less obnoxious to the cord or the sabre, than those of their lords; considerable licence has always been accorded by the Mussel-mans to their women; and their boldness may be cherished, particularly when in a crowd, by the mysterious yashmack or veil. The men avail themselves of these privileges, and whenever popular discontent runs high, they send their wives in troops, to clamour before the gates of government, and to express opinions they themselves could not do with safety. The practice prevails, of course, in the provinces and pashaliks, rather than in the capital. I witnessed a tumult of the sort at Smyrna, a few days after my arrival: a great crowd of women, with every part of their faces covered, except their large angry eyes; and their figures muffled up in loose sheety robes, for the most part of gay though tarnished hues, collected in the open square in the front of Hassan-Pasha's house, to induce the governor to revoke some oppressive or unpopular measure. As they waved their hands in the air, – as their voices rose shrill and piercing, – as they hissed together like a myriad of serpents, – I could not help feeling that the collected wrath of woman is 'a fearful thing'. They might have been taken, as they stood in the enclosed square, for a congress of Thessalian sorceresses, or a sabbat of witches, more baleful than those who beset the ambitious footsteps of Macbeth.

Charles MacFarlane, *Constantinople in 1828*, 1829, pp. 364–5

Lucie Duff Gordon had different feelings about similar actions by Egyptian women.

The Sultan's coming is a kind of riddle. No one knows what he wants. The Pasha has ordered all the women of the lower classes to keep indoors while he is here. Arab women are outspoken, and might shout out their grievances to the great Sultan.

Lucie Duff Gordon, *Letters from Egypt*, 1986 (1st edn 1865),
pp. 52–3

In the next pieces she spoke about the freedom available to women to farm their own land, and a meeting with an unusual woman. Since she lived in Egypt for several years and spoke Arabic, she was able to enter into much more meaningful conversations than a traveller just passing through.

Above Girgeh we stopped awhile at Dishne, a large village. I strolled up alone, *les mains dans les poches*, '*sicut meus est mos:*' and was soon accosted with an invitation to coffee and pipes in the strangers' place, a sort of room open on one side with a column in the middle, like two arches of a cloister, and which in all the villages is close to the mosque: two or three cloaks were pulled off and spread on the ground for me to sit on, and the milk which I asked for, instead of the village coffee, brought. In a minute a dozen men came and sat round, and asked as usual, 'Whence comest thou, and whither goest thou?' and my gloves, watch, rings, etc. were handed round and examined; the gloves always call forth many *Mashallah's*. I said, 'I come from the Frank country, and am going to my place near Abu'l Hajjaj.' Hereupon everyone touched my hand and said, 'Praise be to God that we have seen thee. Don't go on: stay here and take 100 feddans of land and remain here.' I laughed and asked, 'Should I wear the *zaboot* (brown shirt) and the *libdeh*, and work in the field, seeing there is no man with me?' There was much laughing, and then several stories of women who had farmed large properties well and successfully. Such undertakings on the part of women seem quite as common here as in Europe, and more common than in England.

Lucie Duff Gordon, *Letters from Egypt*, 1986 (1st edn 1865),
pp. 253–4

While I was walking on the bank with M. and Mme. Mounier, a person came up and saluted them whose appearance puzzled me. Don't call me a Persian when I tell you it was an eccentric Bedawee young lady. She was eighteen or twenty at most, dressed like a young man, but small and feminine and rather pretty, except that one eye was blind. Her dress was handsome, and she had women's jewels, diamonds, etc., and a European watch and chain. Her manner was excellent, quite *ungenirt*, and not the least impudent or swaggering, and I was told – indeed, I could hear – that her language was beautiful, a thing much esteemed among Arabs. She is a virgin and fond of travelling and of men's society, being very clever, so she has her dromedary and goes about quite alone. No one seemed surprised, no one stared, and when I asked if it was *proper*, our captain was surprised. 'Why not? if she does not wish to marry, she can go alone; if she does, she can marry – what harm? She is a virgin and free.' She went to breakfast with the Mouniers on their boat (Mme. M. is Egyptian born, and both speak Arabic perfectly), and the young lady had many things to ask them, she said. She expressed her opinions pretty freely as far as I could understand her. Mme. Mounier had heard of her before, and said she was much respected and admired. M. Mounier had heard that she was a spy of the Pasha's, but the people on board the boat here say that the truth was that she went before Said Pasha herself to complain of some tyrannical Moodir who ground and imprisoned the *fellaheen* – a bold thing for a girl to do. To me she seems, anyhow, far the most curious thing I have yet seen. . . .

I made further inquiries about the Bedawee lady, who is older than she looks, for she has travelled constantly for ten years. She is rich and much respected, and received in all the best houses, where she sits with the men all day and sleeps in the hareem. She has been in the interior of Africa and to Mecca, speaks Turkish, and M. Mounier says he found her extremely agreeable, full of interesting information about all the countries she had visited. As soon as I can talk I must try and find her out; she likes the company of Europeans.

Lucie Duff Gordon, *Letters from Egypt*, 1986 (1st edn 1865), pp. 96–8

E. W. Lane's sister (such was the name under which her books were published) was surprised one day on a visit to a harem to find the women engaged in a political discussion.

I was surprised, during my second visit to the hareem of Habeeb Effendi, to find the ladies (whom I had not seen for a long time on account of the late plague) immersed in politics, and painfully anxious on account of the difference of opinion which has arisen between the Emperor of Russia and their cousin the Sultan. They earnestly inquired whether England would espouse the cause of Turkey, and were in some measure comforted by a reference to the friendship which England had so warmly manifested for the young Sultan, and the active measures which our government had adopted for the re-establishment of his rule in Syria. I find the feeling very strong in favour of England in the hareems; and I conclude that I hear general opinions echoed there.

The Englishwoman in Cairo . . . with E. W. Lane, By His Sister, 1844, vol. II, pp. 42–3

While travelling in Syria at the beginning of this century, A. C. Inchbold witnessed an incident when her husband tried to make a sketch of a woman standing beside a pool. Although the woman's husband was willing to allow it, she was not to be intimidated into agreeing.

There were peasants by the wayside here, squatting among the stones on the margin of the pool. While the horses were being watered these men and women – not at all of a prepossessing type – gathered around the carriage offering their rings, trinkets, and knives for sale. They were still active in barter, when two newcomers approached the pool – a dark-browed Bedawi, with the thick black agal pressing a purple keffiyeh on his head, and a woman who was leading their horse to drink at the fountain.

She was young and beautiful, also unveiled, her waved, abundant hair growing low over her broad forehead. From the clear, sun-bronzed skin her eyes glowed soft as stars, yet dark as water in a deep well. Her figure was tall and of plastic mould, draped and swathed in a gown of red and white with loose pantaloons skirting her well-shaped ankles. She appeared indifferent to the gaze of onlookers, as she stood with one hand touching the horse's neck, the other holding the halter by which she held him.

Quickly sprang to view the artist's notebook, and then it was evident that the beautiful statue could see out of the corners of her eyes, for she immediately crouched down by the water's edge in the shadow of a bank of stones. The Bedawi, who was her husband, was willing that she should allow her face to be looked upon by the stranger, and expostulated in energetic voice, to which the peasants around added open wonder and derision that so easy a method of obtaining backsheesh was scorned.

'If I were her husband and she did not obey me, I would shoot her,' said a hawk-nosed fellah emphatically.

The beauty peered round at the speaker, then at her husband, who stood scowling but silent near, his old flintlock slung across his shoulder; and she laughed aloud, showing the perfect ivory of her teeth.

'He moved the mountains to get me,' she said simply.

To this remark no one could find suitable comment, for the woman, as was shown by her dress, was from a distant part of the country.

A. C. Inchbold, *Under the Syrian Sun*, 1906, vol. I, pp. 253–4

Later this century Wilfred Thesiger was surprised to meet an unmarried mother of three children in the Arabian desert.

There was a constant passage of visitors to our camping place while we were at Habarut. A woman came over to us and I recognized her as Nura, whom I had met the year before. Her three small children were with her; only the eldest one, aged about nine, wore any clothes. She told me that they were camped four miles away, and that the children had insisted on coming to see me again when they heard I was here. I gave the children dates and sugar to eat, while I talked to Nura. She was unveiled, and like most of the women in this part of Arabia was dressed in dark blue. She had a strong, square, weather-beaten face, and wore a silver ring through her right nostril. I thought she was surprisingly old to have three small children. She talked in a rather husky voice, telling me how she was going down to Ghaidat al Mahra on the coast to get a load of sardines. As bin Ghabaisha had shot an ibex we had meat and soup for lunch. The children fed with us, but Nura was given a dish by herself. Arabs will not feed with women. Later, however, she returned and, sitting a little back from the circle, was given coffee and tea which she drank with the rest of us.

The general belief among the English people that Arab women are kept shut up is true of many of the women in the towns, but not among the tribes. Not only is it impossible for a man to shut up his wife when he is living under a tree, or in a tent which is always open on one side, but he requires her to work, to fetch water and firewood, and to herd the goats. If a woman thinks she is being neglected or ill-treated by her husband she can easily run away to her father or brother. Her husband has then to follow her and try to persuade her to come back. Her family will certainly take her part, insisting that she has been monstrously ill-treated. In the end the husband will probably have to give her a present before he can induce her to return. Wives cannot divorce their husbands, but the husband may agree to divorce his wife if she has refused to live with him, on condition that he recovers the two or three camels which he gave as the bride-price. If, however, he divorces her of his own accord he does not get back these camels.

In the evening someone mentioned Nura. I asked if her husband was dead, and al Auf said, 'She has no husband. The children are bastards.' When I expressed my surprise he said that bin Alia, who was one of our party, was also 'a son of unlawfulness'. I asked if there was any slur attached to being a bastard, and bin Kabina said, 'No, it is not the child's fault'. . . .

I knew that elsewhere in the Arab world a girl who is immoral, or indeed in many places even if she is only suspected of immorality, will be killed by her relatives in order to protect the family honour.

Wilfred Thesiger, *Arabian Sands*, 1987 (1st edn 1959), pp. 193–5

In his journey through Arabia starting in 1792, Niebuhr stopped in Sanaa. Describing the local markets he mentioned that only women sold the bread there. Although many writers recorded the hard work done in rural areas by poor women, I was interested in the odd references made to other activities by women which were rarely followed up in any great detail. The next two extracts concern the labour of women on an archaeological site and as plasterers in house building.

Yusuf's excavations were much more lively and amusing than such works generally are. Their proximity to the Arab camp induced a number of the Tuweyba women and children to gather round their friends and relations. The females in their deep blue and red gowns sat spinning and chattering at the edge of the trench, and the younger part of the community, in dress of nature's own providing, gambolled round them, or stood watching when any object was being minutely examined.

In addition to the enveloped tablets and copper articles, Tel Sifr produced a third novelty – two girls were carrying baskets of earth from the trench. One, a very pretty lass of sixteen or thereabouts, had begged so hard for work to support her old, infirm mother and three young brothers and sisters, that Yusuf could not resist the appeal. The second girl was jealous of the first one earning money, and therefore offered her services, which Yusuf accepted in order to countenance the other. They were great favourites among the men who, with more kind feeling than the Arabs usually exhibit towards their women, picked out for them the smallest baskets, which they never wholly filled. I observed to Yusuf that they carried their loads with infinitely greater ease and speed than the men, and that they discharged three baskets of earth while the men lazily emptied two. Yusuf grinned and declared that he wished all his labourers were women, because they were not only quicker in their movements, but more manageable.

William Kennett Loftus, *Travels and Researches in Chaldaea and Susiana*, 1857, p. 272

If some of our appliances are rough-and-ready, they often possess the merit of cheapness. Plastering, for instance, is an expensive luxury; but the natives have a way of plastering the walls which is nearly as good, and by no means costly. This is entirely done by the women, who come and sift soil, which they mix with cut straw and water, and knead into a paste. When they have plastered the walls and floors with this, they make another with a peculiar, fine white clay, which they dig from certain places in the hillsides, and, mixing this also with finely chopped straw, lay it on as an outer covering.

Laurence Oliphant, *Haifa, or Life in Modern Palestine*, 1886, p. 166

The next group of extracts concerns the economic contribution of women to the family budget. None of this equates with all the usual rhetoric about passive women. In the first piece, by E. W. Lane, the reference to women keeping shops in the towns was a casual remark. W. M. Thomson travelled Palestine relating contemporary life to biblical words, but in this piece he dropped in an important remark about women's earnings. The third writer, E. S. Stephens, was a woman living in Iraq while her husband was employed there. In this piece of writing about the scenery and the women's appearance she mentions the labouring work done by women. The last author in this group, while trying to present a more balanced picture of the family system in Syria and Palestine, talked about a woman he met who organized the family business, even though she had a husband and sons.

The women of the lower orders seldom pass a life of inactivity. Some of them are even condemned to greater drudgery than the men. Their chief occupations are the preparing of the husband's food, fetching water (which they carry in a large vessel on the head), spinning cotton, linen or woollen yarn, and making the fuel called 'gelleh', which is composed of the dung of cattle, kneaded with chopped straw, and formed into round flat cakes: these they stick upon the walls or roofs of their houses, or upon the ground, to dry in the sun; and then use for heating their ovens, and for other purposes. They are in a state of much greater subjection to their husbands than is the case among the superior classes. Not always is a poor woman allowed to eat with her husband. When she goes out with him, she generally walks behind him; and if there be anything for either of them to carry, it is usually borne by the wife; unless it be merely a pipe or a stick.

Some women, in the towns, keep shops, and sell bread, vegetables, etc.; and thus contribute as much as their husbands, or even more than the latter, to the support of their families.

Edward William Lane, The Manners and Customs of the Modern Egyptians, 1860 (1st edn 1836), pp. 198–9

I saw a woman sitting at the door of her hut on Zion, spinning woollen yarn with a spindle, while another near her was twirling nimbly the ancient distaff, and I felt some curiosity to know whether in other things they resembled King Lemuel's good wife, according to the 'prophecy that his mother taught him'.

There are such even now in this country, and in this city, where the prophecy was uttered. They are scarce, however, and their price is above rubies. The very first item in the catalogue of good qualities is the rarest of all: 'The heart of her husband doth safely trust in her.' The husband, in nine cases out of ten, does not feel very confident that 'she will do him good and not evil', and therefore he sets a jealous watch over her, and places every valuable article under lock and key. His heart trusts more in hired guards and iron locks than in his wife. This is mainly owing to two things, – bad education and the want of love; both grievous sins against her, and committed by her lord and tyrant. She is kept in ignorance, and is married off without regard to the affections of her heart; and how can it be expected that the husband can safely trust in a wife thus trained and obtained?

There are numerous allusions to the domestic habits of Orientals in this 'prophecy' of Lemuel's mother which are worth noticing: 'She seeketh wool and flax, and worketh diligently with her hands.' In Sidon, at this day, a majority of the women are thus working in raw silk and cotton instead of wool and flax. Many of them actually support the family in this way, and, by selling the produce of their labour to the merchants, 'bring their food from afar'. A leading Moslem told me that nearly every family in Sidon was thus carried through the past scarce and very dear winter.

W. M. Thomson, The Land and the Book, 1890, p. 681

Another road, beside another creek, led through palm-gardens and a negro village out into the desert, and, branching off to follow a waterway to the left, one arrived at the old Turkish fortifications and walls. Walking through the palm-gardens, through which kingfishers flashed like blue fire, you were sure to meet the comely damsels of Khwat Razna, a village out in the desert, with their nose-rings of turquoise and pearls, their gleaming anklets and silver bracelets.

Their black wimples and garments were sometimes relieved by a soiled scarlet skirt, or a glimpse of pink, and on their turbaned heads they usually bore burdens, a basket, or a copper pot, and if they came from town, perhaps a fish, held so that its tail trailed in the dust. These girls have ready smiles for the stranger, and work in the town as brick-porters, water-carriers, and so on. I employed one of them once to shift some rubbish, and she bore the filth away on her head, walking like a queen.

E. S. Stephens, *By Tigris and Euphrates*, 1923, pp. 143–4

Thus, speaking generally, while it is impossible to exaggerate certain evils inherent in the *nature* of the system, it is quite possible to exaggerate their extent and, to a less degree, their results. Take, for example, seclusion within the harem. This naturally appears horrible to a woman brought up under Western civilization. But women brought up in the harem do not miss a liberty which they have never known. Among the higher Moslem classes charming family life may be found. The spirit of high breeding is in every race the same though conditions of life may differ radically. But even granted that, as a rule, the evils of life in the harem bear hard on the occupants, it should be emphasised that these are confined to the cities, and hence affect only the minority of Mohammedan women. In passing from the towns to the country in Syria and Palestine the traveller cannot fail to note a great contrast. The town women when they go out are swathed in sheets, white or coloured, with their faces hidden by dark veils. The peasant women, on the other hand, appear publicly in their ordinary dress, leaving the face and sometimes also part of the hair exposed to view.... This state of things naturally gives an opportunity to a peasant woman of strong personality to make her controlling influence felt in the household and in the community. Such a woman I once met in a village lying in a deep valley of Mount Hermon, where, during the summer, the inhabitants live in booths. We were encamped not far from each other, and so exchanged calls. This handsome, dignified matron, who serenely kept her face uncovered, had an authoritative air well befitting the sole head of the house. From her little booth she was regulating the varied work of her estates, which brought her in the princely income of twelve hundred to fifteen hundred dollars a year: the herding of cows and goats; the threshing of wheat; the culture of vines and tobacco; the cutting of wood. Her sons, all married or betrothed, obediently worked under her orders. Her husband I recall as a mild man, apparently in total eclipse. Such instances are not uncommon in Turkey.

Frederick Jones Bliss, *The Religions of Modern Syria and Palestine*, 1912, pp. 281–3

Ferdinand Ossendowski, a Polish professor visiting North Africa, described the work done by male and female members of the Uled Nail. In the first paragraph he described the women as parasites, in the second the relative earning power of the men and women.

After luncheon, I visited one of the most characteristic curiosities of Bu Saada. A whole street extending between the native and the French quarters contains almost nothing but houses and *fonduks* crowded with women singers and dancers of all ages belonging to the tribe of Uled Nail which is the most powerful one in the region. It is a strange tribe, from the standpoint of both its origin and its cult and traditions. The men are handsome, with noble, proud features, thin, aquiline noses and statuesque, athletic figures, while the women with light, slightly olive complexions, expressive, enigmatic eyes and beautiful features, are parasites.

The men earn their living as blacksmiths, barbers, doctors and sorcerers; the women as dancers, singers and witches. Were it not for their womenfolk, who by their art often earn considerable sums of money with which they help their fathers and brothers, or bring dowries to their husbands, the men, who do not in the least object to the frivolous, often licentious life of their wives, daughters and sisters, would be beggars and wretches throughout their lives.

Ferdinand Ossendowski, *The Breath of the Desert*, 1927, p. 43

Lieutenant-Colonel Hugh Mulleneux Walmsley of the Imperial Ottoman Army assisted the French in the horrific 'subjugation' of the Kabyles in Algeria. In this extract from his book about his experiences he spoke of the famed prophetess Lalla Fathma, who was taken captive by the French until they were sure of final victory. In the second piece Edward Barker, who edited the writings of his father, a consul-general, included some stories of a famous female leader of the Kurds.

Alexander Knox, in the next piece, made the point that custom is often very different from the written law and gave a picture of the forceful Kabyle women. E. B. Soane travelled around Kurdistan disguised as a Persian and there he went to the house of an extremely powerful woman, Lady Adela. Travelling in 1935, Freya Stark met 'one of the happiest women in the Hadhramaut', a scholar of religion and philosophy.

The men of these mountain tribes had apparently trusted to their mountains and ravines; and, when these failed them, they gave all up for lost. But in one of the far-off villages of the Illiten dwelt a great prophetess. Her fame was spread over the whole Kabyle land. Not a tribe, not a faction, not a village, existed in Kabylia where the divine mission of Lalla Fathma was not known and venerated; and now the infidel, unbelieving foe, was at the gates of her mountain retreat. She could not resist the bright bayonets of the French – the thunder of their mountain-guns reached her ears, and the line of smoke advancing day by day met her sight, as she sighed over her conquered country. The land which had rolled back the Turk, the Roman, the Arab foe, was at length doomed. With all the fatalism inspired by the religion of Mahomed, she bowed to the decree, and sent her brother as ambassador to the Marshal's camp. . . .

Her brother met the conqueror, who agreed to spare her village and the brother in return offered to lead the invading columns. The column marched on, destroying all before them, until one night:

Suddenly the loud challenge of the main-guard sentry was heard, brought by the breeze into the camp itself. What could it be? A moment more, and an officer of the Marshal's staff announced, most unexpectedly, the arrival in the camp of the far-famed prophetess Lalla Fathma, together with the whole Smala, making in all over two hundred prisoners, most of them women, who, with the exception of the priestess herself, uttered continual shrieks. What they expected would happen to them I don't know, but they seemed in mortal fear, more for their revered female chief than for themselves.

The Marshal himself received the prophetess, and as the long train of prisoners marched into the camp preceded by Lalla Fathma, with their strange dresses, their bournous, and the tears running down the cheeks of the women, it was a curious spectacle.

Stately as a queen (though an old and ugly one) Lalla Fathma approached the Marshal, who received her as he would have received some foreign potentate visiting him in his own halls in his fair France, – nay, perhaps, he threw more of politeness and urbanity into his tone as he expressed his regret for her situation.

It is said that Lalla Fathma had for years foretold the subjection of the Kabyle race, not that it was difficult to foresee, but still her reputation as a prophetess had given her predictions weight, and the fulfilment of them had cast a fresh halo of holiness round her head in the estimation of the poor Kabyles her fellow-prisoners. With proud and haughty carriage she replied in the most unbending manner to the Marshal's expression of regret, announcing in a voice which could be heard by her followers, that what had now happened had long been known to her. It was the will of Allah, and as such had long been written in words of fire. A long wailing cry followed her words, and the heavy sobs of the women might be distinctly heard as they closed up round their revered priestess. Behind her were the women of her 'Smala', placed two and two on mules, many of whom had fallen down from sheer fatigue, while in rear of them the male prisoners, their looks cast down, but not abject, came on foot. . . .

Morning dawned, and under a strong escort Lalla Fathma and the female prisoners were directed on the rear. The fate of the prophetess of the land was kept open until the submission of the tribes still in arms should become known. It was a *triste*-looking spectacle enough as the long train of females left Tamesguida on their way to captivity. All seemed cast down except the prophetess, all else showed pale, haggard faces; and as she headed the procession, her large, stout person, adorned with jewellery, a white veil thrown over her face, and a gay scarf hanging from her shoulders, she seemed in no wise abashed or depressed. The native soldiers in French pay showed her quite as much deference as her own people, and the Kabyle loiterers in the camp pressed round her to receive some mark of her favour. He who was allowed to kiss her white fingers, for white they were, deemed himself supremely happy; and though she was of unwieldy make and large size, her piercing black eyes, and undaunted bearing, became well her high fame and sanctity. Hardly had the captive prophetess left the camp, when messengers arrived from the front bearing tidings of the submission of the Illiten; these were followed by others announcing that the Beni Ithouragh and the Illalou had also given in, completely subdued.

Hugh Mulleneux Walmsley, *Sketches of Algeria during the Kabyle War*, 1858, pp. 362–70

He also saw 'the house of the famous Koord heroine, the late Haissa Khatoon [Mistress Eve], who died the previous year (1813), after having governed with great credit for twenty years the whole Koord nation, who inhabit the mountains in that neighbourhood. She was left, when young and very handsome, the widow of their chief, and maintained the authority of her deceased husband till her death.' He saw 'the tomb of one of her servants, who fell the victim of his temerity in making her an amorous overture. She, like all the Koords, rode always armed with a sabre and a brace of pistols at her girdle. The unfortunate man was one day, while assisting her to mount her horse, tempted to make a declaration of his love by pressing her hand, and was instantly shot through the head for his presumption.'

Edward B. B. Barker (ed.), *Syria and Egypt Under the Last Five Sultans of Turkey*, 1876, vol. I, pp. 220–1

It was, unless my memory fails me, just after passing the caravanserai and the turn-off to Dellys that our driver pointed to a tree on the left of the road, and said, '*Vous voilà, monsieur, dans La Grande Kabylie!*' One could begin to look about with some confidence. Here was the Kabyle at home – the thing which we had come out to see. To our eyes, bleared with cockneydom, it was a striking thing to watch these Scriptural-looking figures stalking through the corn-fields, sometimes driving their camels before them, just like pictures which I remember well in the Bible at home when I was a child. As they came near us, these Kabyles seemed to be stout, sturdy, yeoman-looking fellows, apparently stronger than the Arabs.

The women, whose faces were uncovered, were for the most part short and square-built, with flat broad fore-heads and good eyes. I do not think a sculptor would have selected a Kabyle female nose as a model of that feature. They generally – even the poorest of them – wore jewels, that is, Kabyle jewels, not of any great value, but very pretty. They had that appearance of having undergone hard work out of doors, which you see in the female peasantry of France, and were generally in charge of a number of children. No wonder, then, that, what with work in the fields and family cares indoors, they seemed to have gone through hard times. I was told they were married at thirteen or fourteen years of age – so they begin early with life and its cares. They had not, however, an oppressed or injured look as we passed them trudging along or resting by the wayside. On the contrary, we always found on them a good-humoured smile – not to say a grin, which displayed their strong white teeth (could this have anything to do with it?), and a touch of eager curiosity to investigate the details of the stranger lady's dress. As I was afterwards told in the country itself, the ladies of Kabylia (though hardly pressed on by the laws of inheritance, and marriage) have a very good notion of holding their own. They work hard, and expect their husbands to work hard, and have more authority in their households than their Arab sisters.

Custom, or the unwritten law of a country, is of more account than the law which is written, and is nominally supreme. But it is when the powder speaks, or in the midst of warfare, that the Kabyle ladies show themselves in their full vigour. Woe to the faint-hearted sluggard who would loiter in his own hut or devote himself to the care of his own household goods whilst the fight was on! Not only would his gentle helpmate drive him to the front with a stout cudgel, but in case of need, would give him the contents of his own gun. Once in the front, and in a good hot corner, the gentleman becomes the object of his wife's most anxious solicitude. As long as he can pull a trigger she will load for him; if he is down, she will fight for him, and bear him to a place of safety, as fighting is no longer of avail. In fact, they are a race of short, squat Helen McGregors, and had I charge in this matter, it would be my most anxious thought how to get the women on my side. The men would soon be kissed or kicked into submission.

Alexander A. Knox, *The New Playground*, 1883, pp. 222–4

Before proceeding with the narrative, it is advisable to give some note upon the family and tribe of the Jaf, and more particularly upon the extraordinary woman in whose house I was a guest – a woman unique in Islam, in the power she possesses, and the efficacy with which she uses the weapons in her hands.

The Jaf tribe is an ancient one, and has from the earliest history of Kurdistan been powerful, and renowned for the manner in which its chiefs agree and hold together. This trait of character – coherency – so rare among the greater Kurdish chieftains, has won for the tribe wealth and power, so that now various chiefs own such important towns as Panjwin, Halabja, and Qizil Rubat, besides numerous villages and lands, which they have acquired by purchase. . . .

But here we must make a slight digression to bring in Lady Adela, who comes from over the border. The Persian province whose land runs up to the borders of Shahr-i-Zur is Ardalan. This Ardalan was formerly a kingdom under a dynasty of petty Kurdish princes who, though they were virtually independent, yet acknowledged the suzerainty of the Shah of Persia. For five hundred years these princes reigned, holding court at Sina, which is still the capital of Ardalan. . . .

The old Jaf Pasha had been forced to keep upon good terms with the dynasty of Ardalan, and from time to time marriages were effected between the Jaf and Ardalan chiefs and petty chiefs.

These alliances were looked upon with great disfavour and some alarm by the Turks, whose keenest desire is to see the Jaf on bad terms with their neighbours in Persia. Consequently when Uthman Pasha in 1895 announced his intention of marrying into the family of the Ardalan Vazirs, some futile opposition was offered by the Turkish government. However, he proceeded to Sina and brought home to Halabja, then an insignificant village, as bride, a lady of the Vazir family whose father occupied an important position in Teheran.

Once installed at Halabja, Lady Adela proceeded, aided by the prestige of her family, to assert her position, a procedure not opposed by Uthman Pasha. She built two fine houses, finer than any edifice in Sulaimania, upon the Sina model, importing Persian masons and artificers to do the work. Her servants were all Persian subjects, and in Halabja she instituted in her new houses a little colony of Persian Kurds, and opened her doors to all travellers from and to that country, and kept continual communications with Sina, five days' journey away.

Gradually the official power came into her hands. Uthman Pasha was often called away to attend to affairs, and occasionally had to perform journeys to Sulaimania, Kirkuk, and Mosul on matters of government. So Lady Adela, governing for him in his absence, built a new prison, and instituted a court of justice of which she was president, and so consolidated her own power, that the Pasha, when he was at Halabja, spent his time smoking a water pipe, building new baths, and carrying out local improvements, while his wife ruled.

She built a bazaar in Halabja, a square construction having four
covered rows of shops connected by alleys of more shops, all covered
in and domed with good brick arches, and trade flowed into Halabja,
which grew to considerable importance. Such importance did the
place attain that the Turks actually grew jealous, and to obtain a hold
over it, put up a telegraph line, to which the tribesmen objected, and
expressed their objection by cutting down the wire. At the same time
Lady Adela advised the Turks not to repair it, for she too objected to
the incursion of Turks upon her territory, and warned them that as
fast as they built up telegraph wires her people should cut them
down. And so today Halabja possesses no telegraph line, though a
uniformed official lives there and rejoices in the title of Post and
Telegraph Master. Every summer, when the climate of Halabja
becomes oppressively hot, the court of Lady Adela repairs to a little
village in the hills, or to a town in Persian territory, where some three
or four months are passed.

In and around Halabja Lady Adela has instituted the Persian
fashion of making gardens, apart from the gardens around the
houses, and now outside the little town are several of the graceful
and thickly treed gardens which are only seen in Persia, gardens
which are wildernesses of large shady trees, with unsuspected bowers
and flower-beds in their shady depths.

So here, in a remote corner of the Turkish Empire, which decays
and retrogrades, is one little spot, which, under the rule of a Kurdish
woman has risen from a village to be a town, and one hill-side, once
barren, now sprinkled with gardens; and these are in a measure
renovations of the ancient state of these parts. . . .

Most remarkable was the space Lady Adela took up in their affairs
and conversation. She had, in building this bazaar which attracted
trade and was a source of profit to merchants, at the same time done
the best thing for her own pocket that she could possibly have
devised, for she was heavily in debt to the occupants, and had
naturally the widest option as to when she should pay. It was
reported that she always did pay in the end; and for this reason, and
also the excellent reason that makes a tenant submissive to a
powerful landlord, no one attempted to limit her purchases, which in
cloth and stuffs were really enormous. . . .

The floor was carpeted with fine Sina rugs, and at the far end
stood a huge brass bedstead piled high with feather quilts. Before
and at the foot of this lay a long, silk-covered mattress, and upon it

sat the Lady Adela herself, smoking a cigarette. The first glance told
her pure Kurdish origin. A narrow, oval face, rather large mouth,
small black and shining eyes, a narrow, slightly aquiline hooked nose,
were the signs of it; and her thinness in perfect keeping with the
habit of the Kurdish form, which never grows fat. Unfortunately, she
has the habit of powdering and painting, so that the blackened rims
of her eyelids showed in unnatural contrast to the whitened forehead
and rouged cheeks. Despite this fault, the firmness of every line of
her face was not hidden, from the eyes that looked out, to the hard
mouth and chin. . . . Her tones were peculiar, not those of a woman,
and though not deep, were clear and decisive, and abrupt. . . .

We spent all the morning in the bazaar, and returned for lunch,
which appeared about noon. In the afternoon, about the time tea was
being served – for the Persian invented afternoon tea long before
Europe – we went to the divan of Lady Adela. The long room this
time was crowded to its fullest. Near the mattress of Lady Adela two
others had been put, one for Majid Beg, the Pasha's eldest son, a
man of forty-five or thereabouts, and Tahir Beg, both of whom
usually called in the afternoon. The former was already there, a stern
Kurd, totally unlike his rakish-looking younger brother. A much
bigger man, his face was much more of an English cast than any
other Kurd I ever saw, though an immense number of them have the
features and appearance of the Saxon races.

Blue eyes, a fair complexion, short, straight nose, stubby
moustache and square chin, were the facial features one notices at
once; and he sat, hand upon hip, making no remark to anyone,
occasionally nodding in reply to something Lady Adela said. All the
Jaf chiefs have this characteristic of silence, and will sit for hours
sometimes without uttering a syllable. Round the room, squatting
against the wall, were all sorts and kinds of Kurds. Natives of Halabja
and the district were there; two stray Hamavans, on goodness knows
what business, sat there silent and awkward, dark-featured, wild-
looking men, who kept their rifles in their hands and their alert eyes
ever on the glance this way and that, from sheer force of habit. A
black-browed priest from Pava, a village in Persian Kurdistan, three
peasants from Sina, and various merchants, went to make up a
collection of all sorts of southern Kurds. Everyone, even to the
shopkeepers and the priest, carried the large Kurdish dagger.
Menservants stood about around the door and by their mistress and
master, and a stack of guns in the corner represented the property of

a number of the assembly. Outside the room in the verandah the overflow pressed their noses against the glass doors and occasionally shouted remarks, often enough in answer to Lady Adela's comments. Rakish-looking handmaids in flowing robes and turbans set askew, stood about, or brought cigarettes, fanned Lady Adela – for the room and the day were warm – or fetched scissors and tape for the silk cloth she was inspecting. A Jew of the bazaar was displaying to her his wares, taking huge orders for all kinds of stuffs, and squatted before her, making notes in Hebrew on a dirty scrap of paper. The maids advised, criticised, and chose cloth and stuff for themselves, which Lady Adela would promptly refuse, or occasionally grant them, for she treated them remarkably well. The audience made remarks upon the proceedings, often enough chaffing Lady Adela regarding her purchases, when she would retort in quick Kurdish with the best humour, everyone joining in the laugh which not infrequently was against her. A shopkeeper arrived with a bill long overdue, and she endorsed it on the back, making him the owner of a quantity of wheat when the harvest should be in, for she possessed no hard cash, or professed to none.

E. B. Soane, *To Mesopotamia and Kurdistan in Disguise*, 1912,
pp. 216–34

As we sat there, a message came from a learned widow of Sewun to ask me to call. A handmaid took me, trailing her green surplice through a sandy palm garden up other whitewashed stairs to where, in a pleasant room, columned and carpeted, about twenty ladies with amber bracelets and flowered cotton gowns sat in the formation of a square round their spiritual leader. It was very like the learned ladies of Molière. The widow was young, plumpish, and bright-eyed, with a gay little curl on either side of her face. When she saw me coming, she was hastily absorbed in a copy of Bokhari propped on a stand in front of her on the floor. She read from it with the expressionless drone of the expert, too much absorbed to notice my presence, while her flock moved restlessly, torn between their docile listening habits and the fact that they were dying with curiosity to see me.

I approached; skirted the sitting ladies; and bent and kissed my hand to the mistress of the house, who welcomed me with an affectionate oration into the sisterhood of learning. She did not rise to it gradually, but turned it on like a tap, holding me with one hand and the corner of her eye while she exacted the attention of her flock with the other. She punctuated her periods with pretty little hennaed fingers, quoting the Prophet, the Quran, and the poets – for she was a poetess herself, and had entered open competitions, and once won a complete tea-set as a prize. Every day, she said, the ladies gathered here and listened to one of the five books – the Quran, Bokhari, Muslim and two other traditionalists I have forgotten. I happened to know a little Bokhari and got half-way to a sentence about him: it carried her, with not a second's hesitation, into the realms of philosophy and the excellence of religion. 'Why do you not live here?' she said. 'Every day we would meet and meditate.'

I was meditating as it was, for I had no talking to do: but the flock, which had the privilege of listening to the Sayyida every day, but had very few chances of seeing a female European, now began to show signs of insubordination, and finally sent a message across the room by the green-gowned maid to ask if I would mind removing my hat: they would look if they could not listen. I took it off and smiled towards them: several opened their mouths, but none quite ventured to interrupt the second sentence, which with flowers of eloquence and fancy was winding on its way. Before it closed, I had to rise, for the afternoon was waning: I left the Sayyida with friendly feelings in my heart, for her pedantry bubbled out spontaneous and gay, as artless, in those arid theological pastures, as a mountain stream in rocks. There were other learned ladies in Sewun, she told me – for it and Tarim are cities of religion and learning – but they were 'very bigoted'. She was not so: her arms were open to the Christian listener, and she was full of genuine friendliness: when I came back through Sewun, she came to see me. Her husband was dead, she had lots of children, and she lived in a house of her own: she was, I imagine, one of the happiest women in the Hadhramaut, for she did what she liked doing, and was virtuous and important as well, and people told her that she was so all the time.

Freya Stark, *The Southern Gates of Arabia*, 1982 (1st edn 1936), pp. 201–2

Finally, Sir Valentine Chirol in his book *The Egyptian Problem* gave a partisan account of the new ideas and aspirations of Egyptian women and the part they played in the political demonstrations against the British in 1919. Not surprisingly, he believed that men were the main force behind the women's participation but he does give some interesting details of women's lives.

One of the most striking features in the political turmoil of the last twelvemonth has been the conspicuous part played by the women of Egypt.

In Egypt, as in most Oriental countries whose domestic institutions have brought about the seclusion of women, the influence she nevertheless wields behind the sheltered walls of the *hareem* is apt to be often underrated. Polygamy in Egypt is rare, and generally regarded with disfavour, except perhaps as a luxury for the rich. In her own home the Egyptian woman, in spite of the proverbial contempt in which the superior sex holds her, is not infrequently a very despotic mistress, both as wife and as mother, and her counsels and commands go abroad with husband and sons after they have crossed the threshold of their house into the outside world which is supposed to ignore her very existence. Until recently the Egyptian lady of the upper classes knew no society outside her home except that of her own sex, but the collective influence exercised through *hareem* society on the habits and opinions of male society was, and is, an important factor. In the old days of the Khedive Ismail, the Princess Mother, who had a vast establishment of her own, was a power in the land, and an almost greater power was the chief eunuch of her palace, a pure negro from the Sudan, who was her trusted and extremely unscrupulous confidant. Even in much later days the source of many political intrigues could be traced to the recesses of some great personage's *hareem*. Native wit and feminine charms went a long way to make up for lack of education. For a good many years past, however, many Egyptians of position have begun to give their daughters a semi-European education, sometimes even having European governesses to reside in their houses, and there are today a certain number of Egyptian ladies who are as well fitted to preside over a *salon* as was, for instance, Princess Nazli, when twenty years ago she alone ventured to open her house to a small circle of male visitors. Increasing opportunities of European travel, and even the close contact maintained by many Egyptians of the better classes who are of Turkish origin with Constantinople, where the revolution of 1908 produced a great feminist ferment, imported new ideas and new aspirations into the Egyptian *hareem*. There was not, until recently, any breach on a large scale with the old traditions, but they no longer inspired the same unquestioning reverence.

The *fellaheen* could never seek to impose similar restrictions on their womenkind, for girls and grown-up women have to go out and do their share – and a very heavy share – of work in the fields. The *fellah* indeed too often treats them as mere beasts of burden, and whilst the husband jogs along at his ease on a donkey, the wife toils behind him carrying a big load on her head. Nevertheless, in most cases, she rules in her own home, especially if, as is often the case, she develops considerable business capacity. It is she who generally markets all such produce as cheese, milk, eggs, etc., and she even becomes an expert in the sale of cotton. In an interesting paper read before the Cairo Geographical Society two years ago, Sir William Willcocks has described how many wives of *fellaheen* have profited by the rising tide of agricultural prosperity to start a little money-lending on their own account, and not infrequently to their husbands. In one well-to-do village where the value of the land held by the *fellaheen* amounted to about a quarter of a million sterling, mostly in quite small holdings, and they had cleared off the whole of their indebtedness except £25,000, some 80 per cent of the women had small sums of money out on loan, and their husbands were found to have borrowed from them altogether no less than £6,000, and often at very high rates of interest. The profits at least remain in the family instead of going into the pockets of Greek and Coptic usurers, and the woman's hold upon her husband is substantially strengthened – a very important consideration in a country where, according to Mahomedan custom, he can divorce her by a mere word.

The proportion of illiteracy amongst the women of Egypt is still appalling. Not one per cent yet know how to read or write. But the movement in favour of female education which started in the upper classes has begun to spread down to the humbler classes, and the old prejudice against it is dying out even in the rural districts. Amongst the Western-educated middle class especially there are many who feel the lack of intellectual fellowship in their own homes which must continue until their womenfolk have a larger share in the advantages of education. It was just at this stage of social and intellectual transition that political agitation suddenly opened to the women of Egypt an unexpected opportunity of emerging *en masse* from their seclusion. To those in whom an incipient spirit of revolt against the artificial life in which they had hitherto been cribbed, cabin'd and confined was already stirring, the cry for 'complete independence' naturally made a strong appeal, for even if they knew little of the larger political issues which it raised, was it not enough that it generated ideas of freedom which could not possibly stop at the outer doors of the hareem? Many of them, doubtless, were keen to ingratiate themselves with their lords and masters; others snatched greedily at new forms of excitement that broke the monotony of their lives. They all worked themselves up into a frenzy of patriotic indignation.

In the stormy days of March and April 1919 they descended in large bodies into the streets, those of the more respectable classes still veiled and shrouded in their loose black cloaks, whilst the courtesans from the lowest quarters of the city, who had also caught the contagion, disported themselves unveiled and arrayed in less discreet garments. In every turbulent demonstration women were well to the front. They marched in procession, some on foot, some in carriages, shouting for 'Independence' and 'Down with the English!' and waving national banners. They flocked to the houses of the Extremist leaders, and the leading Egerias of Nationalism addressed impassioned orations to them from their windows. They followed in large crowds the coffins of the rioters killed in the street affrays, and their shrill lamentations were an eloquent appeal for vengeance. They took a hand in the building of barricades, and though they generally dispersed when fighting actually began, some of them, it was noted, returned to gloat over brutal deeds of violence perpetrated by the men. When the Government officials went on strike excited groups of women acted as pickets outside the gates of the Ministries to hold up those who wanted to return to their duties.

In the *fellaheen* rising the women, embittered perhaps by the hardships they had suffered through the ruthless requisitioning of war supplies and the arbitrary recruitment for the Labour Corps in their villages, 'by order of the British Government', as they were told, joined with the men in tearing up the railway lines and destroying the telegraphs, and in the pillaging and burning which took place up and down the countryside. Women were again equally prominent in all the noisy demonstrations against the Milner Mission, one of their favourite devices being to take possession of the tramway cars at some terminus and drive through the city – without, of course, paying any fares – yelling 'Down with Milner!' and other patriotic amenities, and flaunting little paper flags in the faces of any Europeans who ventured to claim their right to travel in public conveyances.

Still more serious is it that the infection spread into the girls' schools. These, like the boys' schools, went on strike to mark their disapproval of Lord Milner and his colleagues, and children of eleven and twelve concocted passionate telegrams of protest to the Minister of Education, and even to the Prime Minister. Members of the Cabinet themselves complained bitterly that they could not restrain their own daughters. The girls were indeed more violent than the boys, and some of the few English women teachers had an extremely unpleasant time at the hands of their mutinous pupils. Much of this may seem childish, but it would be wrong to make light of the widespread bitterness that underlies this feminine upheaval. For the women of Egypt, though they may be politically powerless, reflect, perhaps in an exaggerated but none the less alarming form, the general uprising against authority produced by the Extremist campaign against the British usurpers.

Participation in turbulent street demonstrations may not have been the healthiest form of emancipation, but so sudden and violent a change is bound to leave a permanent mark upon the women of Egypt. Whether the men of Egypt were wise to encourage it may be left to them to discover. Anyhow, it has imported a new and very potent ferment which is likely to affect social life more deeply than political life.

Sir Valentine Chirol, *The Egyptian Problem*, 1920, pp. 165–9

While it may have been very new for women from rich households to go out on the streets demonstrating, it should be remembered that seventy years earlier Lucie Duff Gordon reported that the lower-class women had been ordered off the streets during the Sultan's visit because Arab women were considered to be outspoken and might have shouted out their grievances.

In these few passages, then, authors may have opened up to their readers the possibility that the passive, subservient life described with such authority by the majority of travel writers was not necessarily the experience of all Oriental women.

Chapter 11

VERY QUESTIONABLE SOCIETY

The Hon. Lewis Wingfield, whom we encountered earlier recommending rape as the best way of pleasing an Arab woman of the desert, obviously believed that Western travellers had a God-given right to go wherever they pleased in order to see whatever they wanted. And in this he was not alone. Europeans often displayed great rudeness and believed that their right to gain the information they wanted was without bounds. In fact, they were the predecessors of today's tabloid press journalists. In the first extract Lewis Wingfield, seeking a good place from which to make a sketch of a street, barged into a house, took a good look at the women's dress, and then ran out describing the women as 'very questionable society'.

Being anxious to obtain a sketch of one of the quaint streets of the upper town, I wandered one morning up its dark alleys and intricate by-ways; and wishing to establish myself at a window (sitting in the narrow street was quite impossible), knocked at a promising-looking door, and was answered by a mysterious voice from behind a lattice above; the door opened of itself, and I marched up the stairs, unmindful of evil. In the upper court I was instantly surrounded by a troop of women, in the picturesque private dress of the Moorish ladies, unencumbered now with veil or yashmak. This dress consists of short pantaloons and jacket of bright material, hidden about the neck and bust by gauzy scarfs and filmy nothings; the hair is plaited in tails with gold and silver cord, whilst a band of gold pendants, mixed with pearls, encircles the brow, and the arms and neck are heavily loaded with chains and bracelets and strings of sequins. It is a very rich dress, and well suited to the lavish magnificence of oriental beauty. These ladies dragged at my watch chain, and pulled my hair, until, finding myself in such very questionable society, I beat a hasty retreat, flying down the stairs six steps at a time, first slamming the doors in the faces of the houris, and eventually reached the street in safety.

The Hon. Lewis Wingfield, *Under the Palms in Algeria and Tunis*, 1868, vol. I, pp. 12–13

Another artist, Henry Blackburn, referred to this incident in his own book, *Artists and Arabs*. He described this behaviour as part of an English invasion of North Africa:

It is pleasant to see with what good tempered grace, both the Moors and French take this modern English invasion. We settle down for the winter here and build and plant vineyards, and make merry, in the same romping fashion that we do in Switzerland. We write to England about it, as if the country belonged to us, as if we had been the discoverers of its charms. (pp. 193–4)

This behaviour may have been, as Blackburn put it, less than polite, but other visitors went to extraordinary lengths to achieve their ends.

C. S. Sonnini, whom we have also met earlier referring to the immoral and murderous habits of Egyptian women, made a plan which he called 'very daring to anyone who knows the inhabitants of Egypt'. Not deterred by this, the intrepid M. Sonnini paid a family to have their daughter circumcised in his room, all in the interest of scientific research. Here he recounts what took place that day in the 1790s.

Everybody knows what male circumcision is and there is no one who does not know that the Jews and the Muslims are circumcised. Among the ancient Egyptians the practice was obligatory. Why was it, in fact, in their climate? This is a question which I will not try to resolve here, although it seems to me to be almost proved that circumcision here is, if not necessary, at least extremely useful among people who are uncivilized and careless. It is also practised by the

Copts who, not sure that they will get into paradise by virtue of the baptism which they are given as Christians, count circumcision – in the same way as the Mohammedans among whom they live – as one of the precepts of their religion. What a strange religious practice, that is disavowed by nature and about which one cannot speak without offending modesty. The details of an operation which is the same for all who follow the religion of Mohammed, can be found in the account of my journey in Turkey. But in Egypt it is not unique to men – there is also one for women.

This type of circumcision was also in use among the people of ancient Egypt, and has been passed on to their descendants only. For the strangers who have come to live in this country are not circumcised, they do not need to be. I know how difficult it is to discuss subjects of this nature, without awakening other ideas than those which the naturalist follows in his research. But this point of the natural history of man is too important to be passed in silence and nobody, before me, has examined and determined it with precision. I will only make use of expressions which are accepted by anatomy. If it is allowed to be unclear to the majority, it is certainly in a matter as delicate as this.

It is known that Egyptian women are circumcised but there has been disagreement over the reasons for it. Most people who have written on the subject have looked at it as cutting the labia minora which, they claim, grows in an extraordinary way in these countries. Others, among whom we can single out the famous traveller James Bruce, have thought that it was nothing less than the amputation of the clitoris whose extension, according to the same authors, was somewhat deformed and disgusting. This is what M. Bruce called excision, an expression his translator passed into our language and which is indeed difficult to replace.

Before an occasion arose when I was able to ascertain the nature of the circumcision of Egyptian girls I was also of the opinion that it consisted of the amputation of the surplus part of the labia minora or the clitoris, given the circumstances and given that these parts were more or less extended. It is even very likely that these operations took place, not only in Egypt but in many other countries of the Orient, where the hot climate and other causes can produce an excessive growth of these parts; and I had more reason to believe this having consulted some Turks who lived in Rosetta on the subject of the circumcision of their women. They had given me no other idea than that of these types of painful mutilations. They also explained to me their reasons for it. We have seen how much importance is attached to having a body that is smooth and glossy. Therefore, any protuberance or unevenness is an offence to their eyes. On the other hand, they claim that after such an operation the women lose some of their passion and, therefore, the ability to enjoy illicit excitement. It is a barbarous refinement of tyranny and the lowest possible degradation of one half of the human race that by these cruel means the other half creates for its own pleasures and because of its jealous despotism. . . .

I guessed it must concern something other than an excessive growth in these parts; an inconvenience which is not found in all women and could not therefore have been the object of an ancient and widespread practice. I resolved to settle this question for myself and made a plan which was very daring to anyone who knows the inhabitants of Egypt. I decided not to paint a picture of a circumcised woman, but to have one circumcised in my room. M. Fornetti, whose enlightened help I had used so many times, was very keen to help me in this enterprise. Through the intervention of a Turk who acted as a broker for French merchants at Rosetta, I was able to have in my room a woman whose job was to circumcise others, and two young girls – one who had been circumcised two years before and one who was going to be now. M. Fornetti, the Turkish broker, and the janissary of the consulate, were, with me, the only men present at the ceremony.

First I examined the young girl who was to be circumcised; she was about eight years old and of the Egyptian race. I was very surprised to see that she had a thick outgrowth of plump flesh covered over with skin. This growth began below the corner of the large lips and hung down the length of half an inch all along this same corner. You will get a near enough idea if you compare it for thickness and shape to the hanging caruncle of a turkey-cock.

The woman who was to do the operation sat down on the floor and made the little girl sit in front of her. Without any preparation and using a very poor razor she cut off the peculiar growth which I have described. The child showed no signs of being in great pain. A pinch of ashes was the only remedy applied to the wound, although there was a lot of blood pouring out. The woman did not touch the labia minora or the clitoris and these parts were not visible in this girl nor in the older one who had been circumcised previously.

This, then, is how Egyptian girls are circumcised. It is believed to be a necessary operation since this kind of caruncle becomes larger with age, and if it was left it would cover over the opening of the vulva. The woman assured me that by the age of twenty-five the growth would be longer than four inches. It is unique to women of Egyptian origin. All other women, even though they belong to the groups of people who are domiciled there and are naturalized, are exempt.

Generally they do not wait for the age of puberty – which is earlier than in our northern countries – to circumcise the Egyptian girls. They remove this troublesome growth at the age of seven or eight. It is the women of Upper Egypt who are in the habit of doing this operation, which is not very difficult as far as one can judge. They go around the towns and villages crying in the streets to advertise their services. There is an old superstition which says that circumcision must be performed when the Nile begins to flood. Here was a great difficulty for me, to find a family who would agree to have their daughter circumcised at a time so far away from that accepted to be the most propitious. For we were in winter. However, some money easily removed this obstacle, as it did all others.

C. S. Sonnini, *Voyage dans la haute et basse Égypte*, 1798, vol. II, pp. 32–9

The next two pieces are descriptions of a trip to a market to view some merchandise. Not too intrusive perhaps, a visit to a public market, except that the goods for sale were slaves and the authors (Alexandre Dumas and A. Dauzats followed by A. W. Kinglake) used the visit merely as an opportunity to describe the women's bodies.

We entered the courtyards and found the merchandise that we wanted to examine, completely naked so that we could first appreciate its quality, then sorted by colour, nation and age. There were Jewesses with a serious countenance, straight nose and long, black eyes; Arabs with swarthy complexions and golden bangles on their legs and arms; Nubians with their hair in very fine plaits divided in the middle of the head and falling to right and left. They were all black and among them were two classes and two prices; this is because some belong to a race which, however great the heat, maintains a skin as cool as that of a snake – which is a priceless quality for the master in this scorching climate where every living thing spends ten hours of the day looking for coolness. Finally there were the young Greek girls, abducted at Scio, Naxos and Milo, and among these there was a child of such ravishing grace and beauty that I asked the price, and was told 300 francs.

All the slaves appear happy at all times because, badly fed by the slave-dealers, beaten for the slightest fault they make, or rather at the slightest caprice of their masters, nothing could be worse for them than to remain in the bazaar. How many grimaces, smiles and silent, lascivious promises these unfortunate girls make to the purchasers who examine them. The merchants treat them like cattle; there is not a horse in the market on whom the curiosity of the lover could exert itself in a more ingenuous and far-reaching manner than on these unfortunate creatures. Moreover, in this fiery climate a woman is no longer young at twenty.

Alexandre Dumas and A. Dauzats, *Quinze jours au Sinaï*, n.d.,
pp. 61–2

I went round the Bazaars: it seemed to me that pipes, and arms were cheaper here than at Constantinople, and I should advise you therefore if you go to both places to prefer the market of Cairo. I had previously bought several of such things at Constantinople, and did not choose to encumber myself, or to speak more honestly I did not choose to disencumber my purse by making any more purchases. In the open slave market I saw about fifty girls exposed for sale, but all of them black, or 'invisible' brown. A slave agent took me to some rooms in the upper storey of the building, and also into several obscure houses in the neighbourhood, with a view to shew me some white women. The owners raised various objections to the display of their ware, and well they might, for I had not the least notion of purchasing; some refused on account of the illegality of the proceeding, and others declared that all transactions of this sort were completely out of the question as long as the Plague was raging. I only succeeded in seeing one white slave who was for sale, but on this one the owner affected to set an immense value, and raised my expectations to a high pitch, by saying that the girl was Circassian, and was 'fair as the full Moon'. After a good deal of delay, I was at last led into a room, at the farther end of which was that mass of white linen which indicates an Eastern woman; she was bid to uncover her face, and I presently saw that though very far from being good looking, according to my notion of beauty, she had not been inaptly described by the man who compared her to the full Moon, for her large face was perfectly round, and perfectly white. Though very young, she was nevertheless extremely fat. She gave me the idea of having been got up for sale, – of having been fattened, and whitened by medicines, or by some peculiar diet. I was firmly determined not to see any more of her than the face; she was perhaps disgusted at this my virtuous resolve, as well as with my personal appearance, – perhaps she saw my distaste, and disappointment; perhaps she wished to gain favour with her owner by shewing her attachment to his faith: at all events she holloaed out very lustily, and very decidedly that 'she would not be bought by the Infidel'.

A. W. Kinglake, *Eothen*, 1844, pp. 160–1

Dr Moritz Wagner on his travels through Persia in the 1850s was most shocked to discover that European male residents entered into temporary marriages with local women. This was similar to the *mut'a*, the Shi'i temporary marriage, but according to him the cases he heard of were between Christian Nestorian women and European men. He attributed this lack of moral scruple by Western men to the fact of having lived in the East so long!

The domestic position of the European residents is not without interest. Some of these Greeks were married men, but had left their wives behind at Constantinople. Most of the members of the Russian Embassy had also come here as bachelors. In both cases, the new comers had followed a long established practice of Europeans in Persia, and contracted temporary marriages with Nestorian women. The Christian sect of the Nestorians, which is even more numerous than the Gregorian–Armenian in Aserbeidschan, has a remarkable partiality for Europeans, and its members have not the least scruple, on religious, national, or ethical grounds, to give their daughters in marriage to Europeans, for a limited period, (be it six years or six months,) and for a stipulated sum. The affair is generally arranged in the most regular and formal manner, always in the presence of the parents and the nearest relations of the girl, and often under the sanction of a Nestorian priest, acting, perhaps, as a notary. In fact, there is a complete competition for a preference of every newly arrived European, who is supposed to be about to take up his residence for some time in the country. The wealthiest strangers have naturally the best selection. As soon as they have agreed about the duration, and the terms of these *matrimonie alla carta*, the bride is brought to her husband with due ceremony, by her relations. It is usual for the family of the lady to take up their residence in the house of her temporary lord, who must naturally maintain them all. This arrangement is often expressly stated in the marriage settlement. Not only all the Greek merchants, but most of the members of the Russian General Consulate, were married in this manner, and the practice is so usual and long established, that public morality is not at all shocked at it. The persons concerned ask each other, without the least embarrassment, how their wives and children are. Each of these gentlemen had set apart a portion of his house for the women, and called it the harem. The ladies retained the mode of life, and costume of native females, covered their faces when strangers appeared, kept away from table when guests were invited, filled up their leisure hours like Turkish women, with devotion to the toilette, and visiting the baths, and when they went abroad, appeared like the other women, in long envelopes, extending from head to foot.

It cannot be disputed that these females are faithful and affectionate to their children, but being totally deficient in cultivation and refinement, notwithstanding their beauty, they cannot compensate for the life of intelligent female society in Europe. It was evident, from the regrets expressed by the gentlemen, for the tender reminiscences in the West, that these Perso-Frankish weddings did not satisfy the affections and the imagination. Young M. Mavrocordato longed for Parisian grisettes, M. Osserof, for the refined females of the Petersburgh salons. The physical beauty of these Nestorian women, which is quite undeniable, was lost sight of, in comparison with the delicacy and spiritual refinement of the cultivated class of European women.

So soon as the interval, specified in the contract, has elapsed, another agreement is made, unless the gentleman is tired of his partner, when he forms a new one. The deserted lady is sure of a settlement at home, because she brings a good sum with her, whereas most Nestorians have to pay dearly in purchasing a wife. The children, the fruit of these short-lived marriages, almost invariably follow their mothers, and I was told that the Nestorian females love

them almost more than those born in subsequent alliances. The step-
fathers are, also, said to treat them very kindly. Nor is it less
remarkable, that the European fathers are said to feel no scruple in
abandoning their offspring, without taking a farther thought about
their destiny. A long residence in the East appears to blunt the sense
of duty, honour and affection, even in the most upright characters.

Dr Moritz Wagner, *Travels in Persia, Georgia and Koordistan*, 1856,
vol. III, pp. 112–15

Wandering around and peering into village houses was clearly
considered by many visitors to be part of the general tour of
the Middle East. The surprising thing about these accounts is
the civility with which such intrusions were apparently
received. The same could not be said of the intruders. The
slightest sign of irritation shown by a woman in the house was
liable to be explained as dislike of foreigners or fear of the evil
eye – as in the first piece by William Arthur Bromfield
published in 1856. Arthur Copping, visiting the Holy Land at
the beginning of the twentieth century, 'made bold' to enter
someone's house and then proceeded to liken the scene inside
to a biblical story.

We never molest the pigeons in the villages, but to shoot any stray
birds outside, however near to the houses, is considered perfectly
fair, and is never objected to by the people, who invariably behave to
us with civility, as we stroll amongst their huts of mud or unburnt
brick. The children it is true, sometimes run way at the sight of us
giaours, and the dread of the evil eye is occasionally manifested by an
expression of impatience from the women, if we indulge in a stare of
curiosity or speculation at them or their occupations, but the dread
and dislike of the Frank is fast wearing away, not in Cairo only, but
all along the river.

William Arnold Bromfield, *Letters from Egypt and Syria*, 1856, p. 66

We made bold to enter one of the forbidding dwellings, where we
found, asquat on the floor, two cats, one dog, and a woman. She
smiled no welcome, nor betrayed any resentment at our intrusion.
Replying in sluggish monosyllables to Solomon's questions, she
continued to pound pease in an earthenware vessel – with a view, as

we learnt, to the making of pastry. If externally the walls presented
an uncouth aspect of dried mud, they were lined evenly enough
inside with a surface of cement.

An interior so simple and primitive suggested a deep interest. For
this apartment could scarcely be different, one supposed, from that
other chamber in Shunem where, years ago, a faithful woman set a
bed, and a table, and a stool, and a candlestick, to serve the needs of
Elisha.

Arthur E. Copping, *A Journalist in the Holy Land*, 1915, pp. 171–2

Other authors, having gone to observe the people, were
irritated when the people came to observe them. Gertrude Bell
found the women particularly annoying.

The rest of the afternoon was devoted to society and to fruitless
attempts to escape from the curiosity of the townsfolk. It was a
Friday afternoon and no better way of spending it occurred to them
than to assemble to the number of many hundreds around my tents
and observe every movement of every member of the camp. The men
were bad enough, but the women were worse and the children were
the worst of all. Nothing could keep them off, and the excitement
reached a climax when 'Abd ul Hamed Pasha Druby, the richest man
in Homs, came to call, bringing with him the Kadi Muhammad Said
ul Khani. I could not pay as much attention to their delightful and
intelligent conversation as it deserved, owing to the seething crowd
that surrounded us. . . .

'Abd ul Hamed said:

'Please God the populace does not trouble your Excellency; for if
so we will order out a regiment of soldiers.'

I murmured a half-hearted refusal of his offer, though I would
have been glad to have seen those little boys shot down by volleys of
musketry, and the Pasha nodded reflectively:

'The Emperor of the Germans when he was in Damascus gave
orders that no one was to be forbidden to come and gaze on him.'

With this august example before me I saw I must bear the
penalties of greatness and foreignness without complaint.'

Gertrude Bell, *The Desert and the Sown*, 1987 (1st edn 1907),
pp. 186–90

Again, Lucie Duff Gordon saw events differently.

A little below Thebes I stopped, and walked inland to Koos to see a noble old mosque falling to ruin. No English had ever been there and we were surrounded by a crowd in the bazaar. Instantly five or six tall fellows with long sticks improvised themselves our body-guard and kept the people off, who *du reste* were perfectly civil and only curious to see such strange 'Hareem', and after seeing us well out of the town evaporated as quietly as they came without a word.

Lucie Duff Gordon, *Letters from Egypt*, 1986 (1st edn 1865), p. 44

In the next piece, also by Lucie Duff Gordon, she relates the behaviour of some Englishmen in the house of a sheikh.

At first I thought the dancing queer and dull. One girl was very handsome, but cold and uninteresting; one who sang was also very pretty and engaging, and a dear little thing. But the dancing was contortions, more or less graceful, *very* wonderful as gymnastic feats, and no more. But the captain called out to one Latifeh, an ugly, clumsy-looking wench, to show the Sitt what she could do. And then it was revealed to me. The ugly girl started on her feet and became the 'serpent of old Nile', – the head, shoulders and arms eagerly bent forward, waist in, and haunches advanced on the bent knees – the posture of a cobra about to spring. I could not call it *voluptuous* any more than Racine's *Phèdre*. It is *Venus toute entière a sa proie attaché*, and to me seemed tragic. It is far more realistic than the 'fandango', and far less coquettish, because the thing represented is *au grande sérieux, not travestied, gazé*, or played with; and like all such things, the Arab men don't think it the least improper. Of course the girls don't commit any indecorums before European women, except the dance itself. Seyyid Achmet would have given me a fantasia, but he feared I might have men with me, and he had had a great annoyance with two Englishmen who wanted to make the girls dance naked, which they objected to, and he had to turn them out of his house after hospitably entertaining them.

Lucie Duff Gordon, *Letters from Egypt*, 1986 (1st edn 1865),
pp. 99–100

The next three travellers, writing between 1867 and 1890, spoke of their attempts to persuade women to sell their jewellery. When the request was refused, there does not seem to have been any thought by the writers that they were at fault in approaching women trying to buy the jewellery they were wearing.

There was one charming creature about five-and-twenty, who seemed to be the oracle as well as the life of the party. She had bright cheeks and lips, large grey eyes, beaming with intelligence, and a frank, broad brow that told plainly enough how very little education would fit her for the very best kind of civilisation. There was not a hint or shadow of shame in her bright face as she compared our European garb to her own, and evidently our condition too; for she turned to one of her companions and seemed to sum up a hasty verdict, whether in our favour or her own, we could not tell.

It amused her immensely that we should be so amused, and she plainly thought us a little impertinent for trying to buy some of her necklaces. Sell her jewels, forsooth, and, least of all, the brooch she wore in honour of having borne her husband a male child; what were we good for, to dream of such absurdities? This was said as plainly as looks can say rather cutting things.

Matilda Betham Edwards, *A Winter with the Swallows*, 1867,
pp. 69–70

Then the sheikh introduced us to his wife, who was accompanied by her sister and cousins, some of whom were very handsome and covered with jewels, but abominably painted. We in vain tried to purchase some of their ornaments, but they replied, 'If we were to sell them, we should no longer belong to our husbands.' They showed us the circular brooches given to them by their lords and masters when they gave birth to a male child. Some are flat, with coral and green enamel let in, and others are with knobs set in a circle.

These poor women are regularly *bought* in fact, the ordinary price being from 200 to 300 francs; but the pretty ones are much dearer. They do all the hard work, carry wood and water, labour in the fields, grind the corn, and weave the stuff that forms their burnouses and haiks. The labour of bringing the water from the deep ravines and gorges below up to the very tops of these hills is something fearful, and the water, even when brought, is brackish and bad. They are married at thirteen and fourteen, and by dint of toil and ill-usage become old women at thirty. But they have some of the finer elements of a mountain race, and often accompany their husbands to war.

Lady Herbert, *A Search after Sunshine*, 1872, pp. 146–7

I stopped also at the *Fountain* of the Annunciation, according to the Greek tradition, and, among other things, attempted to purchase one of those singular rolls of old coins which the girls of Nazareth bind around their foreheads and cheeks; but I could not succeed in my negotiations, for they refused to sell at any price. Most travellers speak of the beauty of these girls, and not altogether without reason. To me, however, they appear unusually bold, and their obvious want of modesty greatly depreciates their good looks.

W. M. Thomson, *The Land and the Book*, 1890, pp. 431–2

Arriving at Gheneh in Egypt in the early 1840s, the Reverend Stephen Olin was very shocked – and even more shocked to be told that the increase in 'licentiousness' was due to the demand by English gentlemen. Guy de Maupassant, on the other hand, was no stranger to brothels in Paris, so on arriving in Tunis he visited a dancing performance and, later the same evening, a brothel. Coached by Flaubert in the art of writing, he made full use of his skills in this account of the evening's events, giving a highly romanticized description of an Arab prostitute – 'l'idéal d'une conception de beauté absolue' – and of the atmosphere in the brothel.

Gheneh is distinguished, probably beyond any other place in Egypt, for a laxity of manners quite at variance with the laws and customs of a Mohammedan country. We saw a great number of women unveiled in different parts of the city, but especially upon the streets and approaches towards the harbour. They were dressed with much finery, in silks and other stuffs of the gayest colours, and wore a great profusion of metallic and glass ornaments such as earrings and necklaces, and various decorations for the forehead and cheeks, rings upon the fingers and toes, which glittered with these shining trinkets, and very massive bracelets, some gilt and other silver, upon the wrists and ankles. They use the henneh and other colours much more extensively than any other females I have seen in Egypt, tinging not only the eyebrows and lips, but a large part of the face. Several of them had regular, soft features, and would be handsome but for this unnatural disfiguration. They were seated conspicuously by the sides of the streets, or in the houses by open doors and windows. Some we met walking with a bold and impudent air, which is specially revolting in a country where so much reserve is imposed upon females. It is difficult to conjecture what may have given to Gheneh a distinction so peculiar and discreditable. I was told that serious attempts have lately been made here, as well as in other parts of the country, to repress this growing licentiousness. An order was issued by the governor forbidding females of the class to appear on the streets or at the doors or windows, and at one time during the present winter they were absolutely imprisoned in anticipation of a large arrival of travellers. The police, however, found much difficulty in enforcing these new regulations, and quite lately the attempt has been abandoned altogether, for a reason, as it was stated to me, which it is hardly possible to believe – the repeated and urgent remonstrances of Frank visitors, and especially those of Englishmen of distinction and influence who had very recently been at Gheneh.

Reverend Stephen Olin, *Travels in Egypt, Arabia Petraea and the Holy Land*, 1843, vol. I, pp. 275–6

In Algiers the Arab town is full of movement at night, but as soon as the night falls in Tunis everything is dead. The small, narrow streets, winding and irregular, look like the corridors of a deserted city where no one has remembered to turn off the gas.

We have come deep into this maze of white walls to see the jewesses performing the 'belly dance'. This dance is ugly and ungraceful, of interest only for the manner in which it is executed by the artist. Three sisters, all heavily adorned, were performing their indecent contortions under the protective eye of their mother, an enormous ball of fat wearing a head-dress of gold paper. She went around begging for the expenses of the establishment whenever her daughters' bellies had achieved a paroxysm of quivering. Around the room three half-open doors revealed low beds. I opened a fourth door and saw a woman who seemed very beautiful lying on a bed. Immediately, the mother, the dancers, two negro servants and a man hidden behind a curtain all hurled themselves upon me. I was about to enter the room of his lawful wife, the daughter-in-law, the sister-in-law of the three hussies who tried, but in vain, to mingle us in with the family, if only for one evening. That I might forgive them for not allowing me to go in they showed me the woman's first child, a little girl of three or four years who could already give a sketchy performance of the belly dance.

I left extremely digusted.

I was now taken with great precaution to the house of some famous Arab courtesans. We had to look around carefully at the end of the streets, enter into long discussions and even make threats for, if the natives discovered that a Christian had entered, the women would be abandoned, disgraced and ruined. Once inside I saw some dark, stout girls of mediocre beauty, in hovels full of mirror wardrobes.

We were thinking of returning to the hotel when the native policeman offered, quite openly, to take us to a brothel, a place of sex, which he would get us into by using his authority.

Once again we are following him, groping about in the unforgettable, dark, narrow streets, lighting matches to see our way but still stumbling into holes, banging our hands and shoulders against houses. Sometimes we hear muffled voices, strains of music, the murmurs of wild festivities coming through the walls as from far away, a terrifying feeling of deadened sound and mystery. We are right in the middle of the area of debauchery.

We stop in front of a door and conceal ourselves on all sides while the police officer bangs on the door with his fists, shouting an order in Arabic.

From behind the door a frail, old voice replies, and now we notice the sound of instruments and the high-pitched singing of Arab women coming from the depths within.

They don't want to open and the officer becomes angry and shouts out some raucous, violent words. Finally the door is half-opened, the man pushes it and marches in like a conqueror gesturing us to follow.

We follow him down three steps leading into a low room where four Arab children belonging to the house are sleeping on carpets along the walls. An old woman – one of these old native women who look like a bundle of rags tied around something that moves, with an unbelievable head sticking out from the top, tattooed like a witch – tries to stop us going any further. But the door has been closed, so we go on into the first room where some men who have not been able to get into the second one are standing blocking the entrance and listening with a rapt air to the strange, shrill music being played inside. The officer makes his way on into the first room, pushes aside the regular clients and leads us into a long, narrow room where piles of Arabs are crouching on benches along the white walls to the far end.

There, on a large French bed as wide as the room, a pyramid of more Arabs rises up in tiers, amazingly piled up and jumbled together, a heap of burnouses with five turbanned heads sticking up.

In front of them, at the foot of the bed on a bench facing us, and behind a mahogany pedestal table covered with glasses, bottles of beet, coffee cups and small pewter spoons, four women are sitting singing an interminable and drawling song from the south, accompanied by some Jewish musicians.

They are decked out in fairy-tale costumes, like the princesses in the Thousand and One Nights, and one of them aged about fifteen is of a beauty so surprising, so perfect, so rare, that she illuminates the strange place transforming it into something unexpected, symbolic and quite unforgettable.

Her hair is held back by a golden scarf which cuts across the forehead from one temple to the other. Underneath this straight, metallic stripe two enormous eyes open in a fixed stare, indifferent, incomparable – two elongated black eyes, somehow distant, separated by a nose like that of an idol, dropping to a small child-like mouth which opens to sing and seems to be the only part of the face that is alive. It is a face without expression, quite unexpectedly regular, primitive and superb, composed of lines so simple that they seemed to be the natural and unique forms of this human face.

Consider any face and I am sure that you could replace one feature, one detail by something taken from another person. There is nothing you could change on the head of this Arab woman since the design is quite perfect and true to type. This smooth forehead, this nose, these cheeks so delicately moulded, ending in the fine point of the chin, and framing in a perfect oval of faintly brown skin, the only eyes, the only nose and the only mouth that could possibly be there. This is the ideal of a conception of absolute beauty which delights our eyes – and it is only in our dreams that we could feel less than completely satisfied.

Beside her is another girl, also charming but not exceptional, with one of those white, sweet faces that seem to have been made from milk pastry. On either side of these two stars two other women are sitting. They are of the bestial type, with short heads and prominent cheek-bones, prostitutes from the nomadic people, lost souls whom the tribes discard along the wayside, gather up again only to lose once more, then finally one day they leave them trailing behind a group of soldiers who take them to town.

They are singing and tapping on the darbouka with their henna-coloured hands, and some Jewish musicians accompany them on small guitars, tambourines and flutes.

There is no talking, no laughter, everyone listens with an air of majestic seriousness.

Where are we? In a temple of some barbaric religion, or in a brothel?

A brothel? Yes indeed we are in a brothel, and never before have I experienced a sensation so unexpected, so new, so full of colour, as I did when I came into this long low room where these girls, decked out as though for a sacred cult, waiting for the whim of one of these grave men who seem to be murmuring the Koran in the middle of the debauchery.

One of these men is pointed out to me, sitting with a miniscule cup of coffee in front of him, his eyes lifted up in a state of meditation. It is he who has engaged the idol, and nearly all the others are his guests. He offers them refreshments and music, and the chance to look at this beautiful girl until such time as he asks them to go home. And then they will go, greeting him with majestic gestures. He is handsome this man of taste, young, tall, with the transparent complexion of the Arab of the town, enhanced by a silky, glossy, black beard and sparse hair on his cheeks. . . .

Nobody talked to the women, who sat as still as statues, and I began to chat to my two Algerian neighbours with the help of the native policemen.

I learned that they were shepherds and landowners from near Bougie, and that in the folds of their burnous they carried a flute from the country to play in the evenings and amuse themselves. Of course they wanted someone to admire their talent and showed me two thin reeds with holes in, genuine reeds which they had cut from the edge of a river.

I begged that they be allowed to play and everyone immediately stopped talking with a perfect politeness.

Oh, the astonishing and delicious sensation which stole into my heart with those first notes – so light, so strange, so unknown, so unexpected, the two small voices of these two little tubes which had grown in the water. It was so delicate, so sweet, disconnected and jerky; the sounds flew up, fluttered around in the air one after the other, but never caught up with each other, never found each other, never came together. It was a song that constantly faded away, then started up again, weaving its way and floating around us like a breath of the spirit of the leaves, the spirit of the woods, the spirit of the rivers and the wind which these two shepherds from the Kabyle mountains had brought with them into this brothel in the suburbs of Tunis.

Guy de Maupassant, *La Vie errante*, 1890, pp. 160–8

Mme Jean Pommerol travelled around the Sahara trying by any means whatever to meet women whom she could write about. In a piece in an earlier chapter of this book she had 'struggled with her conscience' before telling her readers that these women possessed no moral code at all. In the following extracts she reveals how she set about acquiring the knowledge which enabled her to make such judgements – first, by hunting out 'curious types' and forcing her way into their houses and, secondly, by becoming friendly with the men.

I now went, every morning and afternoon, into the streets and alleys to hunt out curious types. I met women packed up in their veils, followed them, and when they went into their low houses with the tortuous entrance passages, I went in after them without invitation. A pause would then ensue, during which they gazed at me with unveiled faces, either hostilely or with looks of surprise, and I noted everything about them, including the wretched holes, dark and bare, dignified by the name of rooms, opening from the narrow court. All the looms for weaving as well as the cooking utensils are kept outside; and at the end of a kind of den, from which all air is excluded, are the piles of worn stones constituting the hearth, from which issues an acrid reddish smoke. Everything is shewn to me, and even explained, but at the same time there remains a wall of defiance between the women and myself, a wall I found it indeed difficult to break through. The farther I went, whether in the gardens of the oasis or towards the rocks at the foot of the fort, where the nomads pitch their camps, and the tent more and more constantly replaced the *gurbi* or house, the greater did this reserve seem to grow, till it almost deepened into hostility.

My aim was not yet attained. It is true I could see the stuffs in which the women draped themselves, such as the variegated *maliffa* rolled about the body, kept in place on the shoulders by two long silver pins called *richetts*; the white *ougaya* which falls from the headdress, fastened above the breasts with a carved *m'zima*; and the red, green, or blue silk *maharma* draped about their hair; the bracelets on their slender arms and the *khalkhats* on their thick ankles. But their souls were absolutely closed to me. I could not read their very simplest thoughts or understand their most ordinary actions.

Rather discouraged by the ill-success of my efforts, I made up for their failure by interesting myself in the various occupations of the men, who work at their forges, and do their polishing, carving, embroidering, and sewing in public. I made a great many delightful acquaintances amongst the makers of Turkish slippers, wool carders, leather cutters, etc., and I became quite at home amongst the date merchants and sellers of beans and onions. I had long conversations with the big-wigs, or, as they are locally called, the big *cabousses* of the neighbourhood, who used to stroll about in the sunshine in all the majesty of their *haiks* or long cloaks. And through this quite a new feminine world opened out before me.

In Europe it is through the women that one gets to understand the men a little, and to gain some idea of the working of their minds, with the motives of their actions; the mother, the wife, the mistress are the chief sources of information. In Southern Algeria, or the Sahara, it was, thanks to the Arab and Berber men, that I got to know anything about the women. It was the masculine good-will which won for me the admission to the home life or *heurm* (the harem as we call it), and secured for me a welcome there. This became more and more the case the farther I went from civilized districts, but at the very beginning of my travels it was evident enough that the men must be first conciliated. In the eyes of the notables and of the merchants I was a *taleba*, or a *femme savante*, a sort of hybrid between a doctor and a public writer; one who could concoct grievances or grant favours; in fact, an influential deputy, able to secure showers of decorations and appointments. The benevolent protection accorded to me by the military authorities gave support to these ideas. Hence the desire of many to oblige me, and of the more disinterested hopes of others that they should see me set right the mistakes of my predecessors amongst the *rumis*, as they call all foreigners. Many poured out their own pet theories to me, but at the same time they gave me a chance to verify them. 'You will see things as they really are,' they would say, 'you will recognize how much better they are here than in France.'

To use the popular and very expressive saying, I was free to take it or leave it, and I probably did get a lot of information from these men with hobbies that I could never have gained alone. And if the receptions which ensued, and at which the women evidently had orders to be amiable at any cost, seemed to me unnatural, forced, and artificial, I was generally able by going to the same home again and again to get into something like *rapport* with my hostesses. The confidence of a woman of the Sahara really begins exactly when she leaves off trying to please you and treats you as an unimportant person. She is then perfectly unceremonious and goes on with her usual occupations, or she chatters with her friends, your presence affecting her no more than that of a piece of furniture, until she suddenly remembers you and worries you with offers of *caouah*, or coffee, chokes you with sweets, inundates you with rancid perfumes, and overwhelms you with caresses, exclaiming: 'You are my friend, you are my sister; my house and all that it contains are yours, and so is the life of my children, or my own life if you want it.' And she gazes at you with her great deep eyes, and you feel as if you were watching a soul awakening from a sleep of long-past centuries. The soft orbs seem to be literally melting with passionate affection, a violent intermittent tenderness, lasting a few minutes only, but almost sincere at the moment of expression. At last, however, it is over; the fire goes out, the coffee gets cold, friendship folds her wings once more, and all this love changes at need into hatred, or sullen hostility, the unconscious reaction of over-strained nerves after great excitement.

Mme Jean Pommerol, Among the Women of the Sahara, 1900,
pp. 18–23

Even when Mme Pommerol was able to enter into a

conversation with any women it was highly unlikely to have been rewarding, for although she conceded that they had the 'sensitiveness and reserve characteristic of the highest civilization' she summed up her own feelings:

Were they at all in sympathy with me? No, not in the least. Widely separated races never can be in sympathy with each other in any true sense of the word. And for this particular race which cringes, steals, sulks and shuffles, cheating and deceiving us on every possible opportunity, we feel a latent contempt, such as conquerors feel for the conquered. (*Among the Women of the Sahara*, 1900, p. 31)

Later in her tour of the Sahara she was determined to meet the highly secluded Mozabite women in Wady M'Zab, but was repeatedly told that this was impossible. In this account she reported quite unashamedly how she tried to rip veils off faces, force her way into houses and wedding parties – despite the 'unfriendly' and 'unwelcoming' reception she was given – and coerce men into co-operating with her. At the end of all this the reader would have learned nothing about the Mozabite women and a lot about the code of morals of Mme Pommerol.

Quite impossible to go and see the Mozabite women! I felt not unnaturally incredulous, spoiled as I had been by the kind welcome I had received from all the Arab and Berber women I had visited elsewhere. The more I insisted, however, the greater were the obstacles thrown in my way; and the greater the obstacles, the more eager did I, of course, become to overcome them.

. . . so I resolved on a bold step. One day I watched and waited till I saw one of the bundles of wraps I knew to be a M'zabiya going along in a narrow alley. The bundle, as if suspecting my design, fled tremblingly before me, sliding against the white walls as if entreating those walls to swallow her up and protect her, as she tried to efface herself against them. But I had the advantage over her in my unfettered movements. I caught her up, this 'Faffa' or 'Mamma', and I touched her with my finger. She uttered a cry of distress. I made the usual polite remark in local use, 'How beautiful thou art!' at which she seemed to shudder. Then I tried, very gently of course, to draw aside her veil and I received a staggering blow, which took away all wish to persevere. After this she ran away and disappeared round a corner of the street, whilst I debated in my mind how I should achieve my object by less violent means.

I resolved to go and see the Caid of Ghardaya whom I already knew, for that worthy functionary was the one whose strained ankle had prevented him from going with me to the mosque. There is nothing more convenient in the Wady M'zab than a strain; it gets better or worse just as occasion demands. I found him installed in his administrative office a long way from his private residence, but to my questions about the Mozabite women, he answered never a word. However, he offered to escort me to the chief oasis. His strained ankle was better, much better, he could ride well to-day.

So we started together for the lovely gardens of the oasis, where the plaintive noise made by the pulleys of the wells – resembling the long-drawn-out notes of birds – never ceases day or night. It was spring time, and the trunks of the sturdy palms were draped with creeping vines, whilst beneath the shade of their spreading branches grew numbers of apricot trees, then in full flower, shedding the pink petals of their blossoms in the breeze.

I again spoke to the Caid about the women, and he replied with remarks on dykes and water channels. . . .

I began to question my companion again about the women. Did they and the young girls come out here too? But, alas! the Caid began to dwell on the value of a palm tree, which requires some forty years of care to attain its full development. Suddenly, however, he fell into the trap, walking into it unconsciously, or, it may be, with his eyes open, for at last he began on the subject of which my mind was full by saying:

'We are obliged to have gardens in order to be able to marry our sons. For the first question the father of a girl asks is, "Has he got a good garden to give me as a dowry?" '

I caught the ball at the rebound. 'Why,' I enquired, 'do you marry your daughters so young? I do not think that Allah has ordained the sacrifice of mere children of eight or nine years old.'

He protested that such things do not happen now; girls are not married till they are fourteen. When, however, I expressed my scepticism, he did not press the point, and I fancy he guessed that I was well informed. The fact is, the Caids shut their eyes to the evil, and allow local cadis to take refuge beneath the aegis of the law when such abuses are committed. . . .

'Is it true, Caid,' I asked presently, 'that your women never receive anybody?'

At this point-blank question he poured out a volley of words, of which I could only distinguish a few, such as 'no instructions – I don't know – very unfortunate', and so on.

'But, Caid, I am a friend, you know. You will take me to see your wife, will you not?'

He turned pale; he was evidently annoyed, and when I repeated my request, he said: .

'No, no; it really is impossible. Do you think I would refuse anything to you that I could grant? My wife would weep, and you would only feel uncomfortable.'

Back again at the office, the Caid gave me some excellent coffee to drink, and also presented me with a big box of sweetmeats; but nothing would induce him to alter his determination.

'No, no; with my wife or any other woman at Ghardaya, you would only find it very dull.'

The afternoon of the next day found me in the reception-room of a third Caid – that of Ben-Isguen – amongst piles of stuffs, rusty weapons, baskets, chests, etc. I had not the slightest hope of obtaining what I wanted here. In this dissolute town of rigidly virtuous aspect, hostile, too, as it was to the Rumis, how could I expect that barriers and obstacles would be removed to please me? . . .

Presently I saw him bring forth from a chest a wonderful collection of tinsel finery, a perfect tangle of many-coloured ribbons. He placed the whole pile in front of me, and I made out several decorations, amongst which I recognized the well-known Academic palms.

Evidently my Caid was ambitious. Did he aspire to the honour of wearing the red ribbon? I wondered. Shall I be very much blamed for turning to account his mistaken ideas of my influence with the home authorities? Without the slightest hesitation I said to him:

'I should like to see your wife, oh Caid!'

He gave me a searching look, shook his head, and then disappeared into the *heurm*, or harem. What was going on, I wondered, behind those walls? What orders was the master issuing – what severe instructions? Anyhow, a quarter of an hour later, I had been ushered into the sacred place, in other words, into a semi-covered-in court of considerable size, a kind of atrium, to which air and light are admitted by means of a large bay window, open to the blue sky of heaven.

There she stood, the wife of the Caid, between her daughter-in-law and her sister-in-law, embarrassed but smiling, stretching out her bare arms, loaded with bracelets, towards me. A veil embroidered with a floral design of many colours, fell from the fichu which served her as head covering, and was worn low on the forehead and fastened behind. A quantity of woollen drapery completed the costumes, evidently those of every day of the three women, indigo blue for the wife, dark red for her daughter, and dark green for her sister. This drapery was arranged about their well-formed, robust-looking figures, in wide folds, leaving the neck and shoulders, which were of gleaming whiteness, quite bare; I never saw such milk-white complexions anywhere else, except amongst the women of Sweden, as those of these Mozabites. The effect was heightened by the ebony of the hair and the jet of the eyes.

'Enti zina,' 'Thou are beautiful,' I said to each of the three in Arabic, for I did not know a word of their language, and they smiled at me in a contented way. Then they squeezed my hands and embraced me, pressing me against their breasts, in spite of all the formidable pins they wore, which were not unlike stilettoes. I felt rather as if I were being caressed by amiable panthers, and I should not have been sorry to have had some sure protector beside me, if only my little servant Miloud, who had been turned back at the door with gestures of horror at the idea of his coming in. . . .

Emboldened by my first experience, and shutting my eyes to the fact that it was exceptional, I managed to gain admission to the women's quarter in several other houses. I went on knocking at the barred entrances, bristling though they were with iron, until at last they were opened to me. I slipped in behind the jealously-guarded and half-opened door, taking no notice of hostile or forbidding looks; and in the end I recognized the wisdom of the Caid of Ghardaya, when he said to me in the oasis, 'You would only find it dull.'

Everywhere the reception I met with was anything but pleasant. Several times, indeed, the hostility became active, and I was turned out bodily. In one or two instances I was even in danger.

But I had my reasons for persevering in my efforts, unwelcome though they were. Was I to be content to learn nothing about these Mozabite women, when I had become quite familiar with the rest of their sisters of the Sahara? No, indeed! So I went on, still interested but sad at heart, so very depressing was the hatred I met with on every side, the effect of which was like that of the ice and fog of winter, penetrating to the very joints and marrow.

For all that, however, what poetic pictures I carried away in my memory. One family I remember especially, whom I visited in the twilight. There they were, all gathered together in the atrium, the pungent smoke from the juniper wood burning in the grate rising up to the blue patch of open sky above. Father, mother, several children, including the little *fiancée* of one of them, all putting a great restraint on themselves, holding themselves perfectly rigid, in fact, in their struggle to resist the desire to throw me out into the street. Their silence, their clenched fists, their mute attitudes of defiance, gave to them the fierce beauty of the conquered in the presence of the victorious enemy. Then in another house, a fine large residence, there was a camel in the ante-chamber, stretching out its long shaggy neck in the style of early sacred pictures, and, crouching on the hearth within, bending over a little child, was a woman past early youth, but still beautiful, and pathetic-looking. With a cold, dignified, almost aggressive simplicity, she raised seven of her fingers and uttered the Arab word, *maout* (dead). And her negress servant, as she escorted me out, thought it necessary to translate and comment upon that one word, for she remarked laconically and confidentially: *Morto, sebba mutchatchu fini morto!* . . .

Then I often think of a little Mozabite with small delicately-moulded limbs who had already been married for four years, and was soon to become a mother, yet carried her burden with an ease and grace which were almost aesthetic, and are quite unknown to women disfigured by hard work and corsets. I don't know whether her husband was absent or at home just then, but I shall never forget her pretty attitude as she stood gently driving away the doves which kept coming to perch on her head and on her bare shoulders. This charming little woman was the only Mozabitya who did not tremble at my approach.

'Oh, Allah, what shall we do?' she cried. 'Here is the Rumiya coming into the house!'

But she showed no ill temper about the tiring purifications she would have to see to after I was gone, to wash away the profanation caused by my Christian footsteps.

A less pleasant episode occurred when I intruded on an assembly

of women on the second day of a marriage fête. Whether they were
excited by the games and dancing which had been going on, I do not
know, but they behaved in a brutal way to me, and drove me out
ignominiously. I took refuge on the terrace, where they dared not
follow me, for fear they should be seen in my contaminating
presence. I looked down in fear and trembling from my point of
vantage, thinking how ugly their angry faces were as they gnashed
their teeth at me. Loaded with the tinsel finery of their gala array,
their cheeks painted white, red and gold, the tips of their noses and
their chins touched with pitch, of all things in the world to use as an
ornament, badly curled locks of hair falling along the sides of the
temples, and heavy jewels here, there and everywhere, their
appearance was certainly anything but attractive. Whereas the simple
fichus and massive ornaments of their everyday costumes make them
look like demure saints about to emerge from their shrines.

As will be understood at once, I could not take up my abode for
good in the niches or in the pigeon holes on the terrace. I had to get
down again somehow, and when I set about doing so a terrible scene
ensued. The bride of nine years old began to cry, the chief
bridesmaid to scream! some little wives married the previous year,
one eight, the other ten years old – oh, Caid of Ghardaya, what did
you tell me? – yelled till they were out of breath. Then the rest of the
women, the adults, flung themselves upon me, beating me, pushing
me about, scratching me, and even pulling out a lock of my hair. Did
they want to keep it as a souvenir, I wonder? As for me, my
recollection of them is anything but affectionate or grateful. The
scene is still a nightmare to me, the one nightmare of my journey.
Later, when the night-wind swept as was its wont across the desert, I
fancied that I heard in my sleep the clamouring of the Mozabite
women, and that their malignant hands were shaking my tent as if it
were an old plum tree.

'Oh, Allah! oh, Allah!' I seemed to hear them cry, 'here is the
Rumiya coming into the house!'

Mme Jean Pommerol, *Among the Women of the Sahara*, 1900,
pp. 137–60

Delacroix painted his famous picture *Femmes d'Alger dans leur
appartement* by persuading a man to take him to his home –

whether it was in fact a Jewish rather than a Muslim family has been queried. Artists, like photographers, were prepared to do a lot to see a woman unveiled and thus succeed in their profession. A. C. Inchbold and her husband, the artist, met a Bedouin who agreed to allow his wife to model – but only in secret with no one else present. In order to get rid of the crowd they spread the story that the English artist was so jealous that he would not have people staring at his wife. She was quite happy to go along with this hypocritical story which, as she said, 'was a state of mind for which they [the Bedouins] had every sympathy'.

The women of these gypsy Bedawin of the sandhills cover their faces like Moslem women, but their veil is Egyptian in appearance, trimmed with shells, coins, and beads, and having a curious nose-bag which allows only the eyes to be seen. Our curiosity had been stirred with regard to the beauty of one of the young wives whom Mr. H. had known when she was a small girl, long before her marriage. By dint of a little diplomacy we removed from our first station on the sands to the front of her tent in company with her husband Suleiman, and the mother of her husband, called as is usual, Um-Suleiman (mother of Suleiman).

The rest of the crowd withdrew, for they had been told with many an expressive gesture in the Arabic tongue, of which they knew we were ignorant, that the artist was a man subject to fearful attacks of jealousy, and that he objected strongly to his wife being the centre of a staring crowd. It was a state of mind for which they had every sympathy and proper comprehension, and set Suleiman strongly at his ease, for a Franghi who thought so much of his own wife was not likely to think too much of the Bedawi's wife.

When, therefore, it was suggested that I would like to see Fatme without her ugly nose-bag, Suleiman allowed her to uncover her face in spite of the presence of the Inglizi *khowaja*. Fatme was a darling, with her dear little brown face, tattooed around the pouting lips. She had expressive grey eyes which reflected the sky when she smiled, and she possessed a quantity of finely plaited brown hair looped over her forehead and hanging on both sides to her waist. Her figure was well developed and gracefully modelled. Her baby boy seemed nearly as big as herself, and certainly he must have been the hungriest baby in the whole of Jaffa judging from the zest of his appetite.

Diplomacy was required again to enable the artist to procure her as a model for his brush. It was arranged we should visit the tents on the following day with the tea-basket, hold a picnic in Fatme's tent, and thus make the husband amenable to the proposition. We started for the Bedawin tents under a sky scintillating with heat about three o'clock the next afternoon. The people saw us coming from afar and swarmed over the sand-ridges to meet us and relieve us of the big basket we were carrying.

In honour of the occasion Suleiman and Fatme had transferred their dark brown tent to a clean patch of sand, emptied the interior of everything but a few cushions and the usual wooden chest, opened the front of the woven walls, and spread out the matting that we might sit upon it in a semicircle sheltered from the sun. On the glaring sands without, spectators from the other tents quickly collected and squatted in a second bigger crescent, consisting chiefly of boys and girls, and a melancholy-faced relative of Suleiman.

His presence embarrassed us. No other men came near on account of the previous warning of the Franghi's jealousy; on no account, they had been told, were they to approach the tent where his wife sat in seclusion. Nothing could persuade the intrusive relative that his absence would be more desirable than his company, and it was not etiquette to order him to withdraw. He scented the tea and held his ground until that function was over. Until he retired sketching was out of the question, as it was only on conditions of strict secrecy that Suleiman had consented that his wife should sit for the artist.

A. C. Inchbold, *Under the Syrian Sun*, 1906, Vol. II, pp. 369–70

Hiding on the terrace of a house in order to spy on the women on the adjoining terraces was commonly practised by European men. Sometimes the women and children would turn the tables and stare at the intruders, giggling and with an insolent gaze – as these men complained on occasion. The Reverend E. W. L. Davies reported in 1858 that after the French seized the city of Algiers they used to climb up on the roof of a house with a telescope to invade the privacy of the women even more thoroughly. John Horne, writing in 1925, described similar goings-on in Morocco, this time by two Englishmen. On this occasion the invaders were defeated by the women.

The ladies! Two words to remind me that it is time to invade their stronghold, for they have a stronghold where no man may penetrate save their lord and master. Even he rarely appears there, and when he does there is tragedy in the air – for someone. Let us invade it all the same, keeping well under cover lest ill befall us, and view the world from the women's outlook, the terraces of Fez. There is a story of two Englishmen, ardent students of all things Moroccan, who determined to get a close view of the beauties of a neighbouring *hareem* when they should take their airing on the terrace. Nothing daunted by accounts of the dreadful consequences were they discovered, they hid themselves before dawn under two large market-baskets placed in a prominent position upon their own roof, and prepared to await events. The hours of burning heat passed slowly, and yet the watchers dared not move for fear of discovery or of missing the fair ones of their dreams. Towards evening, when they were almost baked, a tiny door leading from a staircase opened and two women appeared. Soon they unveiled. Alas that the world should contain such ugliness! From other doors came other women, each older and less charming than the last, laughing and pointing mockingly towards the market-baskets on the only empty terrace. This went on till at last night hid all from view. Then the gallants emerged from their hiding-place faint and feverish, though it was no fever of love that consumed them. They had thought to be amused, but the laugh was with the ladies, for news travels only too swiftly on the terraces.

John Horne, *Many Days in Morocco*, 1925, pp. 117–18

The Duke of Pirajno, an Italian doctor living in Libya, has also contributed to this book earlier, giving a description of the body of one of his woman patients. This present extract might well have been placed in other chapters, but the pornographic nature of this description of his visit to a scorpion charmer, written in overtly sexual language, merits its inclusion here.

She became silent and relaxed her posture, closing her eyes; she seemed to fall asleep, but her shoulders continued to move to the rhythm of the distant chanting. On the brazier the *bhur* continued to smoke and made a slight sizzling sound. Suddenly, the girl shook herself and with a slow movement of head, breast and hips threw off her *haik*. Seated cross-legged, erect from the hips, she remained covered by the *suriya*, the sleeveless, low-cut Arab shift.

She was a young negress, with thick, purplish lips and a short, only slightly flattened nose. She must have been a native of the Wadhai, or perhaps of some more distant region. Her forehead was strongly convex, her eyes coffee-coloured with yellowish whites; her tight black curls clung closely to her head and left her ringless ears uncovered; her arms and hands were bare of bracelets or rings. Beside her the ugliness of the two old Fezzanese women was repulsive.

She took a wicker basket which they handed to her and lifted the multi-coloured lid. In the bottom of the basket a large scorpion was lashing about in a fury, its tail erect like a sword.

Fusuda looked at it, her lips half-open, her eyes half-closed, and then took it between two fingers and placed it on her shoulder. The creature stumbled there, scrabbling upon the buckle of her chemise, then lost its foothold and slipped down into the hollow of her collarbone. She threw back her head and the scorpion climbed up her neck, across her lower jaw and made its way slowly along her cheek. She closed an eye and it passed over her eyelid on to her forehead and attached itself to her woolly hair.

Fusuda took it in her hand again, stroked it, murmured some words I could not catch, tickled its belly and suddenly popped it in her mouth. Only its tail, quivering and lashing out in every direction, protruded from between her thick lips, its poisonous sting striking the girl's chin and nostrils. A moment later the scorpion, covered in saliva, was frantically twisting about, wild with excitement, in the palm of her hand; she smiled at the little monster, and laid it in her armpit. Then with a swift movement she unfastened her shoulder buckle and let fall her *suriya* so that she was naked to the thighs. She thrust the scorpion between her legs, leaving only the tail obscenely protruding.

Fusuda threw back her head and laughed – with silent, ghoulish laughter, her mouth wide open, her glazed eyes nearly closed.

Meanwhile she started playing with another, yellow-striped scorpion, smaller but more poisonous than the other. She poked it with her finger-nail and blew on its head, and when it lashed out in fury she put out her tongue and used it to fence with the deadly tail, which struck but did not wound her. Both scorpions were now on Fusuda's crossed arms. She watched them. Antediluvian monsters in miniature, they faced each other with all their members and weapons ready. Slowly and clumsily they approached each other; they grappled each other by the legs, their tails lashing and quivering in a frenzy which communicated itself to the girl, who shivered as if she were suffering from a tertian fever. Her lips were drawn back from her teeth and her eyes converged on the combatants in a ferocious squint.

Suddenly she emitted the shrill, piercing notes of the *zagharit*, the war-cry which incites men to battle, and the two monsters in miniature seemed to understand and to respond. Locked together, they wrestled and struggled, clawing at each other, their arched tails waving, seeking the adversary's vulnerable spot; their stings beat against each other's backs as they had beaten against Fusuda's face and tongue and lips. All at once they were still. The thrusts had gone home; the poison had struck them motionless. There was a spasm or two in the tails still inserted in the wounds; a pincer let go, slowly, painfully; a leg stretched out in a spasm, and the two reptiles, still interlocked, rolled dead on to the mat.

Fusuda's body slumped forward, and she clasped her hands round her knees, shuddering; she was foaming at the mouth, and her breasts and belly were running with sweat.

Duke of Pirajno, *A Cure for Serpents*, 1985 (1st edn 1955), pp. 42–3

By their own accounts, then, these travellers were indeed 'very questionable society', forcing and bribing their way into private lives, encouraging prostitution and producing accounts of women's lives which were remarkable not only for their criticism, arrogance and hypocrisy but also, by definition, for the absence of information.

To conclude this chapter, a piece written by Arthur Copping in Palestine where he was forced to confront the effect of his own presence there. We can guess how easily this account might have ended after the second paragraph, giving readers one more bit of disinformation.

Leaving Samaria behind us, we rode across lovely hills and dales where throve the olive, the fig, and the pomegranate; and at one time we journeyed beside a rocky glen full of beauty and peace and the song of birds. Instinctively my brother and I paused, that our eyes might take their fill of a delightful scene; and, as we waited and watched, the solitude was suddenly invaded by a muffled uproar that came rumbling up from one direction to awaken eerie echoes from the other. We looked about us in bewilderment. So far in our experience of Palestine the spirit of placidity had everywhere reigned. What din was this that assailed our hearing – here, of all places, at a veritable shrine of peace and repose?

The disturbance grew to be indistinguishable as the strident and urgent shouting of men; and the next minute we were looking down at one of the most grimly grotesque processions I ever remember to have seen. It was a string of mules and horses and donkeys, each animal supporting a swaying heap of bundles, boxes, chairs, tables, and I know not what. Two squatting men were part of the luggage, while other men ran beside and behind the heavily freighted beasts, assailing them with expostulations, blows, and an occasional stone. A company of robbers who had despoiled a village and were fleeing with their booty from avenging justice – to me the affair looked nothing less than that.

One of the fugitives, on looking upward, obviously saw the two horsemen standing conspicuous against the sky. He waved his hand to us; and then, in a flash of understanding, we recognised George the waiter, and our own caravan. So this was what our beautiful camp looked like when travelling along the road! Viewed from a new standpoint, our imported Western civilization was not without a suggestion of primitive barbarism after all.

Arthur E. Copping, *A Journalist in the Holy Land*, 1915, pp. 192–4

Chapter 12

WHICH WAS THE GREATER OUTRAGE?

Although this book has been a continuous illustration of European misogynist, racist and elitist attitudes, writers were capable of producing statements of blind prejudice so outrageous that they can take your breath away. This chapter serves as a way of summarizing the quality of judgement which many travel writers have brought to the task of informing their readers, and is not confined to the nineteenth century. Hopefully, however, an editor today would not pass over a comment such as this written in 1899.

At the present day camels are used for all sorts of domestic purposes in Africa. They may even be seen drawing ploughs in the interior of the Regency of Tunis. You may remark a woman and a camel harnessed to the same plough, and you hesitate to decide which is the greater outrage.

Herbert Vivian, *Tunisia and the Modern Barbary Pirates*, 1899, p. 306

In the extracts below William Arthur Bromfield and William Kennett Loftus suffered from severe gender blindness and, with Charles Tyrwhitt Drake, considered women to be a race apart.

Great consternation prevails at this time along the valley of the Nile, on account of the Pacha's troops being engaged in levying the conscription by seizing men in all the towns and villages. . . . The evening before we had dispatched Mohammed and Achmed on the usual errand on shore to procure milk, when they found the place entirely deserted, the adult male population having fled to the hills to avoid the conscription, the women and children only remaining behind.

William Arnold Bromfield, *Letters from Egypt and Syria*, 1856, pp. 150–1

From Ahwaz our next stage was to Bender-ghil, passing by the way the small Arab village of Wais, where the whole population was busily engaged with the harvest; men and boys, cows and donkeys were assiduously treading out the corn, of which there was an abundant supply. Above Wais the Karun flows through a light alluvial soil, admirably suited for the cultivation of grain, although it is to be doubted if the farmers of Wais were aware of the fact.

William Kennett Loftus, *Travels and Researches in Chaldaea and Susiana*, 1857, p. 292

From these dark passages one suddenly turns into a street with rows of bright-coloured English cottons, native leather bags and pouches, and embroidered goods hung out on both sides; while above, a trellis-work of cane, with vines creeping over, keeps off the intense heat of the sun. Here one is nearly deafened by the clatter of tongues – Moors, Jews, Spaniards, Arabs, and last, but not least, the women wrapped up in their haiks and wearing straw hats about a yard in diameter, all shouting and gesticulating till one thinks it must end in blows; but no bargain can be made without a most unnecessary amount of noise and bargaining, for a shopkeeper always asks a great deal more than he intends to take, particularly when the would-be purchaser is a Christian, for, says he, 'If I don't get it there is nothing lost, and if I do so much is gained.'

Walter Besant (ed.), *The Literary Remains of the Late Charles F. Tyrwhitt Drake*, 1877, pp. 188–9

When M. Guillaume Rey was visited at his camp by some women (Christian as it happened) bearing presents of fruit and cheese he naturally assumed that they had been sent by their menfolk.

This morning when our tents were being taken down we saw two women coming from the town carrying baskets. We thought that they were coming to sell us provisions, but we were mistaken. They were Christian women who, being of the same religion as ourselves, were coming to bring us a present of three large baskets of pears cooked on ashes, grapes and dried cheeses in order to fulfil towards us in some way our rights to hospitality. We were deeply touched by such consideration from people whom we did not know at all but who, simply because we were Christians and strangers, sent to us their wives and their daughters carrying provisions.

M. E. Guillaume Rey, *Voyage dans de Haouran at aux bords de la mer morte exécuté pendant les années 1857 et 1858*, n.d., p. 243

Ardent Christian that she was, determined to save the poor degraded Algerian women from their life under Islam, Mrs Albert Rogers found her aesthetic sense so offended by the appearance of negresses that she made the following preposterous suggestion.

Shopping, and visiting, in the town, which, by reason of the close atmosphere, is always a kind of penance to me. With every feeling of heart and head enlisted against the Darwinian theory, it certainly strains one's fraternal sentiments to the uttermost, at all the corners of the arcades to stumble upon the negresses, enveloped in their invariable blue check *takhelila*. If they would only adopt the Moslem fashion, and hide their repulsive features, it would save one many a shock.

Mrs G. Albert Rogers, *Winter in Algeria, 1863–4*, 1865, p. 71

E. H. Palmer, a fellow of St John's College, Cambridge, made two visits to Sinia and Palestine between 1868 and 1870 in connection with ordnance survey and exploration. Claiming to be an impartial observer, this scholar displayed great ignorance of local conditions and turned the story around to demonstrate that Arab women had no natural feelings.

In Wady Aleyat was an Arab encampment, and during our stay in the neighbourhood a death occurred in one of the tents. The wailing of the women on the occasion was loud and passionate, and would have been touching had it not been too energetic. I saw the mother and sister of the departed sitting by the roadside howling horribly: the old lady especially distinguished herself, and appeared to me as an impartial observer, to be continually watching for opportunities of boxing her own ears unawares, and when she had thus succeeded in arousing herself, she renewed her lamentations, shrieking out, ' *'a b'naiye wain elgak!*' – 'Oh, my son, where shall I find thee?' Within a few hours of his decease, the defunct was decently interred in a *namas* in the vicinity.

E. H. Palmer, *The Desert of the Exodus*, 1871, vol. I, p. 174

Was the author recommending funeral parlours in the desert so that a decent interval should occur between death and burial?

Edward Barker reported a story of a French consul who refused women admittance to the consulate because they annoyed him. Thomas Lyell in the 1920s gave a somewhat similar story, this time a British diplomat 'filled with the idea of chivalry and the sacredness of womanhood'. Unfortunately for him, the woman he had to deal with was not a sweet, passive, veiled creature and misogyny, the reverse side of the chivalry coin, quickly took over.

Monsieur de Lesseps, who was a strict disciplinarian, had ordered that women should not be allowed to come to the Consulate on any pretence whatever, on account of the wearisome importunities of females – a great source of annoyance in the East, for they come to beg off culprits who deserve punishment.

Edward B. B. Barker, *Egypt and Syria Under the Last Five Sultans of Turkey*, 1876, vol. I, p. 194

The following incident throws a strange light on the home-life in Shia' Islam. A certain Political Officer, filled with the idea of chivalry and the sacredness of womanhood, was, early in his career, presented with a petition from a heavily-veiled female which moved him profoundly. It was to the effect that she, Fatima, having no other protector than Almighty God and himself, had fled to him for succour. She was a married woman, who had borne her husband no less than five children, and had then been brutally turned out of her house. She had tried to return, not only to see her children, but also to collect some of her household goods, and had been set upon by her husband and most soundly beaten.

The worthy officer was most profoundly moved. He understood little Arabic, but sufficient to know that he had before him an unfortunate victim of wife-beating. He was determined to make an example, and show these wretched Arabs that if there was one thing more than another that the British Government would NOT stand, it was wife-beating. The husband was summoned and asked what the devil he meant by such brutality. The interpreter tried hard to explain that the woman was a thoroughly bad lot, who had actually been divorced many months back for the crime of barrenness, and that the husband held a most unimpeachable bill of divorcement from the Shara Court and had never seen the woman since the decree, until that very moment. But our friend would hear no excuse: he had before him that most degenerate type of human being, the wife-beater, and passed sentence of three months' hard labour.

Had the Prophet himself suddenly risen up in the bazar of the town, it could not have caused a greater sensation. There was not a doubt that madness had smitten their Hakim. Such was the common gossip in the coffee-shops. It was appalling. The whole of their social life was in a moment undermined. Had not the Prophet himself (and on him be the peace) laid it down in the Quran that unruly wives were to be beaten? The fact that in this particular case the whole charge was trumped up, did not worry them at all. The question was: 'When and how often has each of us beaten his own wife, and will she also send up a petition, and shall we ourselves be doing three months' hard labour? Furthermore, how can we possibly keep a semblance of discipline among our women when such things may happen?'

The interpreter, of course, waxed quite wealthy by means of promises to destroy any such appeals before they reached the Hakim. However, the unfortunate officer found himself snowed under with petitions from the wives of those who had not had the foresight to interview the interpreter. The same punishment was meted out to all, and consternation was everywhere.

But Allah is All Merciful, and in this case He smote the Hakim with an attack of malaria. None the less he made his way down to the office, though his head was bursting.

It was in the middle of the hot weather. The river flowed past the entrance to his office, and the door was kept open for any breeze that might enter. He sank down in his chair, and told the interpreter that he could not see any petitions except those of women who might want his assistance to relieve them of maltreatment. He was really very charitable, considering that his head was opening and shutting with throbs that seemed to be shooting in every direction at once.

A woman came in.

An excitable woman of any race is at normal times a trial, but when that woman is an Arab suffering under a grievance she is a yelling fury, and it is well not to have a headache at such moments. Such a woman was the petitioner. She came in accompanied by her husband, a most inoffensive and insignificant little man. She began to complain, and within a minute she was a raging tornado. Words poured forth, her voice rising higher and higher each moment, till she reached the highest possible note on which she could enunciate, and from that moment the office was filled with one continuous shriek. The Hakim held his splitting head. He groaned, and muttered little exclamations to the interpreter, 'stop her, for God's sake, stop her!' Unavailing efforts were used. True, she stopped for a moment, but it was only to gain more strength to impress the Hakim with the justice of her case. He, poor man, was by this time barely conscious. His temperature was anything up to 104, weird lights were dancing before his eyes. His whole body seemed to be burnt up with the cataclysm that was going on in his head. She paused a moment. He looked up. He spoke. 'Oh Hell! chuck her in the river!' were his first audible words. The husband, of course, thought they were the dreaded sentence; and trembling he asked what the Governor had said. The interpreter gave a literal rendering. There was a shout of 'Al hamdu Lillah'; a confused mass appeared before the eyes of the Hakim; a mass of struggling draperies and shrieks – followed by a significant splash and silence. Great was the rejoicing in the coffee-shops that night. The short reign of feminine power was over, and it was universally agreed that the Prophet was most emphatically and surely the Apostle of God!

Thomas Lyell, *The Ins and Outs of Mesopotamia*, 1923, pp. 158–63

Lady Herbert believed that it was her duty to visit Algerian women languishing at home in order to relieve them from boredom.

But when all is said and done, the position of women in this country is deplorable. To bathe and dress, to smoke and eat, are their sole occupations. Hardly any can read or write, and their time hangs so heavily on their hands that the greatest kindness you can do is to go and pay them a visit, if only to kill half an hour or so.

Lady Herbert, *A Search after Sunshine*, 1872, p. 262

The Reverend G. Robinson Lees chose to pretend a staggering ignorance of his own class-ridden English society in this piece on the importance of dress in Palestine.

This difference of costume might not be so readily understood in England, where dress is meaningless, and it is almost impossible to distinguish one person from another by his outward appearance, as social position is not determined by clothes, and garments are not always a guide to a man's occupation. No one is easily recognised as the member of a particular church or sect by his dress.

In Palestine every man is known by his clothing, his race and creed, the position he occupies, and the part of the country to which he belongs. The infinite variety of costumes that may be found in a street of Jerusalem is full of information of the people who wear them. Those who wear 'soft raiment' are the wealthy, the aristocrats (St. Luke vii. 25); the toilers dress in coarse mantles similar to that worn by John the Baptist. There is never a change of fashion in Palestine, and this is no doubt comforting to the husbands of the land who have wives and daughters.

Reverend G. Robinson Lees, *Village Life in Palestine*, 1905, p. 58

More than one writer claimed magical powers to interpret the thoughts of 'invisible' women, but Mirko Ardemagni, travelling in Libya, surpassed many in his choice of language.

look at the Arab women and you will read on the invisible faces the suffering of their millennial slavery.

Mirko Ardemagni, *Dalla terra di Salambbô ai laghi di cristallo*, 1928, pp. 15–16

As we have seen, feminists have not been innocent of ethnocentrism. While deploring the narrow-mindedness of Eastern women, Trowbridge Hall related a dialogue which took place at a women's conference in the 1920s. Over-reacting, one suspects, to an earlier speech, an American woman explained what freedom meant to a woman in her country – but hardly in feminist terms.

The harem of the East, really *haremlik*, a word derived from the Arabic, meaning sacred and forbidden, which Europe and America consider so filled with wicked mystery as never to be spoken without a leer or a smirk, does not mean a collection of concubines but simply the place where women congregate, and to which no man other than the master of the house is ever admitted. Custom has so firmly rooted a belief in the necessity for the harem that the resultant narrowness of point of view is simply appalling. At a recent congress of women an American speaking of the freedom observed at home, mentioned the fact that her husband would never think of questioning her right to receive a man alone, and that she rarely took afternoon tea without some man friend; upon which, a Persian feminist arose and seriously asked how it was ever determined who was the father of the children.

Trowbridge Hall, *Egypt in Silhouette*, 1928, pp. 58–9

Gertrude Bell was decidedly not in sympathy with Western feminists and showed a staggering lack of interest in Eastern women. They usually featured in her books as shadowy figures flitting in and out of tents serving meals, while she talked to the men. The first two extracts show her indifference at its worst; in the third piece she acknowledged that women did have special problems – but only when they were her own.

Half an hour later my camp was pitched a little lower down on a lovely grassy plateau. We were soon surrounded by Arabs who sold us a hen and some excellent sour milk, 'laban' it is called. While we bargained the women and children wandered round and ate grass, just like goats. The women are unveiled. They wear a blue cotton gown 6 yards long which is gathered up and bound round their heads and their waists and falls to their feet. Their faces, from the mouth downwards, are tattooed with indigo and their hair hangs down in two long plaits on either side.

The Letters of Gertrude Bell, 1947, p. 66

The Zagarit are thoroughly enjoying our visit. They sit in an expectant circle round Fattuh's tent, waiting for any stray handful of dates or cigarettes that he may give them. They bring their needlework and establish themselves for the afternoon. I found the men of the tribe employed upon some new shirts (of which they stood in great need) when I came in for a hasty lunch. 'Don't your women make your shirts?' said Fattuh. 'Wallahi, our women do nothing but keep quiet' they replied. And I'm not sure one can ask more of woman.

The Letters of Gertrude Bell, 1947, p. 237

You know there are moments when being a woman increases one's difficulties. What my servants needed last night was a good beating and that's what they would have got if I had been a man.

The Letters of Gertrude Bell, 1947, p. 179

Before departing to take up a position as consul in Mosul in 1935, Laurence Grafftey-Smith consulted a colonel who had lived there for years. Few Western men would have been as blunt as this military man about their feelings towards Eastern women: 'The only serious advice he gave me, crystallizing long years of experience, was, if ever using a Kurdish woman, to have a Flit-gun by my side' (*Bright Levant*, 1970, p. 180).

In Chapter 1 of this anthology there is a quotation from Michael Asher, who went to the Sudan in 1979 to work as a teacher and subsequently with the UNICEF camel expedition to take aid to the nomads in remote regions. As many Englishmen before him, he fell in love with the desert and on one occasion he tried to explain his feelings to a camel-man who was his comrade on a long and hazardous journey. 'He looked at me uncomprehendingly, then said, "The desert! The desert is a bitch!"' Eastern and Western men were not so far apart, however, for when Michael Asher came to bid his farewell to the desert he summed up his feelings:

I was looking out at the desert, the lonely desert which I had crossed.
Like a woman, it looked its most beautiful at the time of parting. . . .
(*In Search of the Forty Days Road*, 1984, p. 232)

REFERENCES FOR INTRODUCTION

Ahmed, Leila, 'Western Ethnocentrism and Perceptions of the Harem', *Feminist Studies*, 8: 3 (1982), pp. 521–34.

Alloula, Malek, *The Colonial Harem*, translated from French, University of Minnesota Press, 1986.

Altick, Richard D., *Victorian People and Ideas*, New York: W. W. Norton, 1973.

Badran, Margot, 'The Origins of Feminism in Egypt', in A. Angerman, G. Binnema and A. Keuran (eds), *Current Issues in Women's History*, London: Routledge, 1989.

—— and Cooke, Miriam (eds), *Opening the Gates: A Century of Arab Feminist Writing*, London: Virago, 1990.

Bell, Susan Groag and Offen, Karen M., *Women, the Family, and Freedom: The Debate in Documents*, vol. I, Stanford University Press, 1983.

Birkett, Dea, *Spinsters Abroad*, Oxford: Basil Blackwell, 1989.

Bloch, Iwan, *The Sexual Life of Our Time in Its Relation to Modern Civilization*, translated from German, London: William Heinemann (Medical Books), 1930 (reprint).

Brahimi, Denise, *Femmes arabes et soeurs musulmanes*, Paris: Editions Tierce, 1984.

Butler, Josephine E., *The Education and Employment of Women*, London: Macmillan & Co., 1868.

Caplan, Pat (ed.), *The Cultural Construction of Identity*, London: Tavistock, 1987.

Clark, Michael J., 'The Rejection of Psychological Approaches to Mental Disorder in Late-Nineteenth-Century British Psychiatry' in A. Scull (ed.), *Madhouses, Mad-doctors and Madmen*, London: Athlone, 1981.

Conceptual Clothing, catalogue for the exhibition, Birmingham: Ikon Gallery, 1986.

Crepaz, Adele, *The Emancipation of Women and its Probable Consequences*, London: Swan Sonnenschein, 1893.

Djebar, Assia, *Femmes d'Alger dans leur appartement*, Paris: Des Femmes, 1980.

Ellison, Grace, *An Englishwoman in a Turkish Harem*, London: Methuen, 1915.

Fraser, Rebecca, *Charlotte Brontë*, London: Methuen Mandarin, 1989.

Fried, Albert and Elman, Richard (eds), *Charles Booth's London*, Harmondsworth: Penguin Books, 1971.

Gay, Peter, *The Bourgeois Experience*, vol. I: *Education of the Senses*, Oxford University Press, 1985; vol. II: *The Tender Passion*, Oxford University Press, 1987.

Gilman, Charlotte Perkins, *The Yellow Wallpaper*, London: Virago Press, 1987 (first published 1892).

Gissing, George, *The Emancipated*, London: The Hogarth Press, 1985 (first published 1890).

Graham-Brown, Sarah, *Images of Women: The Portrayal of Women in Photography of the Middle East 1860–1950*, London: Quartet Books, 1988.

Groot, Joanna de, ' "Sex" and "Race": The Construction of Language and Image in the Nineteenth Century', in Susan Mendus and Jane Rendall (eds), *Sexuality and Subordination*, London: Routledge, 1989.

Haeri, Shahla, *Law of Desire: Temporary Marriage in Iran*, London: I. B. Tauris, 1989.

Hewitt, Margaret, *Wives and Mothers in Victorian Industry*, Westport, Conn., USA: Greenwood Press, 1958.

Himmelfarb, Gertrude, *Marriage and Morals among the Victorians and Other Essays*, London: I. B. Tauris, 1989.

Hwang, David Henry, *M. Butterfly*, Harmondsworth: Penguin Books, 1989.

Janus, *Why Women Cannot Be Turned into Men*, Edinburgh and London: William Blackwood and Sons, 1872.

Kabbani, Rana, *Europe's Myths of Orient: Devise and Rule*, London: Quartet Books, 1986.

Lambert, Elie, *Delacroix et les Femmes d'Alger*, Paris: Librairie Renouard, 1937.

Llewellyn, Briony, *The Orient Observed: Images of the Middle East from the Searight Collection*, London: Victoria & Albert Museum, 1989.

Magraw, Roger, *France 1815–1914: The Bourgeois Century*, London: Fontana, 1988 (reprint).

Menefee, Samuel Pyeatt, *Wives for Sale: An Ethnographic Study of British Popular Divorce*, Oxford: Basil Blackwell, 1981.

Moscucci, Ornella, *The Science of Woman: Gynaecology and Gender in England, 1800–1929*, Cambridge University Press, 1990.

Neff, Wanda F., *Victorian Working Women*, London: Frank Cass, 1966 (first published 1929).

Parkes, Bessie Rayner, *Essays on Woman's Work*, London: Alexander Strahan, 1865.

Pinchbeck, Ivy, *Women Workers and the Industrial Revolution, 1750–1850*, London: Frank Cass, 1969 (first published 1930).

Poovey, Mary, *Uneven Developments: The Ideological Work of Gender in Mid-Victorian England*, London: Virago Press, 1989.

Said, Edward W., *Orientalism*, Harmondsworth: Penguin Books, 1985.

Shirreff, Emily, *Intellectual Education and its Influence on the Character and Happiness of Women*, London: Smith, Elder, 1862 ed.

Showalter, E., *The Female Malady: Women, Madness and English Culture, 1830–1980*, London: Virago Press, 1987.

Spark, Muriel, *Mary Shelley*, London: Cardinal, 1989.

Thompson, E. P. and Yeo, Eileen (eds), *The Unknown Mayhew: Selections from the Morning Chronicle 1849–50*, Harmondsworth: Penguin Books, 1973.

Thornton, Lynne, *La Femme dans la peinture orientaliste*, Paris: ACR Edition, 1985.

Vial, Charles, *Le Personnage de la femme dans le roman et la nouvelle en Egypte de 1914 à 1960*, Damascus: Institut Français de Damas, 1979.

Warner, Marina, *Alone of all her Sex: The Myth and Cult of the Virgin Mary*, London: Picador, 1985.

Weideger, Paula, *History's Mistress*, Harmondsworth: Penguin, 1986.

Wright, Sir Almoth E., *The Unexpurgated Case against Woman Suffrage*, London: Constable & Company, 1913.

Yonge, Charlotte M., *The Clever Woman of the Family*, London: Virago Press, 1985 (first published 1865).

SOURCES

L'Algérie de nos jours, Algiers: J. Gervais-Courtellement et Cie, 1893.

Amicis, Edmondo de, *Constantinople*, translated from the 15th Italian edn, 2 vols, Philadelphia: Henry T. Coates & Co., 1896.

—— *Morocco: Its People and Places*, translated from Italian, London: Cassell, Petter, Galpin & Co., n.d.

Aponte, Salvatore, *La vita segreta dell'Arabia Felice*, Milan: A. Mondadori, 1936.

Ardemagni, Mirko, *Della terra di Salambbô ai laghi di cristallo*, Milan: Casa Editrice Alpes, 1928.

Armstrong, Sir W. G., *A Visit to Egypt in 1872. Described in Four Lectures to the Literary and Philosophical Society of Newcastle-upon-Tyne*, Newcastle-upon-Tyne: J. M. Carr, 1874.

Asher, Michael, *In Search of the Forty Days Road*, Harmondsworth: Penguin Books, 1986.

Barker, John, *Syria and Egypt Under the Last Five Sultans of Turkey: Being Experiences During Fifty Years of Mr Consul-General Barker*, ed. by his son, Edward B. B. Barker, 2 vols, London: Samuel Tinsley, 1876.

Belgiojoso, La Princesse de, *Asie Mineure et Syrie*, 2nd edn, Paris: Michel Lévy Frères, 1861.

Bell, C. F. Moberly, *From Pharaoh to Fellah*, London: Wells Gardner, Darton & Co., 1888.

Bell, Reverend Charles D., *A Winter on the Nile, in Egypt and in Nubia*, London: Hodder & Stoughton, 1888.

Bell, Gertrude, *The Desert and the Sown*, London: Virago Press, 1985 (first published 1907).

—— *The Letters of Gertrude Bell: Selected and Edited by Lady Bell*, London: Ernest Benn, 1947.

—— *Persian Pictures*, London: Ernest Benn, 1928 (first published in 1894 under title *Safar Nameh*).

Bernard, Marius, *D'Alger à Tanger*, Paris: Librairie Renouard, n.d.

Blackburn, Henry, *Artists and Arabs: or Sketching in Sunshine*, 2nd edn, London: Sampson, Low, Son, & Marston, 1870.

Blakesley, Reverend Joseph William, *Four Months in Algeria: with a Visit to Carthage*, Cambridge: Macmillan & Co., 1859.

Bliss, Reverend Edwin M., *Turkey and the Armenian Atrocities*, London: T. Fisher Unwin, 1896.

Bliss, Frederick Jones, *The Religions of Modern Syria and Palestine: Lectures Delivered Before Lake Forest College on the Foundation of the Late William Bross*, Edinburgh: T. & T. Clark, 1912.

Blunt, Lady Anne, *A Pilgrimage to Nejd: The Cradle of the Arab Race*, London: Century Publishing, 1985 (first published 1881).

Bradley-Birt, F. B., *Through Persia*, London and Glasgow: Collins, 1909.

Bromfield, William Arnold, *Letters from Egypt and Syria*, London: printed for private circulation, 1856.

Burnaby, Fred, *On Horseback Through Asia Minor*, 2 vols, London: Sampson Low, Marston, Searle & Rivington, 1877.

Burton, Isobel, *The Inner Life of Syria, Palestine and the Holy Land: from my Private Journal*, 2 vols, London: Henry S. King & Co., 1875.

Burton, Sir Richard F., *Personal Narrative of a Pilgrimage to al-Madinah and Meccah*, 2 vols, 3rd edn, London: George Bell & Sons, 1907 (first published 1855).

Calverley, Eleanor T., *My Arabian Days and Nights*, New York: Thomas Y. Crowell Co., 1958.

Chirol, Sir Valentine, *The Egyptian Problem*, London: Macmillan & Co., 1920.

Clayton, J. W., *Letters from the Nile*, London: Thomas Bosworth, 1854.

Clement, Clara Erskine, *Constantinople: The City of the Sultans*, Boston: Estes & Lauriat, 1895.

Cleugh, James, *Ladies of the Harem*, London: Frederick Muller, 1955.

Colette, *Notes marocaines*, Paris: Mermod, 1958.

Conder, Major C. R., *Palestine*, London: George Philip & Son, 1889.

A Consul's Daughter and Wife, *People of Turkey: Twenty Years' Residence among Bulgarians, Greeks, Albanians, Turks and Armenians*, ed by Stanley Lane Poole, 2 vols, London: John Murray, 1878.

Cook's Handbook for Algeria and Tunisia, London: Thos. Cook & Son, 1913.

Copping, Arthur E., *A Journalist in the Holy Land: Glimpses of Egypt and Palestine*, London: The Religious Tract Society, 1915.

Crawford, Mabel Sharman, *Through Algeria*, London: Richard Bentley, 1863.

Davies, Reverend E. W. L., *Algiers in 1857: Its Accessibility, Climate and Resources Described with Especial Reference to English Invalids*, London: Longman, Brown, Green, Longmans & Roberts, 1858.

Davis, Reverend N., *Evenings in My Tent; or Wanderings in Balad Ejjareed. Illustrating the Moral, Religious, Social and Political Conditions of Various*

Arab Tribes of the African Sahara, 2 vols, London: Arthur Hall, Virtue & Co., 1854.

Denon, Vivant, *Voyage dans la basse et la haute Égypte, pendant les campagnes du Général Bonaparte*, 3 vols, Paris: L'Imprimerie de P. Didot L'Ainé, 1802.

Des Godins de Souhesmes, G., *Tunis*, Paris: Gustave Guérin, 1875.

Devereux, Roy, *Aspects of Algeria, Historical, Political, Colonial*, London: J. M. Dent & Sons, 1912.

Doguereau, Général Jean-Pierre, *Journal de l'expédition d'Égypte*, Paris: Perrin et Cie, 1904.

Douglas, Norman, *Fountains in the Sand*, Oxford University Press, 1986 (first published 1912).

Drake, Charles F. Tyrwhitt, *The Literary Remains of the Late Charles F. Tyrwhitt Drake, FRGS*, ed. Walter Besant, London: Richard Bentley & Son, 1877.

Duff Gordon, Lucie, *Letters from Egypt*, London: Virago, 1986 (first published 1865).

Dufferin and Ava, Dowager Marchioness of, *My Russian and Turkish Journals*, London: John Murray, 1916.

Dumas, Alexandre and Dauzats, A., *Quinze jours au Sinaï: impressions de voyage*, Paris: Calmann-Lévy, n.d.

Ebers, G., *Egypt, Descriptive, Historical and Picturesque*, vol. II, translated from German, London: Cassell & Company, 1898.

Edwards, Matilda Betham, *A Winter with the Swallows*, London: Hurst & Blackett, 1867.

Fagault, Paul, *Tunis et Kairouan*, Paris: Challamel et Cie, n.d.

Fakkar, Rouchdi, *Aspects de la vie quotidienne en Égypte à l'époque de Mehemet-Ali (première moitié du XIXe siècle): d'après Les Souvenirs d'une fille du peuple en Égypte (1834 à 1836) de Suzanne Voilquin*, Paris: G.-P. Maisonneuve et Larose, 1975.

Fogg, William Perry, *Travels and Adventures in Egypt, Arabia, and Persia; or the Land of 'The Arabian Nights'*, London: Ward, Lock & Co., n.d.

Fraser, John Foster, *The Land of Veiled Women: Some Wanderings in Algeria, Tunisia and Morocco*, London: Cassell & Company, 1911.

Gentil, Émile, *Souvenirs d'Orient*, Paris: J. Lecoffre, 1855.

Gleichen, Count, *With the Camel Corps up the Nile*, 3rd edn, London: Chapman & Hall, 1889.

Gordon, Helen C., *A Woman in the Sahara*, London: William Heinemann, 1915.

Grafftey-Smith, Laurence, *Bright Levant*, London: John Murray, 1970.

Grassi, M., *Charte Turque ou organisation religieuse, civile et militaire de l'Empire Ottoman*, vol. 2, Paris: Librairie Universelle, 1825.

Griffin, Ernest H., *Adventures in Tripoli: A Doctor in the Desert*, London: Philip Allan & Co., 1924.

Guerville, A. B. de, *New Egypt*, rev. edn, London: William Heinemann, 1906.

Habesci, Elias, *The Present State of the Ottoman Empire*, London: R. Baldwin, 1784.

Haggard, H. Rider, *A Winter Pilgrimage: Being an Account of Travels Through Palestine, Italy and the Island of Cyprus, Accomplished in the Year 1900*, London: Longmans, Green & Co., 1901.

Hall, Trowbridge, *Egypt in Silhouette*, New York: Macmillan Company, 1928.

Harcourt, le Duc d', *L'Égypte et les Égyptiens*, Paris: Librairie Plon, 1893.

Harris, Walter B., *The Land of an African Sultan: Travels in Morocco, 1887, 1888 and 1889*, London: Sampson Low, Marston, Searle & Rivington, 1889.

Herbert, Lady, *A Search After Sunshine, or Algeria in 1871*, London: Richard Bentley & Son, 1872.

Hesse-Wartegg, The Chevalier de, *Tunis: The Land and the People*, new edn, London: Chatto & Windus, 1899.

Hitchens, Robert, *The Holy Land*, London: Hodder & Stoughton, 1913.

Holbach, Maude M., *Bible Ways in Bible Lands: An Impression of Palestine*, London: Kegan Paul, Trench, Trubner & Co., 1912.

Horne, John, *Many Days in Morocco*, London: Philip Allan & Co., 1925.

Hume-Griffith, M. E., *Behind the Veil in Persia and Turkish Arabia: An Account of an Englishwoman's Eight Years' Residence Amongst the Women of the East*, London: Seeley & Co., 1909.

Inchbold, A. C., *Under the Syrian Sun, the Lebanon, Baalbeck, Galilee, and Judaea*, 2 vols, London: Hutchinson & Co., 1906.

Joliffe, T. R., *Letters from Egypt, Describing a Passage up the Nile to Grand Cairo: Including a Cursory View of the Delta, and the Existing Conditions of the Pyramids, with Conjectural Remarks on the Object Contemplated in their Structure*, vol. II, new edn, London: Partridge, Oakey & Co., 1854.

Keane, John F., *Six Months in the Hejaz: An Account of the Mohammedan Pilgrimages to Meccah and Medinah. Accomplished by an Englishman Professing Mohammedanism*, London: Ward & Downey, 1887.

Kinglake, A. W., *Eothen*, London: Century Publishing, 1982 (first published 1844).

Klunzinger, C. B., *Upper Egypt: Its People and Its Products. A Descriptive Account of the Manners, Customs, Superstitions, and Occupations of the People of the Nile Valley, the Desert, and the Red Sea Coast, with Sketches of the Natural History and Geology*, London: Blackie & Son, 1878.

Knox, Alexander A., *The New Playground, or Wanderings in Algeria*, 2nd edn, London: Kegan Paul, Trench & Co., 1883.

Lane, Edward William, *The Manners and Customs of the Modern Egyptians*, London: J. M. Dent, 1860 (first published 1836).

—— with, by his sister, *The Englishwoman in Egypt: Letters from Cairo, Written During a Residence there in 1842, 1843 and 1844*, 2 vols, London: Charles Knight & Co., 1844.

Layard, Sir Henry, *Autobiography and Letters*, 2 vols, London: John Murray, 1903.

Lees, Reverend G. Robinson, *The Witness of the Wilderness: The Bedawin of the Desert, their Origin, History, Home Life, Strife, Religion and Superstitions, in their Relation to the Bible*, London: Longmans, Green & Co., 1909.

Leon, Edwin de, *Askaros Kassis the Copt: A Romance of Modern Egypt*, London: Chapman & Hall, 1870.

Loftus, William Kennett, *Travels and Researches in Chaldaea and Susiana; with an Account of Excavations at Warka, the 'Erech' of Nimrod, and Shush, 'Shushan the Palace' of Esther, in 1849–52*, London: James Nisbet & Co., 1857.

Lorey, Eustache de and Sladen, Douglas, *The Moon of the Fourteenth Night: Being the Private Life of an Unmarried Diplomat in Persia during the Revolution*, London: Hurst & Blackett, 1910.

—— *Queer Things about Persia*, London: Eveleigh Nash, 1907.

Lorimer, Norma, *By the Waters of Carthage*, rev. edn, London: Stanley Paul & Co., 1925.

Loti, Pierre, *Egypt*, translated from French by W. P. Baines, London: T. Werner Laurie, n.d.

Lott, Emmeline, *Harem Life in Egypt and Constantinople*, 2 vols, London: Richard Bentley, 1865.

Lyell, Thomas, *The Ins and Outs of Mesopotamia*, London: A. M. Philpot, 1923.

McCoan, J. C., *Egypt As It Is*, London: Cassell Petter & Galpin, n.d.

MacDonald, George, 'An Invalid's Winter in Algeria', in *Good Words* magazine, 1864.

MacFarlane, Charles, *Constantinople in 1828. A Residence of Sixteen Months in the Turkish Capital and Provinces: with an Account of the Present State of the Naval and Military Power, and of the Resources of the Ottoman Empire*, London: Saunders & Otley, 1829.

Malcolm, Sir John, *Sketches of Persia*, London: John Murray, 1845.

Malmignati, Countess, *Through Inner Deserts to Medina*, London: Phillip Allan & Co., 1925.

Margueritte, Lucie Paul, *Tunisiennes*, Paris: Les Éditions Denoël, 1937.

Martineau, Harriet, *Eastern Life, Present and Past*, 3 vols, London: Edward Moxon, 1848.

Maupassant, Guy de, *La Vie errante*, 13th edn, Paris: Paul Ollendorff, 1890.

Michaud, M. and Poujoulat, M., *Correspondence d'Orient, 1830–31*, Paris: Ducallet, 1835.

Michel, Léon, *Tunis*, 2nd edn, Paris: Garnier Frères, 1883.

Montbard, G., *Among the Moors: Sketches of Oriental Life*, London: Sampson Low, Marston & Company, 1894.

Moore, Thomas, *The Poetical Works of Thomas Moore*, London: Henry Frowde, 1910.

Morell, John Reynell, *Algeria: The Topography and History, Political, Social, and Natural, of French Africa*, London: Nathaniel Cooke, 1854.

Niebuhr, M., *Travels Through Arabia, and Other Countries in the East, Performed by M. Niebuhr, now a Captain of Engineers in the Service of the King of Denmark*, translated into English by Robert Heron, 2 vols, Edinburgh: R. Morison & Son, 1792.

Nightingale, Florence, *Letters from Egypt: A Journey on the Nile, 1849–50*, London: Barrie & Jenkins, 1987 (first published 1854).

Olin, Reverend Stephen, *Travels in Egypt, Arabia Petraea and the Holy Land*, 2 vols, New York: Harper & Brothers, 1843.

Oliphant, Laurence, *Haifa, or Life in Modern Palestine*, Edinburgh and London: William Blackwood & Sons, 1886.

Olivier, G. A., *Voyage dans l'Empire Othoman, l'Égypte et la Perse, fait par ordre du Gouvernement, pendant les six premières années de la République*, 3 vols, Paris: H. Agasse, 1800 (year 9 of the Republic).

Ormsby, John, *Autumn Rambles in North Africa*, London: Longman, Green, Longman, Roberts & Green, 1864.

Ossendowski, Ferdinand, *The Breath of the Desert: The Account of a Journey through Algeria and Tunisia*, London: George Allen & Unwin, 1927.

Palmer, E. H., *The Desert of the Exodus: Journeys on Foot in the Wilderness of the Forty Years' Wanderings. Undertaken in Connexion with the Ordnance Survey of Sinai and the Palestine Exploration Fund*, Cambridge: Deighton, Bell & Co., 1871.

Paris, S. A. R. le Comte de, *Damas et le Liban: extraits du journal d'un voyage en Syrie au printemps de 1860*, London: W. Jeffs, 1861.

Pascal, Louis, *La Cange: voyage en Égypte*, Paris: L. Hachette et Cie, 1861.

Payton, Charles A., *Moss from a Rolling Stone; or, Moorish Wanderings*, London: 'The Field' Office, 1879.

Pirajno, Duke of, *A Cure for Serpents*, translated from Italian, London: Eland Books, 1985 (first published 1955).

Pommerol, Mme Jean, *Among the Women of the Sahara*, translated from French, London: Hurst & Blackett, 1900.

Pye-Smith, Charlie, *The Other Nile*, Harmondsworth: Penguin Books, 1987.

Rey, M. E. Guillaume, *Voyage dans la Haouran et aux bords de la mer morte exécuté pendant les années 1857 et 1858*, Paris: Arthus Bertrand, n.d.

Rhodes, Kathlyn, *A Schoolgirl in Egypt*, London: George G. Harrap & Co., 1937.

Rogers, Mrs G. Albert, *Winter in Algeria, 1863–4*, London: Sampson Low, Son, & Marston, 1865.

Saint-Hilaire, J. Barthélemy, *Lettres sur l'Égypte*, Paris: Michel Lévy Frères, 1857.

St John, Bayle, *Village Life in Egypt, with Sketches of the Said*, 2 vols, London: Chapman & Hall, 1852.

Sandys, George, *Sandys Travailes: Containing a History of the Originall and Present State of the Turkish Empire: their Lawes, Government, Policy, Military Force, Courts of Justice, and Commerce*, London: Printed by Richard Cotes for John Sweeting, 1652.

Ségur, le Vicomte J. A. de, *Les Femmes, leur condition et leur influence dans l'ordre social, chez differens peuples ancien et modernes*, 3 vols, new edn, Paris: Thieriot et Belin, 1822.

Servier, André, *L'Islam et la psychologie du musulman*, Paris: Librairie Challamel, 1923.

Sladen, Douglas, *Carthage and Tunis: The Old and New Gates of the Orient*, 2 vols, London: Hutchinson & Co., 1906.

Soane, E. B., *To Mesopotamia and Kurdistan in Disguise: With Historical Notices of the Kurdish Tribes and the Chaldeans of Kurdistan*, London: John Murray, 1912.

Sonnini, C. S., *Voyage dans le haute et basse Égypte, fait par ordre de l'ancien gouvernement, et contenant des observations de tous genres*, 3 vols, Paris: F. Buisson, 1798 (year 7 of the Republic).

Spry, William, J. J., *Life on the Bosphorous: Doings in the City of the Sultan, Turkey Past and Present, Including Chronicles of the Caliphs from Mahomet to Abdul Hamid II*, London: H. S. Nichols, 1895.

Stark, Freya, *The Southern Gates of Arabia: A Journey in the Hadramaut*, London: Century Publishing, 1982 (first published 1936).

Stephens, E. S., *By Tigris and Euphrates*, London: Hurst & Blackett, 1923.

Thesiger, Wilfred, *Arabian Sands*, Harmondsworth: Penguin Books, 1987 (first published 1959).

Thevenot, M. de, *Relation d'un voyage fait au Levant. Dans lequelle il est curieusement traité des estats sujets au Grand Seigneur, des moeurs, religions, forces, gouvernements, politiques, langues, et coustumes des habitans de ce grand empire*, Paris: Thomas Jolly, 1665.

Thomson, W. M., *The Land and the Book; or, Biblical Illustrations drawn from the Manners and Customs, the Scenes and Scenery of the Holy Land*, London: T. Nelson & Sons, 1890.

Thubron, Colin, *Mirror to Damascus*, London: Century Publishing, 1986 (first published 1967).

Tompkins, Edward S. D., *Through David's Realm*, London: Sampson Low, Marston & Company, 1893.

Treves, Sir Frederick, *The Land That Is Desolate: An Account of a Tour in Palestine*, London: Smith, Elder & Co., 1913.

Vambery, Arminius, *The Stories of My Struggles: The Memoirs of Arminius Vambery*, London: T. Fisher Unwin, 1905.

Van Sommer, Annie and Zwemer, Samuel M. (eds), *Our Moslem Sisters: A Cry of Need from Lands of Darkness, interpreted by those who heard it*, 2nd edn, London and Edinburgh: Fleming H. Revell Company, 1907.

Vaujany, H. de, *Le Caire et ses environs: caractères, moeurs, costumes des Égyptiens modernes*, Paris: E. Plon et Cie, 1883.

Vivian, Herbert, *Tunisia and the Modern Barbary Pirates*, London: Arthur Pearson, 1899.

Vogue, Le Vte Eugène Melchior de, *Syrie, Palestine, Mont Athos: voyage aux pays du passé*, Paris: E. Plon et Cie, 1876.

Voilquin, Suzanne, *see* Fakkar, Rouchdi.

Voisins, Mme de, *Excursions d'une française dans la Régence de Tunis*, Paris: Maurice Dreyfous, 1884.

Volney, C.-F., *Voyage en Égypte et en Syrie*, Paris: Mouton & Co., 1959 (first published 1787).

Wagner, Moritz, *Travels in Persia, Georgia and Koordistan; with Sketches of the Cossacks and the Caucasus*, translated from German, 3 vols, London: Hurst & Blackett, 1856.

Walmsley, Hugh Mulleneux, *Sketches of Algeria During the Kabyle War*, London: Chapman & Hall, 1858.

Warm Corners in Egypt, by 'One Who Was in Them', London: Remington & Co., 1886.

Waugh, Evelyn, *Labels: A Mediterranean Journal*, Harmondsworth: Penguin Books, 1986 (first published 1930).

Wharton, Edith, *In Morocco*, London: Century Publishing, 1984 (first published 1920).

Wilbraham, Richard, *Travels in the Trans-Caucasian Provinces of Russia, and along the Southern Shore of the Lakes of Van and Urumiah, in the Autumn and Winter of 1837*, London: John Murray, 1839.

Wilson, William Rae, *Travels in Egypt and the Holy Land*, London: Longman, Hurst, Rees, Orme & Brown, 1823.

Wingfield, The Hon. Lewis, *Under the Palms in Algeria and Tunis*, 2 vols, London: Hurst & Blackett, 1868.

Wolff, Reverend Joseph, *Travels and Adventures of the Rev. Joseph Wolff, D.D., Ll.D.*, London: Saunders, Otley & Co., 1861.

Zahm, Reverend J. A., *From Berlin to Bagdad and Babylon*, New York and London: D. Appleton & Co., 1922.

Zincke, F. Barham, *Egypt of the Pharaohs and of the Khedive*, 2nd edn, London: Smith, Elder & Co., 1873.